The ART
COMING HOME

Common-Sense Self-Development
Exercises to Educate, Inspire
and Empower You

Suzanne Wylde

lotus
publishing

Chichester, England

First published in 2020 by
Lotus Publishing
Apple Tree Cottage, Inlands Road, Nutbourne, Chichester, PO18 8RJ

Text Design Medlar Publishing Solutions Pvt Ltd., India
Cover Design Alissa Dinallo
Printed and Bound in India by Replika Press

British Library Cataloging-in-Publication Data
A CIP record for this book is available from the British Library
ISBN 978 1 913088 02 6

To Justin,

For all the full burritos, fun and the hours you spent explaining the Monty Hall problem; I still don't get it, but you have convinced me to change doors.

You always light up the room.

Contents

Preface

I didn't mean to become a hippie, it happened by accident. I can't say whether this was an overnight change or more of a gradual unfolding, but I do know that the decision to learn tai chi when I was sixteen was a pivotal point for me. It led me into a world that I had previously known nothing about: the mysterious, wonderful and sometimes eccentric world of alternative health, spirituality and self-development. And yet I remember having strong leanings towards spirituality from as young as five, so maybe the seed was sown earlier. What I am certain of is that I am one of those highly sensitive people who is very attuned to what is going on around them, feeling all the feelings and also very aware of others' moods and their state. Add to that dangerous levels of curiosity and you end up with the kind of explosive mix that leads to a life of wondering about big questions. Why are we here? What does fulfilment mean? How do we heal? On my journey of discovery, I have worked on my own self-development a lot and have supported other people with theirs. So far it has been an interesting, fun, occasionally terrifying, and beautiful adventure.

Some of my biggest allies on this journey of transformation and growth have been books. You never know when you might pick one up in a time of need and read the one sentence that was the exact thing you needed to know. Or when you turn the pages and suddenly find that another person has understood the depths of your soul without ever having met you. Books are a way for one person's mind and spirit to touch another's without judgement or expectation. There is also something magical about information that can be shared far and wide in such an unobtrusive and simple way, quietly waiting for the day you need it. But there was one book I could not find – the one that combined the most important information and tools that I needed to make this epic journey. So (you guessed it) I wrote it.

You have to bear in mind that my clients, like most people, are mainly not weirdy-beardies like me; they are business people, creative types, mums and dads, architects – in short, all kinds of people. They do not have the time to comb through all the many books I have read on different areas of self-development, and many would not want to (I did want to and have loved every moment!). These are the people I really wrote this book for – the people who are getting on with living their lives and just want a bit of guidance on being the most authentic, self-expressed, grounded, compassionate and happy they can be.

Different people have all kinds of different goals for their lives and thank goodness; can you imagine how monotonous the world would be otherwise? So, the information and exercises in this book are to support you in living the life, and being the person, you feel deep down is authentic and satisfying for you. As I have not met you, I clearly have no idea what that is, or what is going on in your life, or what your dreams and difficulties are. But I know that you have all the potential, inner strength, innate talent, desires and instinct that you need for your own unique journey. This work is not about becoming a different person, but about learning to access all the different, brilliant parts of yourself. Often this just requires a shift in perspective, allowing yourself to feel, think or act in a new way, or simply giving yourself permission. Permission to be … valuable, daring, loveable, special, creative, gifted, innovative, intelligent, original or powerful perhaps? Permission to be your true self, completely.

I've been on this journey for a long time, and I am excited to be able to share what I have learned with people beyond my clients in London because I know how transformational this work can be. I like to think that one day someone will be having a tough time and that they will pick up this book and the words will help them somehow, as other authors' words have done for me. It also excites me to think that maybe in some tiny way these tools may help people to step forward into their potential, whether that is by writing a book, creating a beautiful work of art, becoming an astronaut or learning to love themselves. That alone will have made the whole bottom-numbing endurance sport of writing a book worthwhile.

And, of course, writing this ended up being a very long self-development exercise for me: doing each exercise many times, trying to fully immerse myself in the topic of each chapter, and confronting the many fears and insecurities which naturally arise from putting anything out in the world. Unlike my first book, which was very easy going by comparison (though still a lot of work), this one did not let me finish any chapter until I had worked through my own stuff around each topic up to a certain point (although that is not to say I managed to reach guru level, or even guru-light, sigh). I know this might sound strange, but it felt like this book not only wanted to be written, it wanted to be written in a certain way, and that it almost had a will of its own. Now I feel grateful and relieved to have finally written the book that I have been wanting to write for over a decade. For all that it has taken out of me, it has added so much more to my life.

In a restless and sometimes unfriendly world, there is one thing we can all do to help move us forward into a state of harmony, wisdom and love, and that is to be ourselves. Not hiding our gifts, not staying silent when we have something to contribute, and not playing small when we are actually large both in spirit and in heart. Being proactive instead of reactive, loving instead of petty, and seeing the big picture instead of defensively guarding our own small piece of the pie can all be side effects of stepping forward into who we really are – whatever that looks like for us. Beyond our fears and learned limitations there is a whole world of experience and life waiting to be lived, for anyone who is brave enough to explore it. Scary, yes, but tons of fun. And what a ride!

Introduction

It should be so easy to feel at home in ourselves, shouldn't it? It seems like something that would be as natural and inevitable as breathing or falling off a bike while learning to ride. Yet, for so many of us, this is a goal we have to work towards and a huge part of our life journey. It requires not only that we become self-aware, but that we actually like and love the person we find ourselves to be.

The title for this book stems from a long-held belief of mine – that although pushing ourselves out of our comfort zone to move beyond our old limitations can feel scary and unfamiliar, if it is authentic to us then through growing and changing we are actually *coming home* to ourselves. And just like a home, our centre should be somewhere that we feel safe, loved, understood and accepted for who we are. So although the journey may be tough at times, striving too hard and being self-critical will not get us there. Our way home is paved with self-kindness, patience and a sense of our intrinsic worth. And above all it is guided by our own innermost truth and self.

Over the years I have had the privilege of supporting many different people on their unique journeys; sometimes with bodywork, sometimes with energy work, and at other times through teaching new tools for introspection or healing. Working in this way with myself and with others has given my life a depth and meaning that I doubt I could have found in any other way. Many of my clients have courageously moved beyond their comfort zones to explore more of who they are and their potential in this world, which has often paid dividends I could never have predicted.

Certain benefits are quite universal, however, such as an increased ability to laugh, have fun, think outside the box, love deeply, access creativity and intuition, be flexible, be original, stand up for our beliefs, make a difference and find our true north. It is also wonderful when we realise how our own growth can touch others, often starting a chain reaction of increased positivity, love and expansion across the world that we cannot track.

Although I believe that the potential for an amazing experience of life is everyone's birthright, I have noticed that this generally only happens for those who live consciously and grow intentionally, whatever that looks like for them, and self-development is one great way of doing that. On the other hand, if we stay guarded and static out of fear (of the unknown, perhaps, or even of our own potential) then over time we will become rigid, dissatisfied and disconnected from our true self and our authentic power. There are many strengths and talents within us we can only access when we have an open heart and mind, and this is important because there is a big difference between authentic personal power and the pretence of it. Fearful people with the latter may become bullies, try to stop the growth and joy of people around them, be controlling, or create toxic environments. Conversely, people who stand in their power often see the potential and beauty in others, lift people up and empower them, stay open to love, dig deep within themselves, and create collaborative and supportive environments. Isn't it devastating/wonderful to think that this all comes down to our own choice?

In a world increasingly paralysed by fear and controlled by division and inflamed suspicions, we need people with the courage to find the baseline of their true self, feel with their whole heart, think clearly, listen to their intuition and work through their feelings instead of projecting them onto others (especially when those others are vulnerable and need our help rather than our hate). When we find our truth and our talents and bring these into the world, it becomes a kinder, more evolved and more enlightened place. But when we choose to play it safe and stay half in the shadows, our spirits and our communities are diminished. Your unique self and talents are needed, and I know that you will bring with them your own brand of power and truth; I can't wait to see what you do.

What Is Self-Development Work Actually?

Before diving head-first into our self-development work, let's quickly look at the meaning of this slightly vague term and how we use it in this book. The actual self-improvement movement as we recognise it probably started in 1859 with a book called *Self-Help; with Illustrations of Character and Conduct* by Samuel Smiles (randomly, he is also Bear Grylls's great-great-grandfather),[1] but it has also been big at various points throughout history – such as the Renaissance, for example. We could also think of all of the main spiritual texts as the original self-help manuals, so although self-development may sometimes be seen as a modern fad, it is actually a trend nearly as old as society. It makes me wonder how many advances in technology, science and culture have been supported by self-development of some kind, and I think it is telling that many of the greatest thinkers of all time have been introspective, sensitive and of a growth mindset.

The term 'self-development' is often used as a catch-all category for many different subjects, including business skills, mindfulness, self-awareness, thought, relationships, spirituality, punctuality, emotional intelligence and many others. However, the self-development work that I present in this book focuses mostly on your inner experience and giving you tools to access more of yourself. This is intentional, because I am a big believer in getting in touch with your own inner truth and power and letting the benefits of that ripple out, rather than focusing on making lifestyle changes and hoping that will change how you feel inside. We cover most aspects of the self because they are all irrevocably interdependent, and if we want to make a deep and lasting change or get in touch with who we are in a real and 360° way we need to consider all of ourselves, not just the bits we enjoy working on.

The self-development work in this book mainly includes learning tools for becoming more self-aware, finding out how we really feel about things deep down, self-healing, developing a healthy and loving relationship with

---

[1] Smiles 2019

ourself, developing an inner resource, or reflecting on certain aspects of our experience. Of course, any one of the topics in this book (even subsections of topics) could have its own shelf of books written about it, but I feel that I have set out most of what you will need to do this work all in one place.

How to Get the Most Out of This Book

You can either read this book cover to cover, or you can go right to the section or exercise you feel you need right now. If you do that I recommend you still read the first four chapters to start with, because they have important guidance on how to do this work (including chapter 3, which helps us to get an overview of how we are doing at the moment), plus chapter 14, which will help you to apply what you have learned. Almost every chapter has specific exercises to help you to understand yourself better, gain perspective or to heal in some way. They can take a little bit of practice, so do be patient with yourself as you work through them. Note that if you skip straight to an exercise there may be some text right above it that will give you some helpful insights, so you may want to read that also. There are no specific instructions for how often to do the exercises because people's needs differ so much, but, generally speaking, you will want to limit yourself to a maximum of three different exercises in a day, or you may end up doing more than is useful.

The tools themselves are eclectic, and include creative exercises, movement, self-reflection, visualisation, thinking and self-expression, amongst other things. If you are wondering if they fit into one specific discipline – they do not; for the most part I created them from my experience of working on myself and with clients, and this is simply a collection of the exercises that I think will be most useful to you. They tend to work well for people from different walks of life, with different attitudes, ages, genders, political leanings and peanut-butter-consistency preferences (although we all know there is only one correct choice there, right?), but if some part of an exercise does not work for you, you can change it.

I do not think there is only one way of doing self-development that is the best, or any teacher who can tell you more about yourself than you can, other than teaching you how to connect to your own truth. For this reason, I recommend considering whether what I have said on a subject feels true for you and only doing the exercises that feel right. This book is not meant to be prescriptive, but a resource for you to use as you see fit, so it is good to follow your own instincts and take what you need, using this book in the way that works best for you and your world view.

> Absorb what is useful, discard what is useless
> and add what is specifically your own.
>
> —Bruce Lee, *Wisdom for the Way*

A Note Before You Start

I am not a doctor, psychotherapist or psychologist, but I highly recommend that if you need support you do seek out a doctor or mental-health professional. This book cannot replace medication, medical advice or appropriate one-to-one care. In addition, it is important that you do not rush through, push through a lot of emotional pain or try to work out the entirety of your issues in a weekend. It is not possible and you will probably end up feeling overwhelmed, so be kind to yourself and go at your own pace.

Many of the exercises we are going to do require closed eyes and a state of relaxation, so they cannot be done while driving, operating heavy machinery or anywhere else this would be unsafe. Therefore, find somewhere quiet, comfortable and safe to do them.

I also want to note that as well as being (what is commonly defined as) a rational person, I am also interested in a lot of areas that are considered to be alternative; although I think of everything as connected and rational, if it works. In terms of this book, that means every now and then I will mention concepts such as energy or spirit. If you do not believe in these, you can still get a lot out of this book. Feel free to translate it variously as intention, force, effort, being or awareness – whatever is suitable in the context and makes sense to you. I did not believe in energy before I did, and although energy work and spirituality have added a very valuable dimension to my life, naturally it is completely up to each individual to figure out how they feel about these and other topics.

Also, although I was raised religious, I am not now a member of a religion, and I have no vested interest in having people conform to a particular ideology. Of course there are values that I believe are universally important, such as respect for ourselves and others, fairness, equality, and so on, but I am mostly interested in supporting others to find out what is true for them. I know that we can never completely get away from our social and cultural conditioning, but as far as possible I have tried to make this book accessible to people of different cultures and ways of life, underneath which we are all pretty much the same – a fact that seems to be frequently forgotten in our turbulent world, but is very easy to remember as we journey deeper within ourselves, getting closer to that which connects us all: our spirit, our hearts, our fundamental humanity.

I hope that you enjoy my book and find some useful tools to use on your own journey. I have watched so many unhelpful, heavy and sad things move out of the shadows into transformation, and so many gifts, dreams and adventures find the space and light they need to unfold out into the world. Facilitating this is one of my gifts, and one that never fails to give back to me as I am inspired by the success of my clients. Success, you understand – as in being the person you want to be – is not simply gaining money or influence, which can come and go, but a powerful *becoming* that no one can take away from you, bringing with it your own freedom, power and truth. And which, in some large or small way, will mean the world is never the same again.

CHAPTER 1

A Healthy Attitude to Self-Development Work

L ike marmite, self-development can be a divisive subject. People who are against it may believe that it is self-indulgent and navel-gazing, a distraction when there is so much else in the world that needs to be worked on, or that it does not produce real change, but is just fluffy stuff. People who are for it may believe that self-awareness and working on ourselves can lead to being more conscious in the way we live, taking more responsibility for the way we affect others and generally having a more meaningful experience of life.

I have to put my hand up and say that I love self-development, because out of everything it is the thing that has made the biggest difference in my life – I really should not really be writing this book otherwise! Yet at some points the way I have done it has not always been beneficial; for example, thinking it is essential to do it all the time (it isn't), thinking it can fix everything (it can't), thinking of myself as hopelessly flawed (I'm only moderately flawed; the hopelessly part is a bit much), and in general sometimes not giving myself the time and space I needed to integrate new information or insights.

In order to actually progress in our self-development work, we need to do it in a way that actually leads somewhere, with the right attitude and intention. So, this chapter looks at some of the key things to bear in mind before we start doing this work, to try to help us approach it in the most helpful way. Let's begin by having a look at some of the ways that self-development work can be great and some of the ways it isn't.

So, Is Self-Development Good or Bad?

To try and give you a balanced view, we are going to look at the pros and cons of self-development work, starting with the positive. There have been several studies that showed that self-development work can help to improve depression, one of which looked at people who suffered from both depression and type 1 or 2 diabetes (there is a connection between them, unfortunately). The people were split into two groups; one followed an online self-development programme and the other read educational material about depression online. The self-development-programme group showed a much greater improvement in their depressive symptoms than the educational-material group, as well as a reduction in their levels of emotional distress regarding having diabetes (although their self-management of their diabetes did not improve).[2] The fact that a single programme could be uploaded for potentially thousands of people to use and feel better is amazing, as it is such a cost-effective and accessible method.

Another study looked at the effect of practising mindfulness-based stress reduction (MBSR includes mindfulness, body awareness and yoga) on pain levels, quality of life, anxiety and depression in people with fibromyalgia. The researchers found that MBSR greatly improved all of these areas, and a three-year follow-up found that the benefits had been maintained.[3] Looking at positive affirmations (which are designed to give people with low self-esteem and self-confidence a boost), a literature review concluded that they can benefit several areas of life, including education, health and relationships, and that these benefits can last for months or even years.[4]

---

[2] Ebert et al. 2016
[3] Grossman et al. 2007
[4] Cohen and Sherman 2014

Now let's move on to times that self-development techniques have not helped. As I mention later in chapter 6, 'Self-Love and Self-Esteem' (and counter to the results of the study above), repeating positive affirmations can actually make people with low self-esteem feel worse. It does make people with high self-esteem feel better, but obviously they are not usually the target audience.[5] In terms of mindfulness meditation, one study found that right after meditating, people were more likely to form false memories compared with people who had just been letting their minds wander.[6] I am not surprised that people were in a different state of mind right after meditating, but this might be important information for people in professions where a high level of accuracy is needed. The benefits of yoga are widely accepted (including by me), but one unexpected downside is that it may make us more self-centred. A study found that both meditators and yoga practitioners had increased 'self-enhancement' compared with the control group.[7] This draws our attention to the fact that by its nature, self-development makes us focus on ourselves. So, how can we do it without becoming arrogant or self-centred?

I believe a lot of the way our self-development shapes us is down to our intention, the way we practise it and how much we integrate what we learn into 'normal life'. If we like to do self-development because we are addicted to the idea of attaining some lofty ideal, thinking about ourselves a lot, or the feeling of either being virtuous or being broken, then of course we will not move forward, but keep running on a kind of continuous-self-improvement hamster wheel. However, if we are working on a particular aspect of ourselves out of a genuine desire to improve in a way that will benefit us and the people we know, then it should be much easier to integrate these improvements into our personality and life, while still feeling equal and connected to others.

---

[5] Wood et al. 2009
[6] Wilson et al. 2015
[7] Gebauer et al. 2018

Some General Truths about Self-Development Work

Because having the right attitude and method is so important, we are going to look at some of the important things we need to know about doing this work. There will always be differences from person to person, and it is important to decide on the right attitude for yourself, but the following are several things I have found to be true for most people regarding self-improvement work.

1. Some of us need to do more self-development than others

And that is OK. If you grew up in a relatively happy family and feel fairly well adjusted, then you may find it hard to understand why other people might need to intentionally work on themselves. Or if you feel that you have difficulty just doing normal things, like feeling good about yourself in general, having a good relationship or making decisions, you may feel that there is something wrong with you because others seem to have such an easy time, but there isn't. It can be very hard to put yourself in another person's shoes unless you have had very similar experiences yourself. For example, returning to a 'normal', balanced state when you know what that feels like and trying to get there for the first time are two very different experiences, so it is helpful to try not to compare ourselves with others or judge others for doing less or more work.

It is also helpful to remember that we are all at different points on our journey and no two people's paths look the same. We may see someone looking fabulous on social media, yet their inner world might be a desolate and lonely place, while someone else who may seem unsuccessful or unattractive may have one of the most beautiful souls you've ever encountered. Therefore, entering into your own self-development work with an attitude of humility, love and openness is a great idea, and it is always good to have compassion for ourselves and others.

There are also differences in personality which lead some people to do more self-development than others, as some people are more stable and fixed and others have more of a growth mindset. Of course, it is the latter type of person who often embraces self-development with gusto, but I have seen great changes in more fixed people when they challenge themselves a little. Although I think it is positive to push ourselves to grow up to a point, I would also say that it can be equally authentic for some people *not* to. After all, society does need some people who love stability in order to maintain structure and order, and some people with an instinct for change to innovate and improve, so maybe we are meant to have different tendencies, and that is fine – as long as we are not remaining fixed out of fear. It is important to listen to our own inner voice about how much self-development we do, and to avoid trying to force either change or stability on others. It is also important to avoid changing compulsively as a way of avoiding our true self.

2. There is an optimal time, pace and amount

There will be times in our lives when we need to focus on our work, relationships, finances, or other practical and immediate issues, and there will be other times when we may feel called to explore something deeper – our personal growth or spirituality, perhaps. And then we will return to the former again. Life and nature are all about cycles of change and stillness, growth and rest, and we are the same. Listening to our emotional and intuitive feelings can tell us what we need at different times, and help us to honour the needs of our deeper self as well as living a balanced, healthy life.

Sometimes people who have newly discovered a path of learning or growth feel a strong urge to fully immerse themselves, filling themselves up with the new information and experiences. This in itself is not a bad thing, and it is understandable to be excited when we discover something new that we like or need. However, in the long run there is only a certain amount of self-development that we can do at one time. This is partly because changes that we make on one level take time to integrate into the rest of us: our mind, spirit, physicality, beliefs, feelings, self-expression and our life. So it is essential that after a noticeable change we also make space for the rest and integration we need.

There is no need to push forward relentlessly, and it is likely you will not make any progress with that approach. Most of us need a balance between fun, work, friends, family, entertainment, exercise, learning and other aspects of life. Some people may be fine without one or more of these, but they are the aspects of life that are important for most of us. So, if you find that you have put your life on hold to focus exclusively on self-development work and you are missing out on any of these aspects, you should read the section below.

3. Integrating what we learn is essential

Sometimes I feel that it can be hard to find role models for balanced self-development, because people who have done a lot of their own inner work and are living their lives fully are often quietly going about their business and not making a big deal of it. We may only think of the well-known teachers, who we may assume are constantly working on themselves, so we may be forgiven for thinking that full dedication is what is required in order to make progress with this work. However, experiencing life is how we integrate what we have learned. This ties in with the point above, that we need to avoid trying to rush through our self-development and forgetting to live. You can meditate and go to a nightclub later that night, you can work on your self-esteem and then go kayaking, or you can go to a movie with friends and then write in your diary afterwards. Exercise, fun, friends, work and everything else: they all help us to live what we have learned.

Just like a great cyclist who discovers they are awful at running – if you only practise one thing one way, you'll only be good at that one thing. So, if you meditate in a cave for twenty years, then you will be great at meditating in a cave, but you won't know how to apply what you have learned to real life, and therefore you will miss out on really learning about yourself. However, the hermit who pops out to his weekly salsa lesson, watches a movie, spends time with friends and then goes back into his cave could be said to be a whole lot more self-aware and integrated. Applying what we learn to many areas of our life can lead to real change and help us to avoid self-development work that is merely decorative.

4. A lot of our self-development is not going to make sense to other people

You may find that sometimes you realise something, but you don't just realise it – you suddenly know it on a very deep level. It unlocks a part of you, or brings you to a new level of understanding. Rushing to share this revelation with a friend, however, may yield only a shrug or a non-committal comment, as there is a big difference between being told something and having it transform or awaken you. We might assume that by telling someone else it will have the same effect on them – but this hardly ever happens. The reason it affects us so powerfully is that the real-isation arrives at the right time for us and we are at a point where it is not just relevant, but we can know it on every level of our being. However, other people may not be ready to hear it, it may not be relevant to them, or they may already have that understanding. These experiences are often non-transferrable, but maybe this also makes them special. There is no problem with sharing these revelations with others, but it is best not to expect too much back, and not to feel disenchanted when others are at a different place in life to us. Self-development is a very personal thing.

5. The benefits spread out to the wider community

Let's say there is a woman who was defensive and cynical, but she has become more trusting and giving of herself. Let's also say she comes into direct contact with roughly fifty people a month and indirect contact with two hundred people a month, and that her manner has an effect on many of them, to some degree. The way she is in herself has an impact on the world. In addition, there are also changes in how she lives her life. Maybe after becoming more open she starts a relationship, adopts a dog, gives money to charity or inspires three people who look up to her to be kinder. How can we measure the ripple effect that spreads out from one person who chooses to better themselves and how do any of us know what effect we are having on others? This is unquantifiable, but imagine the phrase 'someone else's therapist knows all about you' being used in a positive way. What if we are actively making life better for other people, and do not even realise it?

Doing this intentionally is even better. For our self-development work to be grounded, it is important that we are consciously working towards having some kind of positive effect on the world around us. Be careful not to make other people your project, though! In order to avoid overstepping people's boundaries, we could take an intention such as 'making your son a better person' and switch it to 'working on being a better Dad'. As we work on becoming truer to who we are, we have to allow other people their own experience. I have had many clients who wanted to know how to make other people do things, believing they knew best. However, controlling other people does not come from a place of love, and it will not end up there either.

In other contexts, having a positive impact could mean checking up on our friends, taking shopping to elderly neighbours, mentoring a child, helping children learn to read, being kind to the younger employees in our company (as well as everyone else), sharing useful information, investing in start-ups with something positive to contribute, giving to the homeless, or campaigning or working on a key issue. Basically, it doesn't work if it's just about us, because it can come uncomfortably close to narcissism. Sharing our gifts and time with others can have a deep and lasting impact on others' lives, in a way that meditating in a room never will, and a powerful effect on us. No point doing all that work and keeping it all locked inside us, hey?

6. It doesn't make us better than anyone else

I asked one of my clients a trick question the other day (well, actually, I didn't think it was, but he did!). I asked: 'Out of all my clients, who do you think is the most valuable?' Initially, he answered *the one who came most often*, then *the one who I learned the most from*, and then several other suggestions, but I continued to say 'no' to each. In the end he gave up and I answered that all of my clients are equally valuable – because all people are of equal value. Life may not treat them as if they are, and other people may not treat them as if they are, but there is nothing we can do in this life to become more valuable. Therefore, if we do a lot of self-development it does not make us better than anyone else, because nothing can. We could become more educated, richer, better dressed, more self-aware or famous, but not more valuable.

So, if we are doing more work on ourselves and we start to feel better than others then we are not doing it right – in fact, we're doing it pretty badly. And if we think we are better than others at not thinking that we are better than others, this is another little ego trick to make us pat ourselves on the back for an activity that we are largely doing for ourselves any-way. Because we are not primarily doing self-development work to make other people happier (although this can be a side benefit), are we? Like everything we do, it comes from our self and is therefore selfish. It does not mean it is *bad selfish* – we have no option but to act from our self. But it is good to acknowledge that we are probably doing our inner work to make ourselves feel and live better, rather than having the idea that we are somehow more elevated or worthy than others (which would be a very wonky platform to build our self-development work on).

7. No one else can do it for us

Whether we have just started this journey or have been pursuing self-development for many years, it is common to want a teacher to guide us, someone to look up to – a guru, even. Teachers who hold more knowledge than us can be invaluable, but there have been many situations where the boundaries of what is appropriate have become blurred, sometimes even resulting in abuse. Ultimately, our responsibility for what we do and believe and for how we treat others always rests with us. 'But so-and-so told me it was the right thing to do' may explain the reason why someone did something questionable, yet the responsibility still lies with them. Similarly, the responsibility for our self-development work lies only with us.

The desire for someone to be 'over' us may even signal a hesitation to be the adult, to accept our own power and responsibility, or to live our life fully – all of which can be scary sometimes. If you find that you have put your personal life on hold, you are not developing deep adult relationships, you cannot speak in a way that makes sense outside of a certain group, you are removed from society, you are not making progress or you are revering someone in a way that makes you feel unworthy – you may be giving too much power to another person, instead of investing it in your own growth. Unlike a bank, which holds your money and potentially makes interest for you, you cannot put your self-development in someone else's hands and get a return on that. You will stay as you are or even diminish, because real self-development that makes sense and is integrated comes from the inside, or as Indian philosopher Krishnamurti put it: 'Order imposed from without must always breed disorder.'[8]

So, in terms of our personal development it can be better to be a prodigal son rather than a faithful servant. The prodigal son went off, made mistakes and learned from them, developing wisdom. The other son accepted what he was told without question, martyred himself and ended up bitter. There really is no substitute for living your own life, and one sign of a great teacher is that they know when to send you on your way (if you are interested in this topic, you may enjoy watching the documentary *Kumaré*[9]).

8. Sometimes it is not what we should be doing

If we find ourselves in a situation that is wrong, hurtful or even dangerous in some way, then we should be taking action to change that situation. Whether that means getting help from the appropriate sources, getting to a safe place or sorting out our finances, for example, we should always do this first. There is no self-development in the world that will keep us safe when we are in danger, or make money when we need it – we need to first take care of our most basic needs. When these needs are unmet we cannot make lasting change in our emotions, relationships or spiritual development – because in order to change we need to feel safe.

---

[8] Krishnamurti 2004
[9] Gandhi 2011

For example, quite often when I am treating a client who has come to see me in London, I have to spend at least ten minutes on relaxing chat before their nervous system has calmed down enough to let me work with them in any meaningful way. And this is typically someone who has a good life, but is just a bit stressed from rushing around a city. Imagine how impossible it would be to calm down enough to make a change while you are worrying about survival-level stuff. So I recommend making sensible choices. For example, if you really needed money and had to choose between trying to attract money and going and making it right now – I would choose the latter. Intentions can be very powerful, but being stable now should always be a priority; it is an essential foundation for lasting self-development work. And we do not all need the same conditions or amount of money to feel safe, but feeling safe and secure is the goal.

So, to sum up: when doing this work it is important to remember to go at our own pace and approach the work with the right intention, that there will be times to do inner work and times not to, that we cannot become better than others, that this work can be selfish *and* good, that we are our own gurus, that we should think about our wider community and not just ourselves, and that we should always take care of pressing concerns first.

Just as one final note on this topic, I would like to say that it is best to do this work without treating ourselves like a problem to be solved or as if we are 'broken' or 'wrong' somehow. By looking at self-development as a way to express more of our potential, increase self-awareness, and enlarge our sphere of thought and action, rather than as a means of fixing ourselves, we are much more likely to be able to make real and lasting changes. This is because we need to build on a foundation of self-love and reality, and the reality is that we are full of beauty and potential – regardless of how we, and others, have treated ourselves. If we honour that truth first and foremost, both in ourselves and in others, then we have a much greater chance of getting to know who we are deeply, and expressing that into the world. OK, now let's move on to looking at some of the skills that will come in handy for this work.

CHAPTER 2

Key Skills for Self-Development

We are going to have a brief look at some aspects of doing sustainable self-development work which may help you as you use this book, including having a healthy attitude, certain skills and tools, and how to get the most out of the exercises.

Being Kind to Yourself

This is essential because self-development work can be very challenging at times. Sometimes you may find that you are feeling upset or overwhelmed, and in this case you can just pause what you are doing and do an exercise from chapter 4, 'Grounding and Centring'. An important part of this work is learning how to take care of yourself, and if you feel that you are seriously upset, depressed or vulnerable, it is more important to feel safe than to try to confront difficult emotions. You could reach out to friend, go to a counsellor for help or even see your doctor if needed, as this book cannot replace that kind of one-to-one support. Go at your own pace, maintain an attitude of self-kindness, and if in doubt do less rather than more.

Self-Awareness

Essentially this is knowing ourselves through noticing our actions, thoughts and feelings and making sense of them. This is vital for any self-development work but it can be surprising how little self-awareness we actually have in some areas. Bringing our attention back to ourselves when it would rather be anywhere else (for example, when we are experiencing emotional pain or other hard feelings, such as shame) can yield great benefits in terms of our understanding of our selves. Higher levels of self-awareness have also been shown to improve certain areas of our lives, including our relationships with others and even productivity.[10] Maybe this is because it helps us to be more objective about our feelings and actions, and therefore we can consciously choose healthier ways of expressing ourselves and behaving.[11]

However, it is important to be self-aware in a healthy way, because if we overthink and focus on our problems too much we will start to feel bad about ourselves, have more negative emotions and find it harder to relate to others. As with many things, putting in effort is not enough – having the right attitude is key to getting positive outcomes. Therefore, I recommend aiming for self-awareness tempered with self-compassion and kindness, and remembering that being excessively self-critical or focused on our flaws is not a balanced way of being self-aware.

Keeping a Diary

It can be very cathartic and helpful to write down our feelings and experiences, as well as a great way of integrating what we have learned. Revisiting what we wrote later can also give us a deeper perspective on our journey and how we have progressed. It does not matter if you use a fancy new diary or an old notebook, but it is helpful if your notes are all in one place. When you make an entry, try to present your feelings as well as the full reality, as far as you are aware of it, and be descriptive. Because many of us use our diaries to get negative feelings off our chest, it can be a good idea to also include any positive aspects of your life to remind

---

[10] Sutton 2016
[11] Trapnell and Campbell 1999

you that you have good things going on too, and also to give you a more balanced view when looking back.

Following the Exercises

As some of the exercises in this book are a little longer, it is fine to read and complete one step at a time, rather than trying to remember the whole thing. If you do an exercise several times then you may not need to check the steps, but it will work fine either way. You can find recordings of many of the exercises at www.suzannewylde.com, which will be helpful if you find it easier to be guided through them.

Keeping an Open Mind

Many of the exercises require us to ask open-ended questions and be curious and open about the answers. For example, if you are picturing your inner child and you want to know how they are feeling, you let the information come to you rather than deciding what to picture. This can take a bit of practice, as our mind will often try to dictate the answers rather than letting them arise from somewhere deeper within us. The key is to thank your mind, but ask it to stand to the side as you wait for the answer to arise naturally. This is the mental equivalent of having an open hand which waits to receive instead of grasping, and it can take a little bit of patience and courage.

It is natural to feel resistance towards certain subjects that we feel are uninteresting, but which may also be our weaker areas. I recommend that if you reach a chapter you dislike, you look at the feelings that come up and, as far as it feels right, continue to read and use the tools.

Visualising Things

We are going to use many exercises which include visualisation, and although the term is often used to mean picturing what we want to achieve ideally, in this book we are mainly going to use it to explore a topic, seek out new insights or to change our state in a positive way. As mentioned above, our mind may want to step in and control what we see or the information that comes up. Just thank it and then return your attention to the visualisation you are doing each time you get distracted.

If we are getting closer to an emotion we do not want to feel, we may find it harder to concentrate as our mind tries to protect us from it. Accept any feelings of resistance and, if you are comfortable, bring your attention back to the visualisation again. With practice this can become second nature, but until then just try to relax and approach these exercises with an attitude of self-acceptance and being interested, rather than feeling too goal-oriented or self-critical. After all, most of the easy-to-explore areas of ourselves have already revealed themselves to us, and the other areas are harder to reach for everyone, not just us.

Non-judging Awareness

Depending on the exercise we are doing, we may want to be aware of our physical sensations, feelings, thoughts or other things. When we do this we should try not to judge what comes up because this can scare feelings away or make us categorise them too early, limiting their ability to talk to us (pigeonholes are soundproof, apparently). Therefore, non-judging awareness is very useful for allowing quieter, deeper parts of us to be heard.

And because we can only work on what we are aware of, the more qualities and feelings we can accept having, the more opportunities for growth and transformation we will have. Judgement narrows our perspective, while non-judging awareness opens us up to more possibilities and greater freedom to change.

Acceptance of Our Thoughts and Feelings

On a similar note, acceptance is a vital part of being able to work with something, but it can be tough. For example, it is challenging to allow ourselves to have a thought such as: 'I'm feeling hate right now', rather than instinctively downgrading it to 'I'm feeling annoyed' because we believe that only bad people hate. It can also be hard to acknowledge a feeling without getting caught up in stories we have around it – for example, 'I'm feeling hate because _____ did _____.' Acceptance is taking the emotion or sensation as it comes, without alteration or supporting arguments, even if we do not like or approve of it, and acknowledging our inner feelings and thoughts as completely as possible.

Keeping Going

A common issue for people doing self-development work, especially those who are new to it, is a strong desire to give up. Feeling that we can't change or being scared of what will happen if we do is obviously based in fear – which is natural, but not a great foundation for growth. If you are feeling a lot of resistance (but are not overwhelmed), keep going. Challenge yourself to make just a small next step, and celebrate your progress. Be gentle with yourself; go slowly, but keep going.

If you find yourself self-sabotaging by reaching for a habitual numbing behaviour or substance such as TV, shopping, sugar, alcohol, food, sex or drugs instead of making progress, then it can be a good idea to look at what you are really afraid will happen if you move forwards, including what you may be scared of leaving behind. Of course, we all need a break sometimes, and some shopping or a cake is not the worst thing in the world while we are bridging the gap to not needing it any more, but if your self-sabotage is harmful to you then seek help. If you feel that you are self-sabotaging mainly because you are doing too much, then it is a good idea to set a pace that works for you instead of trying to rush and then crashing.

Knowing When We Have Done Enough

Self-development is absolutely fabulous, but, as mentioned in the previous chapter, without frequent breaks and gaps to integrate what we are learning and actually live our life, it can become forced and unnatural.

Some signs of doing too much are having a glazed expression, not being able to take in any more information, feeling tired, having trouble focusing or thinking clearly, and feeling overwhelmed. If you feel any of these things, this is a great point to stop self-development work and rest, go for a walk, or do the washing up or any other normal day-to-day activity. Do not resume challenging inner work until you feel a genuine impulse to do so – not when you feel that you 'should', but when you feel you actually want to.

Remembering to be kind to yourself and open-minded and to take as much time as you need will help you progress in your self-development in a way that is sustainable and healthy. And, as I mentioned before, this looks different for everybody, so it is important to always be aiming to move closer to yourself, never towards an ideal or someone else's idea of who you should be.

The sweet spot combines being honest, holding ourself accountable and liking ourself all at the same time – but if you find this hard you could always try imagining how your favourite teacher (or another role model) would treat you and doing that. The inner separation we create by being excessively self-critical prevents the full integration of all aspects of ourself that we need in order to move forward. I strongly recommend bearing this in mind as you work through the book, choosing truthfulness over self-criticism and responsibility over self-blame. So, as we start to look at how we are doing across the different aspects of our self in the next chapter, please remember to be kind!

CHAPTER 3

Our State

Before we look at some more specific aspects of self-development, it is great to get an overview of how we are doing in general. Looking at our whole self gives us an idea of which aspects are fairly balanced and which may be getting left behind. It can pay off to do this kind of general evaluation every now and then, as so many of us enjoy working on our strengths and unintentionally put off working on our weaker areas.

We are going to look at our physicality, emotions, mind and spirit, before we go on to consider our way of being as a whole. In the West we sometimes think of these different aspects as separate, but of course they are completely interrelated. For example, any time we are in bad shape physically it has an immediate effect on us mentally and emotionally; or if we are feeling jaded spiritually, then our bodies, thoughts and feelings can feel like lead. That is why in addition to looking at each aspect of ourself in more detail it is handy to take a step back and look at how we are doing as one interconnected whole.

I recommend that as you work through this chapter, you try to be as honest as possible with your answers. You might find it interesting to write the results of the exercises in a diary and redo them after a couple of months of self-development work to see if you have changed and how.

Our Body

Our body is our physicality, our home, our pleasure centre, our transportation, and a way of both gathering information and communicating with others. The state of our body has a huge impact on how we feel, what we can achieve and our experience in all spheres of life. Our body is also the way our emotions make themselves known to us: through our physical sensations. Lastly, the fact that we know our body is mortal can give us a sense of the importance of finding meaning and making the most of our lives.

Exercise 3.1: The state of our body

We all think of, and treat, our bodies in different ways. Looking at how much we agree with the following statements will show us if any areas need some TLC and which are doing better. The aim is to help us to evaluate whether we feel that the state of our body right now is authentic to us; not to compare ourselves to a model or an Olympic athlete.

	Strongly agree	Slightly agree	Neither agree nor disagree	Slightly disagree	Strongly disagree
I feel at home in my body and connected to it					
My body right now is a good reflection of who I am					
My health is at a level that feels right for me					
My physical state allows me to express myself in the way that I want to					

If you identified any areas that have some room for improvement, it might be interesting to note down what you feel could change for the better and how that might be achieved. Bodies like it when we are connected to them and enjoying ourselves, rather than feeling critical of or alienated from them. It is common for people who feel their bodies are letting them down (because of an injury, for example, or how they look) to suffer from that disconnect because it is unpleasant when we dislike part of ourselves and feel critical and down instead of joyful and alive. So it is important to have an attitude of collaboration with and appreciation for our body and how hard it works for us, even if we have some work to do on our physical state. After all, our body cannot be perfect all the time and it is doing its best.

To summarise how your physical state is right now, complete these sentences, writing whatever you feel you need to for as long as you like, without censorship or blame. (Feel free to change the wording of the sentences, as they are just to get you started.)

- 'Currently, the state of my body is _____.'

_____

_____

_____

- 'Ideally, I would like my body to be _____.'

_____

_____

_____

- 'I would describe my connection to my body as _____.'

_____

_____

_____

Please remember that although society may tell you your body should be a certain way, we are not interested in that – we want to get to *your own* authentic physical state. So write what you really want for yourself, including how you want to feel.

Our Emotions

Our feelings are like invisible messengers and their job is to tell us about ourselves and our experience of the world. Unfortunately, many of us reject certain emotions and actively seek out others, so it can be hard for us to feel all of the emotions we have. We discuss this more in chapter 8, 'Recognising Our Emotions', but, generally speaking, the more emotions we can accept having, the more we can learn about ourselves and address any outer and inner issues that are affecting us.

Allowing ourselves to feel a very wide range of emotions does not mean we let them control us, acting however we want to in the moment. It just means we have more access to ourselves and more emotional intelligence, which is very important for our quality of life and our relationships.

Exercise 3.2: The state of our emotions

In this exercise we are going to look at your relationship to your feelings. Take your time and keep an open mind, as it is common to make an assumption that we have a good sense of our emotions. Try to reflect honestly on what is the truest answer as you look through the following statements, and score how much you agree with them.

	Strongly agree	Slightly agree	Neither agree nor disagree	Slightly disagree	Strongly disagree
I find it easy to tune into my emotions and what they are telling me					
I am comfortable feeling and expressing a wide range of emotions, including anger, excitement, hurt feelings or love					
I find it easy to steer my feelings in a more useful direction if they are lowering my quality of life					
I do not lose self-control when I am feeling strong emotions					

If you disagreed with any of the above, it might be interesting to reflect on why that is. If there are any changes you would like to make, write them down with ideas of how you could achieve that change.

While it is common to want to feel happy or 'up' all of the time, a more realistic goal might be to feel content most of the time, tolerating less comfortable emotions that come and go and not chasing a specific state (especially through unhelpful habits or substances, such as shopping, drugs or alcohol, etc.). Some people may feel overwhelmed by their emotions, or let them lead the way in how to behave or speak. But if we see our feelings as messages rather than commands, it is easier to stay centred in ourselves and receive this information and then consciously decide what to do with it, rather than handing our feelings the reins.

To sum up your emotional state, complete these sentences, writing as much as you want to in the blanks:

- 'My emotional state is generally _____.'

  _____

  _____

  _____

- 'I find it easier to feel _____

  and harder to feel _____.'

  _____

  _____

  _____

- 'Ideally, I would like my emotional state to be _____.'

  _____

  _____

  _____

- 'I would like to give myself permission (/to be able) to feel

_____'

_____

_____

_____

There are two pretty big chapters on emotions that you can use if you feel you need to do some work on them (most of us do). One big step in the direction of emotional intelligence is simply recognising what our relationship to our emotions is. From there, we can work on accessing the full range of our emotions and understanding what they are telling us. This helps us to become clear and free from old, stagnant feelings, which can cloud our minds.

Our Mind

A healthy mind is clear, learns easily, remembers things and can focus. A mind that is a little undisciplined or unhappy, however, can get stuck on a recurring theme, worry excessively, have repetitive negative thoughts, or have difficulty remembering or focusing.

As with our emotions and body, it is important to have a healthy relationship with our mind. Even though it may tell us it always knows what it is doing, it is our responsibility to direct and manage our mind so it is in a healthy state. We will look at how to do this in more depth later in the book, but for now we are just going to have a very general look at our mental state.

Exercise 3.3: The state of our mind

Looking through the following statements, score how much you agree or disagree with them.

	Strongly agree	Slightly agree	Neither agree nor disagree	Slightly disagree	Strongly disagree
My mind feels clear and I do not feel that unhelpful thoughts (whether repetitive thoughts or worries) are intruding on my peace of mind regularly					
I find it easy to concentrate on one thing and I can stay with one train of thought until I feel finished, without my mind jumping around					
My memory is great and I can challenge myself to remember things without always needing to look them up online					
If I find that my current thoughts are not useful I can steer them in a more helpful direction					
If there is nothing for me to do I do not need to be entertained or distracted, I am happy doing nothing for a bit					

If you disagreed with any of the above, it means that you are human. If there are any areas you would like to work on, why not have a think about how you might do that?

Now complete the following sentences to sum up the state of your mind and what you would like it to be:

- 'Day to day, my mental state is generally _____.'

  _____

  _____

  _____

- 'If my mindset is unhelpful I find it _____

  (easy/hard/other) to change it.'

- 'My ability to concentrate and remember is _____,

  and these things make it better or worse: _____.'

  _____

  _____

  _____

- 'Ideally, I would like my mental state to be _____.'

  _____

  _____

  _____

Write whatever you feel you want to. Of course, there is a lot of cross-over between our emotions and our thoughts, so do not worry if you find yourself talking about feelings also. The environment in our heads dictates pretty much every facet of our experience in life, so it is worth spending some time on. If you have found that there is some room for improvement, then you may enjoy chapter 12, 'Thinking Consciously'.

Our Spirit

This aspect of ourselves is the most difficult to talk about, and not just because it is intangible and invisible, but because it is not commonly acknowledged in our culture as an aspect of ourselves that we can access directly. In fact, traditionally it has been thought of as something that can only be accessed via religion, if at all.

We can think of our spiritual side as the part of us which seeks to connect to something greater, appreciates beauty, makes us feel alive, yearns for meaning and allows us to feel a sense of wonder. Although our mind, body and emotions all play a part in these too, the spirit is the piece of us that is pushing us to grow and explore, to be ourselves, to try to be better. So, bearing this in mind, why not give the exercise below a try to see how your spirit is doing right now?

Exercise 3.4: The state of our spirit

In this exercise we look at the state of our spirit by looking at our feelings and attitudes, so do not worry if you are having difficulty understanding the exact concept of your spirit, just answer the questions as honestly as you can.

	Strongly agree	Slightly agree	Neither agree nor disagree	Slightly disagree	Strongly disagree
I often feel inspired, a sense of wonder or being uplifted					
My intuition guides me in my day-to-day life					
I feel that who I am at my core shines out in my day-to-day life and is doing well					
I know I am connected to something greater and that my life has meaning					

If you disagreed with a lot of the statements above, it may be time to focus a little more on the spiritual side of your nature; however, this does not mean you have to wear hemp, chant or hug a tree necessarily (although I'm sure the tree would appreciate it). The way that you are spiritual has to be right for you, whether this is more about finding meaning or a sense of wonder in life, following your intuition, or includes a specific spiritual practice.

Bearing this in mind, complete these sentences in the way that feels true for you:

- 'In terms of having inspiration and wonder in my life, right now I feel that _____.'

_____

_____

_____

- 'If my spirit were expressing itself optimally, I would feel/be

  _____,'

  _____

  _____

  _____

- 'I find a sense of purpose and meaning in/through

  _____,'

  _____

  _____

  _____

- 'I want a stronger connection with my spirituality so that I could

  feel _____,'

  _____

  _____

  _____

Do not worry if you found yourself mentioning your body, mind or emotions – our spirit expresses itself through all of these aspects of ourselves also. As the subtlest aspect of our being, it is the hardest to point at directly, and yet it has a huge impact on us as a whole.

Our Overall State

And now, having looked at these four different aspects of ourselves, we can reflect on ourselves as a whole person. We are all of the above and more, as all of the aspects blend into each other and work together to make us the amazing people we are, so now let's just reflect on how we think we are doing overall.

Exercise 3.5: Summary of our state

Reflect on these statements and complete them in the way that feels right to you:

- 'Out of my physical, mental, emotional and spiritual states, my strongest aspect is _____ because _____, and the one that needs more help is _____ because _____.'

- 'My attitudes towards my weaker area come from _____ and are that _____.'

  _____

  _____

  _____

- 'I have developed my strongest aspect by _____ and I can use some of these same attitudes and skills to develop my weaker areas, by _____.'

  _____

  _____

  _____

- 'Overall I feel that I am doing _____, and that in general the state of my whole self is reflecting who I am authentically around _____ %.'

Do not worry about being 100% accurate – this is just to gain a general idea of your state and any biases you may have towards or against certain aspects of yourself. Of course, it is impossible to see ourselves with twenty-twenty vision, so now we are going to try to reflect on how we are perceived by others in order to get a little more perspective.

Exercise 3.6: What other people see

This is not about looking for approval from others, but to use what we think their opinions are as a way of getting perspective on ourselves. Simply read through the statements below and see if you think that people would agree or disagree with them. I recommend reflecting on the likely opinions of your friends, but it is also fine to think of family, partners or colleagues if that is more appropriate to you, and you can do it a couple of times thinking of different people. You may think that they would agree or disagree with just a part of a statement, and that is fine.

- People think of me as positive, upbeat and open.
- People like being around me; I make them feel good.
- I have good energy levels and a good amount of enthusiasm.
- I am healthy and I live a full life.
- I am kind and patient; people feel safe with me.
- I am competitive and focused.
- I am introverted and quiet.
- I am loud and the life of the party.
- I experience many highs and lows.
- People know they can come to me for help.
- I have a good memory and concentrate easily.
- I am great at making decisions.
- I am physically fit and strong.
- I have good, healthy and satisfying relationships.
- I am authentic and say what I mean.

These are just a few of many aspects of ourselves, but a good start to getting an idea of how we are doing in general. If you want to consider any other aspects of yourself, just create sentences for them and add them to the exercise above. Of course, we want to be authentic to ourselves rather than to other people, so it is important to choose the people whose opinions we respect.

Our Authentic Way of Being

Insist on yourself. Never imitate.

—Ralph Waldo Emerson, 'Self-Reliance', [1841]

Our way of being shapes our whole experience of life: how we feel, what we can achieve, how alive we can feel in the moment, the quality of our relationships and more. It is very important that our state authentically reflects who we are, and when this is the case we often find that we are in the flow of life, that good things happen for us naturally and spontaneously and it is easier to form great connections and to collaborate with others. An authentic way of being also makes it easy to express ourselves in a direct and honest way, but it is easier for some of us than others and it usually requires us to be fairly self-aware. So, to help us with this we are going to use the exercise below to have a look at how we see ourselves, in a very open-ended way.

He who knows others is intelligent;
he who understands himself is enlightened

—Lao Tzu, Tao Te Ching, [sixth century BC]

Exercise 3.7: Writing who we are

This is a simple method of self-enquiry, which uses freewriting and an open mind to get in touch with who we feel we are on a deep level. You begin by simply writing the phrase: 'I am', and then you write in a stream-of-consciousness way for ten minutes, without looking back at what you have written or correcting spelling or grammar. If you find it hard to start, or if you ever get stuck, just write the starter phrase over and over again ('I am I am I am I am ...') until you naturally start writing again. After ten minutes you can put your pen down and read what you have written.

You may find that it is very abstract and that is completely fine. On the other hand, maybe you have tried to define yourself in terms of how you are seen from the outside – for example, your job, car, gender or age. In this case, I recommend having another go and writing from the heart. It doesn't matter if you say, 'I'm a blue dragon with a toy train,' but you don't want to be limiting yourself to things like, 'I'm an accountant from Bromley.' (By the way, if you are that's quite a coincidence! Do you have also a toy train?) I am not sure who first came up with this exercise, but it is a great tool.

This exercise reminds me of the part of *The NeverEnding Story* when the hero, Atreyu, must come face to face with his own reflection.[12] As Engywook the research-scientist gnome explains, seeing ourselves as we truly are is the most terrifying test of all because it shatters any illusions we hold about who we think we are. Although this exercise is not so confronting, it can help us to broaden our idea of ourselves and to refocus on the important aspects of who we are, beyond roles, status, gender, age, and so on. This is key to our self-development because the foundation we are building on is who we actually are, not who we believe we are or should be. So having a clearer idea of who we are also helps us to gain a truer understanding of the world around us, because we can see the lens we are looking through more clearly.

Now that we have looked at how we are doing across the main aspects of our being and the general state we are aiming for, let's move on to learning how to ground and centre ourselves. The exercises in the following chapter will be useful tools for you whenever you need to feel comfort after difficult emotions come up; to feel balanced, calm and strong within yourself; and to integrate what you have learned. This helps us to progress in a balanced and healthy way and get back to our centre whenever we need to.

---

[12] Petersen 1984

CHAPTER 4

Grounding and Centring

You may instinctively know what it is to feel *centred* (calm, peaceful, feeling ourselves) but being *grounded* may be a new term for you. It basically means having our feet on the ground emotionally and energetically, and we are covering this topic early on in the book for a couple of reasons.

The first is that, in order to make meaningful progress, we need to be present in the here and now and aware of our bodies and how they are feeling. Doing self-development work while ungrounded is a bit like trying to complete a jigsaw puzzle with only half of the pieces. This is because if we are spaced out, daydreamy, disconnected or mostly in our heads it is much harder to connect to our emotions and deeper thoughts and to make sense of them, whereas if we can stay present it is much easier to think clearly, be attuned to our senses and feelings, and integrate things. So, if you do sometimes feel spaced out, disconnected or 'a bit funny', it is a great idea to use grounding exercises to bring you back into your body. You can add to this by also spending more time in nature and away from devices, exercising, breathing slowly and deeply, avoiding blood-sugar highs and lows, and taking care of things that are weighing on your mind and distracting you.

Another reason that we are covering this topic first is that if you start to feel overwhelmed and that you need a break, you can use one of the exercises below to centre yourself. As discussed, sustainable self-development work is not about relentlessly ploughing forward no matter what, but taking time to integrate our feelings and insights. Ending with a grounding or centring exercise can help you to feel comfortable again even if you have addressed some strong emotions, and return to day-to-day life. You do not need to do this every time you do an exercise, but it is something that it would be better to do too much of, rather than too little.

In this chapter I also mention the energetic aspect of both grounding and centring, but if you are not into that you can still use the visualisations because focusing on being fully present, connected to your physical feelings and breathing will have a great effect either way. We are going to cover a few different exercises and you can just choose whichever you feel is best at the time. Although grounding and centring exercises have a lot of similar effects, I recommend that you mainly use the former to feel more present and the latter if you want to feel calmer.

Grounding Ourselves

The physical, mental and emotional aspect of being grounded is that we are in tune with our body and emotions, have mental clarity, and are present and aware. However, if we are ungrounded all of these qualities are diminished and we may even feel physically and emotionally numb. The energetic aspect of being grounded means that our energy is rooted in our body and the earth. When we are ungrounded we tend to have more energy in the top part of our body, and if we are very ungrounded then often much of our energy and consciousness is outside our body (which is where the 'out' in 'spaced out' probably comes from).

If you are someone who sometimes spaces out I'm sure you are aware that, although your imagination may be boundless while you are in this state, your access to your feelings, ability to think and conversational ability is very limited. We are mainly alerted to our emotions through our physical sensations, so if we are unaware of these we will also be unaware of how we are feeling emotionally. This is great as a defence mechanism in the short term, but it means we are effectively 'on pause' until we get back into our bodies. For those who have experienced trauma and find themselves feeling spacey or disconnected, feeling safe is essential to coming back into the body, so I recommend approaching the work with a lot of kindness to yourself and taking your time, as well as getting professional help if you need it.

To make our work effective and lasting we need to help it integrate across all of the parts of ourselves – emotional, spiritual, physical and mental – and into the way we live. And because everything that we are while we are alive is rooted in our body, bringing ourselves fully back into our body is one of the most effective ways to integrate changes into all the parts of us. We do not need to have experienced trauma to be disconnected: living out of sync with nature, overworking, obsessing and worrying, living in our intellects, having a lack of appreciation or connection to our bodies, eating unhealthy foods, too much screen time, unnatural light, lack of sunshine, lack of fresh air, lack of exercise, and a lack of physical self-expression can all lead to disconnection from our physicality and the foundation of who we are.

Many physical, mental, emotional and spiritual issues can be lessened or even resolved simply through grounding ourselves. This is perhaps one of the reasons that nature therapy (also called ecotherapy) works, so much so that the National Health Service in the Shetland Isles has started permitting doctors to prescribe it to people with diabetes, mental health issues and chronic illnesses, in addition to their usual treatment.[13] Being in nature has been shown in various studies to alleviate stress-related symptoms, reduce risk of depression, and improve memory and attention span.[14] Therefore, we will be including some time spent in nature in this section. Speaking of which, I am going to put a tree-hugging exercise in here; I just wanted to warn/excite you in advance. But first let's start by thoroughly grounding ourselves.

In the exercise below we will use a simple visualisation to ground our energy into the earth. I have incorporated the grounding technique that was taught to me directly by Anna Hunt, a London-based shaman,

[13] Carrell 2018
[14] Frist 2017

mentor and author of sixteen years' experience,[15] with her permission. I recommend that you try doing this once or twice a day, every day for a week and seeing if you notice a difference, after which you can do it less often. However, I recommend you still do it regularly as it is so helpful for maintaining a balanced state.

Exercise 4.1: Grounding

I prefer to do this barefoot in nature if possible, but if that is not convenient you can still get great results inside or with shoes on. You will want some downtime and somewhere quiet for this exercise.

a) Sitting or standing, breathe in a relaxed way, letting tension fall away from your body, and, if it feels right, close your eyes.

b) Have a sense of your whole body and the weight of your feet on the floor, right where they touch the ground.

c) Sensing the energy in your body, visualise it extending down through your feet into the earth. Let this connection be so strong that you can feel the earth as your energy reaches down into it (picture the earth as it would feel in your environment, whether that is cool and moist or warm and dry, or other). Now feel your energy extending even further down into the earth, all the way to the earth's core and picture it connecting to the red-hot magma flowing there.

d) Breathing in, pull that red-hot-magma energy up into your body through your feet, and, breathing out, relax. Continue to pull that energy up into your body from the earth's core each time you breathe in, filling your whole body, making you feel heavy, solid and grounded.

e) When you feel that the magma has completely filled your body and you feel grounded and solid, send a feeling of gratitude and love from your heart down into the earth, and sense your connection to her. When you feel ready, slowly open your eyes.

---

[15] https://www.annahunt.com

A simple grounding exercise like this can really help to bring us into a calm, present state. I don't know about you, but I feel very calm after I ground myself, solid and with a sense of connection to the world and all the positive force within it, so it's not a bad thing to do. How do you feel?

The next exercise is a little reminiscent of forest bathing, or Shinrin-yoku, a practice from Japan which helps people to relax and connect to nature, putting their day-to-day habits and worries aside for a while. The exercise I have created is a little different to this, drawing on my experiences in nature and with clients. Feel free to adapt it to suit your needs. There is an optional tree-connection exercise in here, but if you do not live near any trees, perhaps you could substitute a mountain, a special place, the ocean or the sky, using the alternative exercise below this one.

Exercise 4.2: Remembering ourselves in nature

We all come from nature and are natural beings. It is easy to get caught up in the day-to-day, intellectual, electronic and virtual worlds, however, so in this exercise we are going to practise returning home to our roots for a bit. You may feel some resistance, which might come from feeling like you ought to be busy (which can be an addiction), not wanting to be off your smartphone (also an addiction), not wanting to feel lonely (we use many strategies to avoid facing feelings of emptiness), feeling stupid, thinking nature is too far away (a park or garden is OK in a pinch, even a pot plant will do if needed, although rolling hills, beaches, mountains or a forest are better) or not enjoying the discomfort of the unfamiliar. We are all born of nature even if we are city dwellers, and although it can feel a little unfamiliar at first, you can learn to find your sense of home in it again.

Rather than leaving your mobile phone at home, I recommend that you leave it on silent and keep it with you, especially if you have a medical issue or feel that you might be vulnerable at all. If you have an insight you may want to write it down or record it and your phone will be useful for this. Apart from this use, just keep your phone out of sight and do not use it at all for the whole exercise. You will need a place in nature, some downtime, and comfy shoes and clothes.

a) In the place you have decided to visit, take a moment to notice how you feel, where the tension is in your body, how you are feeling emotionally and what kind of thoughts you are having. If you would like to, you can set an intention for this exercise, such as feeling more relaxed, finding the answer to a certain question, or searching for an idea or inspiration, but this is optional. Once you have stated that intention to yourself, you can set it to one side gently, as we do not want to be in problem-solving mode for this exercise.

b) Look around you and notice the smells, the colours, the temperature, the textures and shapes, what is moving and what is still, and the ambience in this place. Breathe in a relaxed way, naturally and also slightly more slowly and deeply than usual if you tend to be a busy person. Nature generally moves at a slower pace than society and there is an interconnected sense of *being* that pervades it. Whether activity is constant and gentle or more noticeable and sporadic, it is very grounded – can you feel the difference?

c) Find a spot that you like and stand there, relaxed. Breathe in fresh, natural energy and breathe out negative, grey energy, releasing tension from your body as you do so. Enjoy this moment of stillness.

d) Let your senses explore, listening to even the faintest of sounds, smelling the subtlest smells, and let your attention to be drawn where it wants. If your mind tries to take you out of the moment (with stories, worries, etc.), just acknowledge that and return softly to the here and now, noticing everything around you. Keep breathing naturally and keep enjoying observing anything you are drawn to.

This is the first part of the exercise; for the second part we are going to choose a tree to connect with. If you do not have trees around you, you can skip to the exercise below ('4.3: Connection to Nature'), where you can choose something else instead.

e) Let yourself be drawn to a certain tree, intuitively. This is not about evaluating looks or location but about a feeling, so take your time, let your gaze move around freely, and let your mind take a back seat as your heart and intuition choose a tree.

f) When you have chosen your tree, walk up to it, leaving a couple of meters of space between you, and in your mind ask it if it is willing to do this work with you. If you are intuitive you may have a sense of a *yes* or *no*, but if you do not sense anything don't worry as this ability can come with time, and trees tend to be helpful by nature. Walk up to the tree and stand with your back against it (I know I said tree-hugging, but this way works really well and we can do it in broad daylight with much less embarrassment).

g) As you lean against the tree just pay attention to yourself and the tree, see what you can feel. With a slight bend in your knees, breathe and relax back into the tree and feel its strength supporting you. In your mind say 'hello' to the tree and thank it for helping you.

h) Now start to feel a sensation like magnetism in the tree, feel it drawing you towards it even more, and be aware of your body pressing against it (but without physically pushing yourself, just sensing a pull). At the same time, keep breathing naturally with the sense of everything being OK.

i) Let your attention go to any sore or tight areas in your body and visualise grey energy from that area being pulled into the tree as you breathe out (along with the soreness or tension), and as you breathe in feel the 'tree energy' filling that same area. You may want to spend several breaths on one area before moving to the next, wherever your attention is drawn – go with what you feel is right. Visualise the tree processing and releasing the negative energy by sending it up to the leaves where it is released as pure white light.

j) Allow yourself to feel a sense of oneness with the tree, continue to breathe your energy out into it, and, breathing in, bring its energy into you. Do this for as long as you feel is right.

k) When you feel ready to come to the end of this exercise, have a sense of your energy returning to you clear and fresh, and the tree's energy returning to it, also clear and fresh. When you sense your energy is separated, you can step away from the tree, but before I do this I like to ask the tree if there is anything it needs from me. Sometimes I may have a sense of something it wants me to do energetically, or maybe something more practical like spreading its acorns around, and sometimes it does not ask for anything.

l) Step away from the tree and, when you are a few metres away, turn to face it and take a moment to send a feeling of thanks to it. You can nod or even bow slightly, feeling a sense of love and respect for the tree. You can do this very subtly if other people are around – it is the intention that matters.

m) Continue on your walk, noticing how you feel in your mind, body, feelings and senses, and in your connection to the world around you.

This exercise can be very powerful, depending on the day and how sensitive we are. It may feel a bit silly, but in my experience trees are very kind, helpful and wise and make wonderful allies in our quest for grounded calmness. They are also brilliant at processing and transforming energy – that is what they spend most of their day doing; maybe like us they enjoy helping others through doing something they are good at. Thinking about your intention or question, if you had one, do you feel it has been answered or that you have gained any insight? And do you feel different after doing the exercise? Sometimes I find that I become at once more centred and expansive, as well as more joyful and calm. After spending meaningful time in nature we may realise how fragmented our waking experience has become, with unrelated distractions pulling us in opposite directions and making us react much more than acting consciously and with intention.

Many of us have lost the flow of one sequence of events or thoughts that we follow naturally from a beginning all the way to the end, as well as the time to let thoughts and projects mature fully. This not only makes us ungrounded, it also makes us unfocused and unhappy. So, as much as possible, I do recommend spending more time in nature. And this does not require a trip of several hours to reach a forest or a place of outstanding beauty, we can use a pot plant or another element of nature that we are near, using the alternative exercise below.

Exercise 4.3: Connection to nature

For this exercise you will want to be either out in nature or with something from the natural environment. Choose the most 'alive version' of the type of thing you want to work with, because living things are often more capable of responding to us and processing energy. So, if you have the choice between a piece of wood or a plant, the plant is preferable; but rocks and crystals can also be great because they are alive in a different way to plants and animals. If you choose something larger, such as the ocean or the sky, it may be a little more work, but if that is what you are drawn to it is fine. If you are drawn to an ant or similar, just know that it may wander off, but you do not need to always be physically close to it to do the exercise (although it is easier), you will just need to be able to picture it very clearly and maintain a mental connection with the object (or creature), so it can help to close your eyes. As you do the exercise, just replace the words 'thing' or 'object' with whatever you have chosen to connect with.

a) Breathing naturally and in a relaxed way, let tension drop away from your body. If you are outside, let your attention move around. Have the intention of finding something to connect with and see what you are drawn to.

b) Face the thing you are going to connect with and send the feeling of *hello* to it. You may want to express an intention, such as 'I am here to find more peace,' 'I need more perspective' or similar, and add that you would be very grateful for help with this. Although we would not expect the object of our connection to speak directly back as it might in a cartoon, we may gain perspective or receive an insight. The key to being able to receive this is maintaining a mindset of curiosity and openness.

c) Let your awareness of yourself and the way you feel grow as you keep breathing naturally. Now extend this awareness to the thing you are connecting to, and gain more of a sense of it. It will obviously feel different to 'human', but what feelings are there – coolness, warmth, solidity, movement, wisdom, aliveness, or …? Try not to make assumptions but, again, enquire with an open mind.

d) Feel a sense of love and acceptance growing in your heart, and send this to the thing you are connecting with. Sense any feelings that are extended to you in return if there are any.

e) Now ask the thing you are connecting to if it is willing to help process your negative energy. If there is a feeling of *yes*, allow old grey energy to flow into it on your out-breaths to be transformed and released, and a feeling of healing energy to flow into you on your in-breaths. It is important to ask first, because a pot plant does not have as much processing power as a tree and we would not want to overburden it.

f) Continue with this exchange of energy for as long as you feel is right, and then, when you feel ready to draw it to a close, have the sense of your energy coming back into you clear and clean, and the object's energy also returning to it clear and clean.

g) Send a sense of *thank you* towards the object of your connection and ask it if there is anything it would like. Pot plants and crystals might like to be placed in a different spot, watered or washed, for example, while any part of nature may request you to contribute to an environmental project or spread awareness in some way. Try to let your mind stay open as you listen for the answer, and if you receive one try to meet this request as far as you can.

h) Finally, with a feeling of gratitude, you can nod or bow towards the object of your connection and have a sense of recognition of the work it has done for you.

Now that you have finished this exercise, let your mind return to your original intention if you had one – did you gain any perspective or do you feel differently about the topic in question at all? And how do you feel in your body, mind and senses? This exercise can make an excellent addition to your daily routine, grounding you and renewing your love and respect for nature. Of course, spending a night under the stars is even better – but if you only have access to a pot plant right now then that is a great place to start.

This concludes our look at grounding. As I mentioned before, our day-to-day habits also have a big influence on how present and in our body we are. Exercise is a great way of becoming more grounded, but if you are doing it for this reason then it is important not to disconnect while you do it. Many of us listen to music and just get it done with minimal attention to our physical sensations, but in order to reconnect with our body we have to be aware of and listen to it. Ignoring it during physical activities is probably a bit like going to dinner with someone who only pays attention to their phone all evening – rude! Equally, we could also make an effort to be more present when we eat, wash, move around and more, in order to feel more integrated, grounded and ourselves in our everyday life. The benefits are huge.

Centring Ourselves

Although being centred has a lot in common with being grounded, the focus is on being calm and being in our body in a way that feels safe and relaxed, so that we literally feel we are in the centre of ourselves. We can use these exercises when we feel overwhelmed, overstimulated or off-balance, to return to a balanced and calm state. Once we have learned how to do this for ourselves, we can do it in a few minutes while standing in a queue, on a bus or in a boring meeting. We can also do it for longer if we need to; either way, it is a really handy skill to have in our back pocket.

Exercise 4.4: Centring with our breath

If you want to do this for longer, then a quiet space will help, but other-wise you can do it anywhere that is safe. If you are feeling overwhelmed, then after this exercise you could also take time out for a break, a nap, a walk or anything else that is healthy and calms you.

a) Breathe naturally, deeply and slowly and feel your body respond by relaxing and letting go of tension. Feel your breath flowing in and out of your nose or mouth and your torso (nose is best, unless it is blocked). If your mind wants to engage you in thoughts, worries or stories, tell it thank you, but you are focusing on your breath and your body right now.

b) If you need to let any feelings out, you can breathe the way those feelings tell you to, scream into a pillow if you have one, or write all your feelings down until you feel calmer. Then return to breathing naturally and let your breath slow and deepen a little.

c) As you keep noticing your breath, have a sense of the centre of your body and letting your awareness rest there – notice all the sensations that are present. If this brings up more emotions then revisit the step above, but if not visualise the centre of your body as silent, calm and still. Feel yourself gravitate towards your centre.

d) Within the peace at the centre of your body there is a sense of there being nothing that needs to be done, just a sense of eternal being. As you breathe in, let the feeling of stillness and peace fill your body even more. As you breathe out, let go of tension and the need to do anything. If you feel any resistance to this, just accept that feeling and then return again to your centre and your breathing.

e) When you are feeling very centred, I would like you to set a strong intention that is meaningful to you – for example, 'I am still and at peace,' or 'I am perfect.' When you have your intention, imagine it as a big door or ball of colour in front of you and step into it. Feel it around you, protecting you; breathe this feeling in deeply.

f) Before you end the exercise, know that you can return to this feeling whenever you want to, simply by using this exercise or intention. Take a deep breath in and have a sense of how well you have done, before breathing out and slowly opening your eyes.

Hopefully you are feeling happier and calmer, but if you would like to feel even more centred you can also do the exercise below. As I mentioned in the section on grounding, it can be helpful to go for a walk in nature and this will usually centre us also. Avoiding stress, screens and other things that make us feel off-balance is a good idea until we feel ready to face things again. There may be some things around us that are causing us stress without us even realising, such as watching violent films, having a messy home, admin that is hanging over us or unspoken feelings, so addressing these can often help more than a centring exercise in the long term.

The exercise below centres us in a slightly different way, helping us to feel calm through letting out feelings and energy that might be keeping us off-balance. However, this is a relaxing exercise rather than a wildly cathartic one, so take your time and enjoy it, only doing as much as you feel is right for you and keeping it light.

Exercise 4.5: Light in our centre

You will want a comfy place to sit – I like to do this cross-legged, but if a chair is more comfortable that is fine too. As always, do not make any movements that cause pain or injury. This exercise is harder to do in public than the one above as there are some gentle movements and sound involved, so you may want some privacy. You can have your eyes open or closed at any point, whichever feels better.

a) Sit quietly and imagine a wide circle around you. If there is anything on your mind or causing you stress, ask it to step outside of the circle. Keep doing this until you sense that it is just you inside the circle, which is a space for peace and for restoring your body, mind and spirit.

b) As you breathe in a relaxed way, have a sense of a central 'pole' extending from your tailbone all the way up to the top of your head. Try to sit in an easy way that makes this pole feel unblocked and aligned.

c) Have a sense of knowing that as well as being a physical being you are an eternal being, and part of the universe. Let a sense of calmness and solidity fill your body.

d) Place one hand on your stomach, below your belly button, and the other over your heart. Sense the central pole in your body filling with light with each in-breath, and with each out-breath, breathe out heavy, grey negative energy.

e) Continue to do this, but take slightly deeper breaths and on the out-breath I would like you to make a sighing-out noise, as loud as feels right (it should be a sound that comes out naturally and not be pushed out), as you let any negative emotions out of your body. While you do this, you can move your body gently in the way that feels right to you, maybe leaning to one side, twisting slightly, or turning or rolling your head (do not roll it backwards, but sideways or to the front is fine). You may find you want to do different movements on the in- and out-breaths, which is fine.

f) When you feel that you have done this as much as you want to, just breathe normally, in a relaxed way, and have the feeling of being completely at one with your mind, heart and body. There is no need to do or think anything, just breathe and be with this feeling for as long as you feel like.

g) If your eyes were closed then, when you feel ready, breathe in and then open them slowly on the out-breath. You can put both hands over your lower tummy for a few breaths before finishing this exercise.

After doing this it is good to stay mindful and not jump right back on our phone or into work mode. Taking time to journal or sketch can help us to complete our experience, while thinking about what we want to do next consciously and then doing it in a peaceful, centred way is a great way to preserve the feeling while going about our normal life.

Because our mind can easily get caught up in drama, stress, smartphones or thinking a million thoughts a minute, it can be tricky to stay centred and grounded all the time. However, with conscious intention we can start to deliberately choose a more centred and mature way of being. I am sure that when you think of a wise person you do not imagine them rushing around like a headless chicken. Staying centred can also ensure that we prioritise the right things and then do them well. When we feel and act this way we are much more likely to be happy, make progress and be able to be proud of our achievements. Of course, we all get stressed sometimes – but this should not be our default mode, no matter what seems normal in our culture.

So this completes our look at grounding and centring, which are very simple but powerful tools. Anytime you feel spacey, disconnected or overwhelmed, I suggest that you return to this section and use the exercises to bring you back to earth, the present and your body. We cannot make any meaningful progress outside of these three, and why would we want to be outside them? There's no place like home!

CHAPTER 5

Acceptance and Self-Acceptance

Somewhere between a mindset and a skill, acceptance is an attitude that enables us to roll with the punches and work with *what is* rather than fixating on what we think *should be*. It is essential to living a happy, full life as it allows us to move forward by releasing us from past hurts and setbacks that we have remained mentally and emotionally entangled in, and to accept ourselves as we are. Psychologist and meditation teacher Tara Brach explains how transformational it can be: 'It is the necessary antidote to years of neglecting ourselves, years of judging and treating ourselves harshly, years of rejecting this moment's experience. Radical Acceptance is the willingness to experience ourselves and our life as it is. A moment of Radical Acceptance is a moment of genuine freedom.'[16] Put simply, it means being with what is, as it is, without struggle, and therefore is very close in nature to mindfulness. And it is not antithetical to having good judgement or taking action if necessary, because acceptance does not mean condoning bad behaviour or being a doormat. In fact, when we see reality clearly we are often more likely to take steps to resolve issues.

In this chapter we are going to look at many aspects of acceptance, including accepting ourselves, our feelings, other people and difficult situations. You can go straight to the aspect you need now if you prefer,

---

[16] Brach 2003

but I would recommend also reading the other sections as they may have some information that is relevant for you too.

The Alchemy of Acceptance

According to the logic that most of us have been brought up with, it seems unlikely that simply *being* with something could be essential for changing it. In fact, phrases like 'a watched pot never boils' imply that just by being with the kettle we could delay the whole tea-making process (the horror!). We may think of acceptance as passive – just watching, just being there. However, when you try to fully accept something that you are resisting, you will find that acceptance, although a very still place on arrival, can take a lot of effort to get to. There is something very special about the combination of self-awareness, stillness, attention and acknowledgement that acceptance entails. It is both quiet and powerful.

If we look at this quality from the point of view of the mind, we could say acceptance translates as having clarity, because through accepting the situation we acknowledge what actually happened. From a spiritual point of view, it brings us inner peace because we are not struggling against reality – just being with what is, in stillness. Looking at it from the perspective of our emotions we could see it as kindness to ourselves, because it allows us to rest from intense emotions (such as anger or hate), and relief from fighting against how we feel or the situation. Physically, it means much less tension and probably a healthier level of blood pressure as we stop feeling under threat, because even just remembering or imagining an attack of any kind has a strong impact on us physiologically, even though the danger has passed.

Therefore, through acceptance of negative situations, we give ourselves permission to acknowledge what has happened, how much we've been hurt or disappointed, or how much we've lost. It gives us a moment of stillness with our full awareness of that pain, and this can give us the space we need for transformation and healing to occur. Why, then, if it is so beneficial, would it not come naturally to us? Well, accepting things we like can be pretty easy – it happens without us even thinking about it – but we may experience a lot of resistance to accepting anything we feel is negative. Let's have a look at this in more detail.

Why It Can Be Hard to Accept Things

On an instinctive level we reflexively push unpleasantness in any form away, which is usually great in terms of immediate survival, but often not so great for processing things and moving on. The thought of bringing a certain person or event deep enough into our self that we can accept it can feel wrong or even confronting, and we may experience many defensive emotions, including anger, rage, resentment or fear. These feelings may be trying to help protect us from danger; however, if we always stay in a 'fighting against' or 'denying' state regarding something that we cannot accept, ironically, we stay locked in a pattern *with* that thing, event or person, preventing us from finding resolution and peace and from letting it go.

Another reason that acceptance may be hard is that it may derail a story we are attached to. For example, if we feel we have been wronged it often feels bad but also good at the same time. Our ego enjoys being in a morally superior position and being seen as the 'wronged victim' or the 'goodie', while the other person is the 'baddie'. And while anger is often justified, in some cases people feel an excessive sense of victimhood, which can empower them to feel strong and have permission to feel and express anger without needing to justify themselves. This feeling of strength may be hard to give up, even if it is illusory – especially for those who often feel they are weak. However, true strength comes from self-awareness and being grounded in reality, not from letting ourselves be defined by a hardship. It can be difficult to accept that the person who hurt us is likely to also be suffering, because it takes away from our victimhood, and as our anger lessens we are forced to acknowledge the raw feelings underneath it – often a lot of pain. No wonder that many people choose to keep thinking of the other person as a purely evil or aggressive perpetrator and of themselves as the victim.

Although our emotions about a person or situation may be justified and although we may have been wronged, acceptance is never about giving up, enabling bad behaviour or lapsing into complacency. No – if a situation is wrong in some way, we should instigate a healthy and useful change. Acceptance helps us to do this through allowing us to see the situation, ourselves and other people clearly, without reference to the stories we have built around them. This also allows us to change, moving out of rigid patterns of fear and pain towards more elastic, spontaneous and heartfelt states, so it is definitely worth the effort of looking our feelings of pain, shame, anger or hurt in the face – if we feel ready to. Also, when we have a clearer sense of our own anger (e.g. when it is not entangled with a story, but an authentic reaction to something that is wrong) we can use it to give us the energy to right wrongs or stand up for ourselves. It does take a lot of courage to feel and accept the dark and raw emotions within us and to face our own frailty, but ultimately this can open us up to more life and love, and less hiding of parts of us from ourselves. In this state we are also more likely to instigate change that is positive, moving towards something that is genuine, rather than a defensive reaction that seeks to inflict pain or shame out of a desire for retribution, potentially continuing a cycle of suffering that may be years or even centuries old. It could stop with us. We could do that.

So, as we can see, real acceptance takes a lot of strength, but of a quiet, internal kind. This is not the external display of strength of those who fight fire with fire, or who try to always appear innocent and portray their enemies as pure evil, externalising all their own worst qualities ('tabloid strength'?). It is the strength of someone who has an understanding of human frailty and grey areas, and a sense of where their own responsibility lies. No wonder it isn't always popular – it's really fudging hard.

Working on Acceptance

Like everything, acceptance can be positive when used correctly and unhelpful when used incorrectly. Being too accepting of inappropriate behaviour, for example, can damage the boundaries that protect us, and being too accepting of our flaws might stop us from making an effort to improve. To put it simply, real acceptance is balanced, self-aware and self-respecting, and generally leads to positive outcomes. On the other hand, acceptance that is actually an excuse for avoiding having to confront difficult situations or behaviours may lead to no change or a worse outcome. Therefore, it is a good idea to moderate our acceptance with good judgement in a way that is appropriate for us, and to make sure the intention behind it is authentic.

In this chapter we are going to cover accepting ourselves, our feelings, other people, and situations and things being hard sometimes, and we are partly looking at these separately because, although being able to accept things is one general skill, we can find it a lot easier to do in some areas of our lives than in others. Because this chapter and the following two touch on different aspects of our self-regard (self-acceptance, self-love, self-esteem and self-compassion) which are all interconnected, as you progress with this work you may want to pick exercises from those chapters also and mix things up.

First we are going to start by looking at self-acceptance, which is exactly as it sounds: the acceptance of ourselves as we are, including our limitations as well as our strengths. For many of us this is very hard, in fact Jung went as far as to say that complete self-acceptance is the thing that terrifies us the most. So take your time with it and know that even a small amount of progress in this area can make a big difference to our overall wellbeing.

Self-Acceptance

Do you feel happy with all the different parts of yourself – your body, thoughts, feelings, habits, and so on – or are there some aspects of yourself you dislike or want to hide or change? It is a rare person who loves every part of themselves, but it is a great goal, not least because accepting ourselves is a fundamental building block of lasting self-development work. In certain cultures and groups self-criticism is commonplace, and people may even have learned (most likely not consciously) that it is a viable way of staying humble and growing as a person. However, excessive self-criticism actually leaves us feeling less-than and internally divided (between the parts that are criticising and those being criticised), and real self-acceptance is not at all the same as being big-headed or complacent.

For us to be able to become more self-aware and true to who we are, we need to feel safe with ourselves. This safety allows us to see more of ourselves without feeling defensive and also to be open enough to change. On the other hand, with an inner environment of self-criticism and conditional self-acceptance we tend to feel guarded and tense. It is very hard to create the inner level of safety and calm we need in order to grow in a meaningful way against that harsh backdrop. After all, if we cannot even trust ourselves (because deep down our self-criticism feels like an attack), how can we allow ourselves to be vulnerable enough to be genuine? Put another way, if we push a part of ourselves away, we also push away the key to understanding and integrating that aspect of ourselves.

Therefore, self-acceptance gives all parts of ourselves permission to be just as they are, creating a feeling of space in us. Within this space we can change and grow from the viewpoint of already being enough, which can also help to give us more resilience and more flexibility in our out-look and behaviour. However, it is clear that many of us need to work on this; one survey of five thousand people found that most had scored their self-acceptance levels at around 5.6 out of 10 (10 being the best) and only 5% of people scored 10/10.[17]

Self-acceptance is not just important for our self-development; it can also help to keep us healthy, as perfectionism has been linked to several chronic illnesses and has even been found to shorten our life. Another study found significantly higher mortality rates for people who were more perfectionist and neurotic, but, interestingly, this was not the case for people who scored highly in conscientiousness.[18] Perhaps, although both groups of people had roughly the same amount of work ethic or

---

[17] University of Hertfordshire 2014
[18] Fry and Debats 2009

ambition, their difference in attitude led to very different outcomes in terms of their health and happiness. While perfectionism is extremely conditional self-regard, self-acceptance is unconditional self-regard, and this is what we are aiming for: liking and caring for ourselves regardless of our status or what we achieve.

Self-acceptance from an early age

A fundamental reason that a lot of us struggle with self-acceptance is that it was not modelled for us as we were growing up. Many of our parents were self-critical and also believed that criticism was the most effective way of making sure that we didn't become nasty little miscreants, and this would have been the way their parents raised them also. For example, advice in the 1920s from prominent behavioural psychologist John B. Watson included not showing your children affection as it would damage them:

> Let your behavior always be objective and kindly firm. Never hug and kiss them, never let them sit in your lap. If you must, kiss them once on the forehead when they say good night. Shake hands with them in the morning. Give them a pat on the head if they have made an extraordinarily good job of a difficult task.[19]

Out of his four children, one of his sons committed suicide and his daughter, Mary, made several attempts to do the same. She was described as a rage-filled secret drinker, and her own daughter became suicidal but pulled through with guidance, later helping to create the American Foundation for Suicide Prevention.[20] What a legacy from someone who claimed to have the secret to raising well-adjusted children! Of course, this is an extreme example, but it shows how important connection and

---

[19] Watson 1928
[20] Wikipedia contributors 2018a

acceptance from our primary caregiver(s) are to our mental, emotional and physical well-being.

Many of our issues, both within ourselves and in our wider society, come from using the wrong tools for a certain task. Cold, detached logic cannot replace love, connection or acceptance and lead to healthy, happy adults. Expert in addiction and trauma Gabor Maté says that conditional acceptance is deeply wounding to children.[21] If they are loved only when they act in the way that we want them to, we pass on the message that they are not acceptable as they are, and this can stay with people their whole lives.

Therefore, self-acceptance is not a 'nice to have', but *essential* for understanding that we are enough as we are, allowing us to develop our own unique strengths and enjoy our personality and identity. If you feel that you are not very self-accepting and have in the past tried to change by criticising yourself you may be interested to know that, although your motivation to make a change was probably very healthy, a critical attitude keeps us out of our centre and this is where we need to be in order to grow. But, please don't criticise yourself for that! Accept that it has happened in the past and maybe decide to try a new approach.

In the exercise below I will take you through a very simple visualisation you can use for helping to boost your self-acceptance. As it is very short you can use it while standing in a queue, on public transport or anywhere else that it is safe to meditate.

Exercise 5.1: Self-acceptance meditation

a) Sit (or stand) comfortably and breathe in a natural and relaxed way, allowing tension to drop away from your body.

b) Visualise a bright, shimmering point of light in front of you. Without analysing why, imagine that it is absolutely perfect. It can be whichever colour and shape you like. Feel the harmony in contemplating something that is perfect.

---

[21] Maté 2016

c) Now visualise it moving towards you, this perfection. It keeps coming until it enters your chest and then creates a beautiful, shimmering field all around you: a field of perfection. Bathe in this feeling, there is nothing different that you have to do or be.

d) Give yourself permission to feel perfect in this moment by saying to yourself, 'I am perfect in this moment; I am more than enough.' Feel a warmth spread out through your body as you think that, and let yourself feel the self-love that accompanies it.

e) Keep feeling this for as long as you like, and when you want to stop, just bring your attention back to everything around you, and if your eyes were shut, softly open them. Allow yourself to recall this feeling of being enough whenever you want to as you continue with your day.

You can do this exercise whenever you like, several times a day even. Doing this exercise does not mean that we do not have flaws, or that we have to ignore them. Rather, it means that we accept our whole self completely as we are *right now*.

Self-acceptance and our flaws

It may seem as though being able to accept ourselves and looking at areas for improvement are opposite states. However, self-acceptance and self-love mean that we care about ourselves enough to be discerning, while unhealthy habits can often stem from a lack of self-acceptance, not an excess of it. So, if you are worried that being accepting of yourself means having low standards, that is not the case – in many ways they are higher, they are also just more realistic and kinder.

For example, if someone was taught that they were unloveable from a young age, they may fill themselves up with food as the next-best substitute for love. If they gain a lot of weight then other people in society may also reject them, hurting their self-worth even more and fuelling a self-perpetuating cycle. In order to become more discerning for themselves they will have to believe they are valuable and that they deserve love, which will also bring up the pain of acknowledging that they were not really loved and valued before. If they can accept feeling that pain as well as their worth, then they can progress to choosing the type of behaviour that befits someone who has value (which is everyone, regardless of their past, bodyweight or anything else).

Self-acceptance is interconnected with self-love, self-worth and self-respect. Coming from a place of being grounded in all of these qualities means we can examine our flaws constructively and realistically. And although finding the sweet spot between self-criticism and being discerning can be a little tricky (and we will usually be sliding around the spectrum), this is what we are aiming for, ideally. In the exercise below we are going to look at areas of ourselves that we have a hard time accepting, the feelings around them and a way of looking at them more positively. I recommend you do it with a sense of kindness to yourself.

Exercise 5.2: Things we do not accept

This is a simple exercise, but it requires a fair amount of introspection. If the answers do not come easily at first, just be patient and keep going. It is interesting because it can end up being a bit more nuanced than you expect, so please keep an open mind. You will need a piece of paper and pen, preferably, but a device is fine too.

a) Firstly, I would just like you to think of a couple of things that you do not accept about yourself, whether they are personality traits, preferences, habits, physical attributes or anything else. What are the things you most actively dislike, avoid, hide or distance yourself from? You can write them down in the first column of a table as in the example below; I recommend a maximum of five things – for example, 'I have weird feet,' 'I talk too much,' 'I'm overweight' or 'I get angry too easily.'

b) Going down the list one by one, you may notice that there is an internal sense of a fight or struggle as you read each item. What other emotions do you sense and how does it make you feel about yourself as you read the thing you are resisting? Write those feelings in the second column.

For the next three steps we will work on one area at a time, doing all of the steps for that one thing we dislike before moving on to the next one, as it is easier to stay with one issue and explore it more deeply, rather than moving back and forth between different ones.

c) So, looking at the first dislike or thing you are resisting, I would like you to try to identify the reason for your feelings about it. Take your time and stay open-minded – there may be several reasons and they may be in the past or present. Write as much as you like. Look at the example table below if you need some ideas about the kind of things to write.

d) Now I want you to write the positive side of what you are resisting – not the positive side of resisting it, but of the thing itself. Keep your mind open and if you feel there is nothing good about it, just try to accept your resistance, whilst knowing that there will be at least one positive because there is always a good and a bad side to everything.

e) And now I would like you to write an affirmation for this thing you have found hard to accept about yourself. I believe you will know it is the right affirmation for you because your body will feel neutral or good. However, if you still feel a lot of resistance that is OK because it can take a long time to really accept all parts of ourselves, and you may want to use this exercise again in the future. As you can see from the example below, you can accept the thing you dislike and yourself, but still have the intent to make a change for the better if appropriate. If there is something about yourself you don't need to change, or can't, then you could say something along the lines of: 'I accept my eye colour, even though society says it is not the most beautiful, it is right for me and is part of what makes me who I am.'

Things I dislike about myself	How it makes me feel	Reasons	Something positive about it	Affirmation
I have weird feet	Embarrassed, annoyed at my family genes, upset I can't wear sandals	Everyone else takes it for granted they can walk around barefoot at a pool, for example, but I can't The media portrays an image of beauty that is very homogenised, and variations are not really tolerated My friends tease me a lot also	My feet are very strong and they do not cause me any issues It is also a viable excuse to wear comfortable shoes all the time as I can't wear heels	I accept and love myself even with feet that look outside of the norm I have strong, healthy feet I do want to get pedicures more regularly, so I can connect with my feet more, because I have spent years hating them

f) Now go down to the next thing you are resisting and complete the above three steps, and then repeat this until you have finished all the steps for each dislike.

Now that you have done this exercise, do you have more insight into what you have been resisting and why? I recommend that you reread what you have written a couple of times and just try to have the sense of making space inside yourself for the parts you don't like, making them feel welcome and looking forward to expressing them in the most positive way. Maybe anger can become focused healthy action, or feeling ashamed of being overweight can become self-acceptance and addressing our needs healthily. Or maybe the thing we are resisting does not need to change at all, just our perspective on it.

You don't need to wait for someone else to notice your talents before nourishing them. You don't need others to accept you to feel accepted. You don't need to wait. You can

begin, at any moment, to work on noticing, nourishing, and
accepting yourself. You can work on being a better friend to
your reflection. You can start listening to yourself like you
wish other people would. You can become curious about who
you are. You can begin to learn the language of your mind
and body so that you can decode it, understand it, speak it.
You can work on understanding yourself instead of always
trying to make yourself into someone else.

—Vironika Tugaleva, *The Art of Talking to Yourself*

Self-acceptance and the feminine principle

Although most of us are not aware of it, many of our attitudes have their
roots in the history of our culture and family. When people are raised in
a certain way they pass many, if not all, of the same beliefs and feelings
that were imparted to them on to their own children. Although Victorian
morality gave birth to the self-improvement movement, it was very low
on self-acceptance. This makes much more sense when you understand
that some of the things they did not accept included slavery, child labour,
cruelty to animals and transportation of criminals to Australia. However,
there is a saying that culture is first a solution and then a problem, and
although Victorian morality was brilliant for ending many cruel practices,
it was not so great at fostering self-acceptance or accepting others, which
was reflected in the lack of gender equality, amongst other things. Even
nowadays, if you look at people with very strong, 'traditional' views, you
will often see echoes of this gender bias.

However, throughout history there have been many very strong
women. For example, one of the Prophet Muhammad's several wives
was a wealthy independent merchant who provided financial assistance
to her family and helped the poor, while another was highly respected
for her scholarly knowledge and rode into battle on a camel to avenge
a caliph who had been assassinated.[22] This was around AD 600, so long

---

[22] Wikipedia contributors 2018b

enough ago to be considered 'traditional'; however, if some choose to cherry-pick the more patriarchal bits of history and call only that *tradition*, this may point to a lack of acceptance of the feminine principle, both in themselves and in others. Although this book is not concerned with politics, or gender really, this rejection, suppression and condemnation of the feminine is something that has had far-reaching effects on people and their relationship with themselves.

I believe that hatred and suspicion of the feminine principle have their roots in shame and self-loathing (the antithesis of self-acceptance), and are often expressed as a need to control and to force others to submit to power. Like all unhealthy power-wielding, it can hold some people under a kind of perverse, mesmerising spell. If we were living in a long-standing matriarchal society, we might equally be fearful of the masculine. But, actually, fear and mistrust of either the masculine or the feminine will damage both, because they need each other. Strong people implicitly understand that we all hold the feminine and masculine principles within us, and that men and women should be free to live the lives that are right for them, accepting both themselves and others, and being comfortable with who they are.

A need to control and dominate, on the other hand, always stems from fear – 'I must make people live in a certain way in order to validate my beliefs and fears' – whether this is expressed as a desire for inequality between genders, races or other groups. Authentic values do not see us wanting to control others, but to celebrate people's potential and uniqueness. Therefore, I would be wary of any school of thought which tells you that you have to be a certain way because of your gender. This kind of thinking can be seductive to some because it provides a sense of identity (which should come from our authentic self, not from the outside in) and is also often based on a power imbalance, which, for some reason, we humans can go for like a moth to a flame. However, we are so much more than only our biology, and although it is good to understand where we have come from, it is important to intentionally look forward to who we want to become, both individually and as a society.

The reason I am going on about this is that understanding the feminine is crucial for having a deep understanding of acceptance. Because our mainly patriarchal culture is based on goal-oriented progress and problem-solving, the feeling of *not enough* often underlies much of what we do. For example, if men display vulnerability and emotion they are 'not manly enough', if women get frustrated at the battle to be seen as more than the sum of their biology they are 'not feminine enough', or if someone does not earn a good living they are just 'not enough' in general, and underneath it all there is often a sense of perpetual striving and very conditional love. While the masculine is about action and going out and getting what we need (and therefore great for motivation and achievement) the feminine is about everything that we need being right here, and includes the ability to receive, to just be with ourselves and to feel enough as we are. At the end of the day, what kind of person we are is up to us, but cultivating an appreciation of and ability to be in both states as appropriate makes us very balanced people. It gives us more access to the different parts of ourselves, and means we have a full enough personality that we do not need to define ourselves solely according to a narrow societally prescribed role. On the other hand, if we try to make women express only the feminine and men express only the masculine, or confine people to very gendered roles, we will block many people from achieving their potential as individuals.

So what is the feminine principle, then? It can be harder to pin down than the masculine because it is mysterious, wild, creative, unpredictable, deep, spontaneous and powerful. This may be quite at odds with certain beliefs about the feminine that some of us have been brought up with, such as pink things, pretty dresses or being scared of things. I have noticed that people who start to connect more deeply with their feminine aspect often become more centred, have more access to their deeper feelings and innate wisdom, and have more of an appreciation of nuance, as well as a more developed sense of humour. I do not know why, but I think it stems from connecting to ourselves at a much deeper level, gaining an understanding of subtlety and shades of grey, and being more able to see the funny side of things. There is also a greater ability to accept and heal ourselves and others.

Because, as mentioned above, the feminine has been less widely advertised and many people find it harder to understand, I have created the exercise below in order to help you practise tuning into your feminine aspect – enjoy!

Exercise 5.3: Embracing the feminine

In the first stage of this three-stage exercise we are going to look at our attitudes towards the feminine and see if anything may be blocking our ability to access it, so it is important that you let your feelings come out without interruption, censorship or judgement. Do not write what you think you should say (you already know that) or what you think is correct based on what I have spoken about above, but try to connect with how you feel on a deeper level. Do not edit or correct yourself, hesitate, or write out anything that you do not feel is genuine or from deep within you, even if you think it is a bit nasty. You will need a pen and paper and something to time yourself with.

First step

a)   You are going to write for five minutes in a stream-of-consciousness way with the starter phrase 'the feminine is'. To start with, just write the phrase out repeatedly until you naturally feel like writing something else, and then just go with that wherever it leads, without correcting it, reading it or stopping. It is fine if you run out of things to say – any time you get stuck just go back to writing the initial phrase over and over again until you feel like writing something else, and then continue with that as before.

b)   Now read back what you have written and see if there are any themes, or interesting clues to your relationship with the feminine. Does anything remind you of opinions held by your family or friends, or does anything feel charged, odd or out of balance? There is no need to explain anything right now, just being curious is enough.

Second step

c) Now we are going to do a visualisation in order to experience femi-nine energy – an experience is worth a thousand words, after all! Sit somewhere comfortable and quiet and breathe in a relaxed way.

d) I would like you to visualise all of the knowledge and creativity in the world, squashed into a shape that is hanging in space, right in front of you. You may see it as a dark shape or a black hole, perhaps. All of this knowledge is in its potential state, which means that it is not currently being explored, developed or expressed – it is pure being, stillness and perfect in itself. Within that there is a sense of mystery, of divinity and of eternity. You may experience this as heavy, like magnetism, gravity or solidity. It is 100% just *being*, not doing, and is peaceful and still. Can you feel the power in this?

e) Now visualise this shape moving towards you until it is centred in your torso. Feel its gravity and perfection filling your body. Can you feel that in this state you are whole, complete and self-accepting without question? Do you also feel as though you could draw whatever you need towards you, as the magnetic pull of it is so strong? Just be with this feeling for a few minutes before moving on to the next step.

f) I would like you to take a moment and reflect on how you feel about yourself while you are in this state. If you come out of it and start to feel self-critical, just take a moment to return to the feeling of being immersed in this energy and then reflect on how you feel again. Stay in that feeling for as long as you like and then, when you feel ready to open your eyes, take a few deep breaths before opening them slowly.

Third step

g) For the final part of the exercise I would like you to do the free-writing again, using the same phrase 'the feminine is' to get you started, and write whatever you feel you want to. Do not worry if you are writing more slowly, or if you come to a natural conclusion before the time is up. A large aspect of the feminine principle is mystery, so you may feel that you have less to write! If you would like to, you can also do some writing on how you see yourself when you are connected to the feminine within you. Try to maintain this connection as you write.

Having done the exercise, I would like you to compare your first piece of writing with the second. Has your understanding of or feeling towards the feminine changed at all? Also, did you feel a sense of acceptance for yourself during the visualisation? If not, that is absolutely fine, it is something you can work towards slowly, accepting the place you are in right now and knowing that you are enough even while aiming to improve. This attitude is one example of a perfect balance of the feminine and masculine.

Self-acceptance vs success

A common fear is that if we accept ourselves as we are then we will lose our motivation and desire to succeed. I like this one because it is literally the fear of being happy and finding that certain things are no longer important to us – it is like saying, 'But I want to want it!' Could this be because we are attached to a certain idea of what happiness should look like: a bigger house, better career or better-looking partner? Maybe for some of us the thing that scares us about 'enough' is the fact we might have a lot more time and space for self-reflection and we will see parts of us that we do not want to – we will see ourselves just as we are.

Because acceptance is one of the key foundations of self-development work, if we approach the work with an attitude of *not being enough* and thinking we will only ever become enough with loads of concerted effort, we are 100% guaranteed never to get there. It is one of those catch-22s and I think Yossarian would appreciate the irony of that! If we want to work towards more, then we think we must be experiencing less now – it's not our fault if we think this, it's the logic most of us have been raised with. However, being able to entertain the paradox of accepting ourselves and also having the desire to improve is essential to sustainable self-development work. 'Less' is a wobbly foundation to build on, while 'good', or at least 'OK', is something we can really work with.

So, while some use self-criticism to drive them, in the long run it cannot replace healthy self-motivation and self-love. We may achieve a lot in this state, but we won't feel satisfied with our success or ourselves. People in this trap instinctively know they need more of something, but unfortunately they often assume it is more of the same thing they have been chasing, rather than more love or self-acceptance. For many this becomes an endless cycle of creating exterior success without inner understanding or joy – a very expensive and lonely shell. If you find yourself in this position, I recommend redirecting a lot of your ambition towards self-acceptance and self-love instead.

Accepting our darker side

When we do not accept ourselves completely, the aspects we reject often end up in our *shadow*. This a part of ourselves that we are not aware of, but which colours our perceptions, feelings, words and actions. Everyone has a shadow, but some people are more afraid of it than others, fearing that if they acknowledge a part of themselves they see as scary or destructive it may take over. An example of this is when we repress our anger because we fear that it could hurt people or destroy something. Many of us have not been taught how to deal with strong or negative emotions in a healthy way, and have learned to either fight against them or push them down, rather than work through them.

Naturally, we should always seek out help if experiencing uncontrollable emotions that could be destructive to ourselves or others. It is important to remember that feelings often become heightened when we are not accepting of ourselves because we feel more vulnerable and unsafe. In addition, when we reject something within us we may cause it to seek expression in unhealthy or destructive ways that we find harder to control. So, by accepting our darker side, but also being aware of our feelings and discerning in our actions, we can stay more balanced and centred.

Accepting Our Feelings

Depending on what culture and family we were raised in, we will have had different emotions marketed to us differently. Happiness, success, generosity and humour may have been given out in colourful, glossy brochures, brought out and shared around and generally celebrated, while anger, rage, bitterness or grief may have been scribbled on used bits of paper, screwed up, and thrown at people or hidden away, never to be spoken of. This metaphor illustrates how we learn to seek out some emotions, but to feel shame or worry about others. Unfortunately, at the age we are learning this, we do not even know we are learning it, which makes it really hard to question later. We just take it all in like very absorbent little sponges.

And these habits do not always make sense – in some groups, excitement may be suppressed and rage glorified, for example, or people may express normal emotions in an unhealthy or odd way that puts us off them. By the time we are old enough to be autonomous and set out in the world on our own, many of us have a set repertoire of emotions we accept, some we aim for, some we reject and some we hide. This limits our whole experience not only of the world, but of ourselves.

For example, if we think about someone brought up to mistrust excitement who has an amazing opportunity fall in their lap, their natural first impulse might be excitement, but because it feels unsafe they push it away – thinking about problems that could happen or minimising the size of the opportunity in their head. Although this attitude may feel safer to them, they will never get to experience natural feelings of joy or delight and may even turn away from new possibilities in order to stay within their emotional comfort zone.

It may be interesting to contemplate which emotions, if any, you push away: happiness, excitement, anger, bitterness, jealousy or others? We all have at least a couple of emotions we do not enjoy feeling. This section is about learning to accept all of our emotions, not only the attractive ones, which may help us to experience more range in our lives. Rumi, a wonderful thirteenth-century Sufi poet, wrote his poem 'The Guest House' about accepting our feelings:

This being human is a guest house.
Every morning a new arrival.

A joy, a depression, a meanness,
some momentary awareness comes
as an unexpected visitor.

Welcome and entertain them all!
Even if they are a crowd of sorrows,
who violently sweep your house
empty of its furniture,
still, treat each guest honorably.
He may be clearing you out
for some new delight.

The dark thought, the shame, the malice.
meet them at the door laughing and invite them in.

Be grateful for whatever comes.
because each has been sent
as a guide from beyond.

—Jalāl ad-Dīn Muḥammad Rūmī [Rumi][23]

He writes about accepting not only the unpleasant emotions that pass through us, but the parts of ourselves we dislike. None of us can truly know ourselves without being able to tolerate the sometimes painful awareness of our darker feelings and impulses, because they are often a message from a part of us. Through screening these out we also lose access to a part of ourselves as a result.

In this section we are going to look at two broad areas of accepting our emotions: the first is accepting our feelings in general and the second is accepting emotional pain. As with all areas of acceptance, if it

---

[23] Rūmī 1997

was easy to accept then we would have done so already. It is the hard things we are left to work with, so go at your own pace and take it easy on yourself.

Accepting all feelings

There are pros and cons to being as self-aware as humans are, and one of the downsides is our tendency to judge everything. We sort things into good and bad, and make generalisations and rules. However, there is not one thing in the universe that is solely good or bad – and this includes emotions. If we have a rule that anger is unacceptable, for example, we severely limit how we can act and live as people. Or if we are always chasing happiness and running away from disappointment, I'm sure you know which state we are more likely to be in. Research has shown that avoiding negative emotions is a cause of many psychological problems. For example, men who suppress their feelings are more likely to suffer from depression.[24] On the other hand, learning to tolerate negative emotions can lead to resilience and good psychological health.[25]

Because emotions often bring messages from our deeper self, through being able to fully witness them we become more connected to ourselves. In the exercise below we will practise creating a feeling of space into which we can allow our feelings to emerge and be, without trying to change them. You can then use this visualisation the next time you are feeling a difficult emotion and do not want to trap it inside you.

Exercise 5.4: Spacious welcome

a) Sitting or standing where you are, with your eyes closed, I would like you to be aware of the inside of your torso. Sense its state and whether there is any tension or pain, and then just breathe and accept those sensations being there.

---

[24] Flynn et al. 2010
[25] Shpancer 2010

b) Now imagine that your torso is a spacious room, full of light. It has a lovely breeze blowing through open windows, filling the room with fresh air. Maintaining that sense of spaciousness, have the intention of accepting the way you feel right now, in body and mind. Just allow everything you feel to be there, with a sense of welcoming and space.

c) If you have an urge to struggle or resist, just keep breathing and accept that urge also. Do not try to fight it but have the sense of saying 'welcome' to the struggle while you continue breathing in a relaxed way and visualising the light, spacious room. If any emotions come up, let them be there also, without trying to change them – just accepting everything that comes in.

d) When you feel that you have done enough, take a few deep breaths and have a gentle move around and stretch of your body before slowly opening your eyes.

How do you feel after doing this? If you felt a lot of resistance you might just want to leave it for a bit and come back to it again later. This is something we need to practise day to day, and for many of us it will be a work in progress as it can take a lot of courage to feel an emotion or sensation we think of as negative (and even some positive ones) without trying to change it. I recommend that if this happens, you stay with the feeling as long as you can, but if you really feel the need to process an emotion, you can use an exercise from chapter 9, 'Processing Our Emotions', and then try this exercise again afterwards.

I want to stress again that accepting a feeling does not mean accepting a situation that is wrong or a boundary that is crossed. At the other extreme, it also does not mean feeling entitled to behave irresponsibly or vent our emotions recklessly onto others. It does mean accepting our feelings enough to let them fully develop and express themselves safely. Only acceptance gives an emotion the space it needs to communicate everything it wants to say, and we often find that when we have understood it, it resolves itself completely, leaving us feeling clearer and lighter.

Accepting our pain

In addition to being able to accept our emotions as they are, we also need to learn to accept our pain; however, this is the feeling that most of us want to push away more than any other. We may do this by numbing or distracting ourselves, or even by causing a different kind of pain that is easier for us to bear. However, being present and accepting of our emotional pain is essential in order for it to heal, because pain always contains within it the key for its own resolution. That means there is no way to move past our pain but through it.

> If I thought I could help you by putting you into an enchanted sleep and allowing you to postpone the moment when you would have to think about what has happened tonight, I would do it. But I know better. Numbing the pain for a while will make it worse when you finally feel it.
>
> —J. K. Rowling, *Harry Potter and the Goblet of Fire*
> (spoken by Albus Dumbledore)

Generally, the deeper our pain, the deeper the message and potential for growth and self-knowledge, but if you feel that you need a break or help from a friend or professional do not hesitate to get it; we all need support and guidance from time to time. The exercise below shows one way we can approach accepting these feelings of pain and hurt.

Exercise 5.5: Accepting our pain

Although feeling our pain is, well, painful, it is worse to repress it because then we hold it inside us indefinitely, like a fly trapped in amber. We might be forgiven for thinking it is neutralised then, but even in this state and even if we are not conscious of it, it is always affecting us. It may feel like a warning not to be open in a certain way again, not to dare to try or not to love. However, feeling hurt does not mean this; in most cases it is trying to tell us something essential about ourselves, such as 'You are precious, make sure you put your trust in the right people,' or 'The pain you feel at losing someone is a sign of how much you loved them.' If we are in great pain it means that we have been hurt right to the core of who we are, and this is the exact place that we want to get closer to, not to shut down.

Below, we are going to call to mind a painful feeling and just be with it without expectation, so you will want a little time and space for this. Although this pain would have arisen from a specific situation, we will not be thinking about the details of that, just focusing on the feelings. In addition, you may find that different parts of you, such as your inner child, are involved with the pain and want to be heard and included. If this happens, try not to shut them down, but welcome them. If you feel you cannot manage complete acceptance today, that is absolutely fine – just give it a go and take it easy on yourself.

a) Sit or lie comfortably, breathe in an easy way, and close your eyes. Pay attention to your body as you breathe, noticing your ribs and abdomen expanding and the feeling of air moving through your nostrils. As you do so, let tension fall away from your body and try to feel a sense of inner stillness and space.

b) Call to mind whichever painful feeling naturally comes to mind first and notice how your physical sensations shift. You can let any feelings come up but avoid engaging in any stories around your hurt, just feel your physical sensations and emotions and let them be as they are.

c) Continuing to breathe, stay with your feeling of pain as long as feels right to you (but feel free to skip to the last step if you feel overwhelmed). Although it is natural to experience resistance to your pain as well as strong emotions such as anger or anxiety, try to let those feelings be there without judging them and keep breathing. Part of you may also want to protect you from your pain by using defence mechanisms, such as creating a story around you being a victim or feeling superior and judging the people involved. However, we just want to feel our feelings, not to allow our minds to get caught up in stories or blame.

We are just being with our pain, accepting it without needing it to change.

d) When you feel that you have done as much as you want or need to, start to bring this exercise to a close by letting a feeling of love and appreciation for yourself grow in your heart. If the feeling of pain is still there, let the love expand around that, letting it know it is loved and included. Have the intention of knowing that while our pain may be deep, we have the strength and love we need to heal and grow from it and that there is no part of ourselves that we need to reject. When you feel ready, you can slowly open your eyes.

Well done, this exercise takes a lot of effort. It can be empowering to allow ourselves to feel pain without needing to change it and to realise that we can feel both pain and love for ourselves at the same time. Do not worry if you find that you could not release your pain through being with it; there are usually many layers to our feelings so this process can take time and sometimes other tools. In chapter 8, 'Recognising Our Emotions', and chapter 9, 'Processing Our Emotions', you will learn some exercises for processing your feelings, which may help you to work through your pain, so you can use an exercise from one of those chapters and then revisit this exercise and see if it has changed. As you do the work of accepting the hardest-to-accept parts of yourself, it is important to take your time and be kind to yourself. Acceptance cannot be forced; it is about allowing more than completing.

Accepting Other People

It is natural for us to make judgements about others; it is how we navigate the world and our relationships. However, when these judgements become too rigid or automatic they can create walls between us, inhibiting natural and authentic interactions. There are so many different types of people in the world, from bikers to birdwatchers, rock stars to astrologists. There seems to be no shortage of differences in personality, sexual preference or attitude to food, let alone the question of race. Is it really possible to accept everyone as equal? It is very common for people to begin to identify with a particular group as they grow up, and start to see other people as outsiders. Sometimes there is trust and understanding within the group but mistrust and misunderstanding of everyone else. Many of us may assume that we accept everyone, but if we notice our reactions to people when we are out and about, they may be different for different people. So although it is natural to have preferences, we should always be challenging our prejudices.

> There's no beauty without difference and diversity.
> Love unconditionally.
>
> —Rasheed Ogunlaru, coach-speaker-author

Prejudices can have quite a far-reaching impact on our life, both practically and in our personal development. In terms of emotional intelligence, thinking that certain people are beneath us creates space for some very unpleasant thoughts and attitudes to grow within us, fostering negativity where there should be self-awareness and love. Generally speaking, division between people that is based on fear is bad for our world and for us in many ways: it reduces our connectedness, humanity, potential for collaboration and mutual emotional support. The ego boost it gives us to feel different from and better than others is short-lived because it is not genuine at its root, and if some use this method to bolster their self-esteem or sense of identity they will probably need to have these thoughts frequently because they have a tendency to fade, revealing a sense of lack or emptiness within. On the other hand, if we want to have a really good time, then it is better to see the good that is present in others. After all, the more people we can relate to, the more people we can have fun with and learn from, leading to a much freer and more interesting life.

Rather than rejecting our judgements, if we temper them with acceptance we stand a much better chance of being able to think and act appropriately and compassionately. I have met people who fall too much on one side or the other and both can cause problems. Too much judgement and too little acceptance can alienate others, leaving us feeling isolated and alone. On the other hand, too much acceptance and too little judgement can lead to unbalanced relationships or being taken advantage of. Getting the balance right means that we can be open and safe, while not making assumptions about people's natures or intentions based on little information.

Exercise 5.6: Reading through statements of acceptance

This is a very simple exercise – I would like you to just read through the following statements and mull them over. If you have a reaction to any of them, make a note of it.

- I am not in a better position to judge others than they are to judge me.
- Other people are not trying to be the person I want to be, or to live life the way I want to live it.
- All adults are responsible for their own lives and happiness.
- All people have the right to be free to be themselves, whether I approve of their choices or not.
- It is too much responsibility to make choices for other people as well as for myself (except for children or other dependents).
- When other people are being 'difficult', there may be more going on – approaching them with compassion may help.
- Some people may have mental-health issues – how can we judge them for something that is never a choice? They may be suffering, so I should be kind.
- Some people are not as clever as others, but their strengths may lie in different areas. Remembering that many people are more intelligent than I am can bring a bit more humility to the equation.
- Some other people judge and reject me while I am being the person I want to be.
- If people are extremely overweight, remembering that they may be in pain and understanding they would be exactly the same person inside if they were thin can help me to relate to them as equals.

- If people have an obvious fault such as an addiction, it is likely that they are in need of compassion.
- People have an equal right to be happy and to be treated with respect.
- I cannot become better by imagining that others are worse than me.
- I can accept other people even when they don't like me.

Did any of the statements above feel difficult, or create an emotional reaction, even if logically it seemed to make sense? There is no *one* way to work on this, but through bearing one of these statements in mind the next time you find yourself with, or thinking of, someone you find hard to accept, it should be easier for you to challenge whichever judgement comes up. If you find yourself feeling oddly biased against someone, pay attention to your reaction and emotions: they may be reflecting back to you a part of yourself that you dislike.

Although it can be hard to think of ourselves as having prejudices, we all have them; the key is to be conscious of our prejudices and then challenge them. Many will be inherited from family, peers and culture, or created by experiencing something negative. Part of self-awareness is looking at our thoughts and beliefs and making sure they reflect who we are at the deepest level. One clue that a belief about someone may not be authentic to you is if it feels very charged or different from your normal state somehow. And it really helps if we remember to feel compassion – both for ourselves and for others – as it reminds us that we are all similar underneath the surface and all fallible and special in our own ways.

Accepting Situations

Sometimes a situation will come up that we just cannot stomach – it may feel irreconcilably wrong or unfair, perhaps. Our reaction to it and any anger are designed to give us the impetus to act, and many worry that feeling acceptance will diminish the power we have to do this. However, if we can accept what is going on whilst simultaneously harnessing the power of the anger or dismay we feel, we will have a much better chance of being clear-headed and acting intentionally. This is because acceptance helps us to be more self-aware and have a balanced view of the situation, rather than reacting reflexively and making a big old mess of things.

In general, I have found that people who have to endure difficult situations for a long time face a choice: to become consumed by it, or to protect themselves with a measure of acceptance. This allows them the kind of peace of mind that lets them sleep, stay healthy, recharge, communicate effectively, think creatively and make conscious choices. Allowing our feelings about a situation to take over can be exhausting and lead to illness, obsessive thoughts, poor communication or bad decisions. To put this in a nutshell: being controlled by our reactions puts us in a weaker position, while acceptance and being self-aware put us in a stronger position.

Depending on the situation, one tactic we could try is embracing the challenge that the situation presents. Whether it is forcing us to speak out, act, move, make a change or just to endure something unavoidable, each difficult situation presents us with an opportunity for learning and growth. This may sound flippant if something terrible has happened, and it may be years before you can see any gift at all in the situation, but I believe that for many people there will eventually be one. If you have had a terrible experience that you are having difficulty coping with then I strongly suggest counselling, but if it is somewhere between just a slightly annoying situation and a bad one then this section may help.

Exercise 5.7: Embracing the challenge

For this exercise you will need one difficult situation and a pen and paper.

a) Firstly, write out the whole situation, including any details you think are important and also how you feel about it. If you want to do something more creative, you can even draw it.

b) Now, when you have written or drawn everything you want to, try to step back and see the situation as a whole. If it helps, you can imagine being far above it. Write down the first things that you notice.

c) Picture yourself in the situation and, with an open mind, ask yourself what you can learn from this, or how you might grow. If you feel yourself being drawn back into the situation, it might be easier if you use the third person (he/she/they) when you consider yourself.

d) Wonder to yourself if there is one thing (or several) that might make the situation better, whether it is realistic or not, and write it down.

e) Now, with a very open mind – whimsical even – wonder: what would a really wise person do in this situation?

Take your time with this exercise – it is not always easy to work on things that are emotionally charged. If you ever notice yourself getting drawn back in to the drama or stories around a situation, just 'zoom out' again as if you were an eagle flying overhead. Hopefully this will help you to derive some benefit from a difficult time, possibly giving you more insight into yourself or helping you to grow in some way.

Accepting that Some Things Are Just Hard

An important ingredient of the alchemy of creating something great – whether that is a painting, an expedition, a relationship or a family, for example – is the ability to face difficulty and persevere. So many things in our world are geared towards avoiding difficulty that I feel many of us are unprepared for this level of exertion; and yet without it we will never achieve anything great. For example, speaking about the difficult process of writing, comedian Jerry Lewis said there is no way around the tedium of writing but through it.[26] This is a great description of the fact that the only way for the writing to evolve into something brilliant is if the author can accept that it is hard work and stay with it anyway, keeping going until the transformation is complete. And yet even though this is an essential

---

[26] Lewis 2018

part of the process of doing anything worthwhile, hardly anyone talks about the importance of it.

For many of us, if we are finding something difficult then we might start to think that it is not meant to be, we are not good enough, it is not the right time, we are coming from the wrong angle or we have not taken the right class, for example. In short, we may start to have quite far-fetched thoughts about why it is so hard. But, actually, some things just are hard; they are meant to be because if they were low-hanging fruit they would be commonplace instead of real achievements. Therefore, we are going to try a brief exercise in embracing things being hard and all the resistance and feelings that can arise as a reaction to that.

Exercise 5.8: Accepting things being hard

For this exercise we are going to look at one thing we find or have found hard, something that we have not managed to achieve in the way that we want because of our resistance to the amount of effort required. This could be anything from writing your book or exercising regularly to self-love, for example. You may find a pen and paper helpful.

Before we begin I want you first to acknowledge that you are a valuable person, and if you have found certain things hard to achieve that just makes you human. This exercise is not about criticising yourself, so if you find yourself doing that maybe come back to this after doing some of the self-esteem and self-love work in this book for a bit.

a)   First, think of something that stands out as a thing that you have found hard to achieve or complete.

b)   Now write out all of your reasons or excuses that have come up around not achieving this goal. For example, if you were aiming to exercise but then realised you have a work deadline, you just ate, you haven't eaten or you can do it later – include all of these types of thoughts. When you have done that, sit with a feeling of acceptance of your resistance and 'reasons' and the fact that you have not yet achieved your goal. Breathe naturally.

c) In this step I would like you to write out the feelings that came up when you attempted this goal but felt resistance. For example, still using the same example of not exercising, you might feel disappointed in yourself, fearful, annoyed at the energy that would be required, or something else. You may find that some of the emotions are younger, even from your inner child. Again, sit with a feeling of accepting the feelings you had in response to your goal and not achieving it yet, and self-compassion.

d) Now picture pushing through this resistance and achieving your goal, what would that look like, how would you feel and what would have changed for you in your life? Accept that this is possible, that you are not a 'failure' for not having done it yet, but that you are someone with the potential to achieve it. Feel a sense of making room for this achievement inside yourself.

e) Again, visualise yourself having accomplished your goal in the future, but now imagine looking back at how you did it, including the mental and emotional state, the amount of effort, and the actions you needed to achieve it. Make a note of these – you may want to reread them when working towards your goal.

f) Now give yourself permission to achieve your goal. You could phrase this as 'I accept my strength and ambition and I give myself my full permission to achieve [the goal] – this is what I am wholeheartedly choosing.' Allow yourself to feel a sense of expansiveness in you, as you make even more room for this achievement, and a sense of joy, purpose or resolve – whatever arises naturally.

The next time you take a step towards a difficult goal you can remember this exercise, accept the feelings that come up, stay with them and then take as much of a step forward as you are able to. However, if you do not feel any joy or a sense of purpose about achieving a goal but only dread or resistance, then you might want to reconsider whether it is authentic for you.

Sometimes we may be scared of being strong, capable or creative, because these qualities can push us out of our comfort zone. Many of the perimeters we create in our life are determined by our tolerance of change, vulnerability, looking stupid or hard work, in addition to what is right for us personally. I have noticed that a lot of people who are truly happy have expanded out into the fullness of their potential, while many who are bitter or narrow have not dared to. Seen in this light, it is clear that it is better to try and either succeed or fail at something we are interested in than to live within the shadow of our fear of trying. A large part of acceptance is accepting ourselves as we are, including our strengths, aspirations and potential. Although this is often uncomfortable, it can make the difference between a mediocre life and an exceptional one, as well as giving others the inspiration and permission to do the same.

I hope you have enjoyed this chapter on acceptance. This quiet and powerful attitude is surprisingly tricky to embody fully, but even just small increases in our ability to do this benefit us tremendously. I will leave you with one last quote from someone with an experiential understanding of the power of acceptance:

> My happiness grows in direct proportion to my acceptance,
> and in inverse proportion to my expectations.
>
> —Michael J. Fox, interview in *Esquire*, 2007

CHAPTER 6

Self-Love and Self-Esteem

As a baby you would have had immense confidence in your innate worth and loveability. When you needed something you would have demanded it (sometimes very loudly), rather than quietly waiting for someone to notice, and you would have expected love as your birthright, rather than hoped for it. Life, however, often has other plans and after a few bumps and bruises on the road we may be left with a much more fragile level of self-love and self-esteem than when we first arrived. For many of us the idea of self-love may seem over the top or self-indulgent even, because we may think of it as narcissistic or excessive self-regard. It is not over the top, however, but vital to our health and happiness, as is a good level of self-esteem.

Our levels of self-love and self-esteem have a huge impact on how we experience and treat ourselves, which in turn shapes how others see and treat us. The consequences for our quality of life are profound. You could take two people with equivalent skill levels, looks, background, intelligence and lifestyle, yet if one has low self-esteem they are much more likely to suffer from negative thoughts, psychological issues and illness, and may even have a shorter lifespan than the other. And although we all have worth, our views of how much of it we hold vary wildly from person to person, partly because of differences in personality and partly due to differences in upbringing. A common issue for many is finding it hard to get their level of self-worth exactly right. We may wonder why some amazing people seem to be hollowed out by low self-worth and harsh self-talk, while other people with questionable values or average skills may walk around as if they are the best thing since penicillin.

Whether someone is a famous actor, a leading author, absolutely beautiful or has a ginormous brain, without healthy levels of both self-love and self-esteem they will never be able to find the joy in their success and it will never feel like enough. It is only through accepting and loving ourselves and believing that we are worthwhile that we can stay present with ourselves long enough to know who we are deeply and get comfortable enough to enjoy ourselves. This is at the core of all self-development work: liking, loving and accepting ourselves and believing we have worth. From that strong core, many positive expressions of our self may radiate outwards, including our natural talents, creativity, power, love for others and the ability to stand up for our values.

In this chapter there are a variety of exercises you can use to work on self-love and self-esteem. I recommend going with whichever ones you are drawn to and choosing just one or two to start with, so you have time to process the results. Try doing them on a fairly regular basis – daily works well for most people. But, before we jump in, let's clarify what some of these terms centring on our self-regard mean for us.

The Differences and Similarities between Self-Love and Self-Esteem (and Self-Acceptance, Self-Compassion and Self-Confidence)

There is a lot of crossover between these concepts, but there are also key differences. Self-acceptance means being at peace with who we are, self-love is having unconditional love for ourselves, self-esteem is the belief that we have worth and self-compassion is extending compassion towards ourselves. This interconnectedness means that it is very difficult to completely do one and not another (e.g. accept ourselves completely and not love ourselves at all), but we may find we are better in certain areas than others. Although different, all of these qualities contribute to a feeling of being internally solid, integrated and 'ourself'.

Self-esteem and self-confidence are also very interconnected, of course, but self-confidence is more about believing we have the ability to do particular things well.[27] Self-esteem, on the other hand, is about believing we have worth, without the emphasis on specific achievements. So it is possible to be very competent and have high self-confidence in some areas, yet behind the scenes still feel that we are not worth much due to low self-esteem. Now let's look at the difference between self-love and self-esteem in more detail.

When we have self-love it is unconditional: we love ourselves as we would a baby. Not many adults can run around naked, weeing and pooing everywhere and still be loved, but a baby can, and that is a bit what self-love is like. It comes with truckloads of acceptance and no need to prove anything or even have bladder control. Author and psychologist Deborah Khoshaba defines self-love as 'a state of appreciation for oneself that grows from actions that support our physical, psychological and spiritual growth'.[28] So, although we do not get it from the outside world, the act of choosing healthy and positive things for ourselves reinforces our self-love.

On the other hand, because self-esteem is about us thinking that we are good and valuable, it does have more of an element of evaluation in it. For example, someone with healthy self-esteem may feel that they are attractive, competent, interesting or worthwhile, amongst other qualities. With good self-esteem we look at things in a way that confirms our value, rather than looking for proof of the opposite, as with low self-esteem. Also, with healthy self-esteem it is our own opinion of how we are doing that matters, rather than other people's – a much stronger position to be in.

I feel that self-love is centred more in the heart and self-esteem more in the mind, and this is reflected in the following exercises. If you are not sure whether to start with self-love or self-esteem, I would say it does not matter too much as after your first exercise you will probably have a feeling of where to go next, but that working on self-love is always a good bet. Let's start by looking at why it is so important.

---

[27] Burton 2015
[28] Khoshaba 2012

Self-Love

Why we need it

Self-love is essential for self-care, healthy relationships and accepting ourselves no matter how we act or what we are doing. This does not mean that we do not need to take responsibility for our actions, but it does mean still loving ourselves even if we make a mistake, do not fit into society's idea of what is pleasing, or fail to reach unattainable standards of wealth or beauty, for example.

If we love ourselves then we naturally make choices that reflect our personality, values and boundaries. We are not thinking of what to do externally to prove that we are loveable, or of ways to get love and hold on to it. Rather, we so completely feel our love for ourselves that it fills us up and attracts more love towards us. So, to love ourselves is to be present with who we are and not ashamed or apologetic, but celebratory of our true nature.

Working on Self-Love

Sometimes when working towards unconditional self-love, memories and feelings of not having had it in the past may come up and emotions such as anger, rage, shame or grief may surface. There is no way around these feelings but through, if we want to heal on a deep level. On the plus side, this pain is likely to be the part of ourselves that knows we are deserving of love telling us that something is, or was, wrong. If you feel you need to work through some of these feelings, you can use one of the exercises from chapter 9, 'Processing Our Emotions', and then come back to this one; or if you feel that you need to take a break or get some professional help, that could be a great idea too.

Working on self-love with our inner baby

Before we start I would like you to think: 'Wow, I am amazing,' and notice your reaction. Is it internal laughter, discomfort, complete agreement?

With self-love there is nothing to prove, nothing you could possibly do to get more love. You are just enough as you are. An advertiser's nightmare; a tiny baby's reality. And for that reason our first exercise is going to centre on that part of you (not the advertiser).

Some of us have seen photos of ourselves as babies; a few of us even remember being a baby – I do. There was a feeling of calm, and an awareness of everything and everyone around me, without the need to judge anything. Everything was enough – and so was I. You may not remember that feeling, but we have all had that experience, that way of being inside us, even if it has been filed away for a long time. And that is what we are going to be getting in touch with in this exercise.

Please note that if you are triggered at any point it is fine to stop. People who have suffered the loss of a baby, had a tough time giving birth or who were mistreated as a baby may find this exercise too hard to do, in which case you can try another instead. This exercise focuses on a 'tiny baby' because this is when we were new, untouched and in a pure state. However, even if you had a rough start (chemical dependency or illness at birth, for example) you can still visualise this little baby as pure and completely deserving of love – as all babies are.

If you feel a little uncomfortable with the amount of love created in this exercise, you can stop or just visualise the amount of love you can handle, and this will likely increase as you repeat the exercise in the future. In this exercise we are going to use a visualisation to create a slightly different world, so please use your imagination to make it very real, as real as you can – even if it seems silly, try to go with it because it is a lovely exercise. There are quite a few steps so I recommend reading one paragraph at a time and completing it before going on to the next, rather than trying to remember the whole thing.

Exercise 6.1: Inner-tiny-baby love

Find somewhere quiet and comfortable for this visualisation, and you may want a pen and paper. If at any point you feel worried that you are not doing the exercise correctly, just know that you are fine and trust yourself, because excessive self-criticism is a block to self-love. It is important to approach this exercise with an attitude of self-kindness.

a) Close your eyes and, taking a few deep, slow breaths, let any tension fall away as you feel more and more centred and at peace. When you feel ready you can start the visualisation by following the steps below.

b) In this scenario we live in a world where we can give birth to ourselves, the self we were as a baby (our inner baby), and both men and women can do this. The delivery was ridiculously easy (in whichever way your imagination likes) and your inner tiny baby is being cleaned up and weighed and cared for in a nearby room. You are waiting, peacefully, yet with a strong sense of anticipation to hold your inner baby in your arms.

c) You want your inner baby to come into a very loving environment, so before they are brought in, I would like you to visualise any old negative feelings or emotions easily draining out of your body into the earth, being absorbed and disappearing deep underground. You can visualise this on each out-breath, if that helps. When you have done that for yourself, do it also for the room you are in. This does not have to be a sterile hospital room, it can be beautiful, homely, full of light – whatever makes you feel relaxed and happy.

d) Now that you have cleared the room and yourself, it is time to fill the space up with love. You can imagine angels, ancestors, animals you like, cartoon characters – anyone who is very loving – being in the space and surrounding you with love. You can see it pouring out of their hearts like a warm glow, filling the room. Anything that is not love can be asked to leave your space for this exercise and you can feel it go (it is common when feeling this much love that you become very aware of anything that is out of harmony with that).

Please note that if ever you feel you do not deserve this much love, or are struggling to visualise and feel such a large amount, the thoughts that 'the tiny baby deserves it' and that 'there is plenty of love in the universe for each person' can really help, or you can try saying, 'I give myself permission to feel, give and receive all this love.'

e) When you and the room feel completely full of love, you know it is time for you to meet your little tiny inner baby. The door opens and someone enters, carrying your inner baby with care. They are wrapped in a blanket and you notice a crystal on the centre of their forehead. It shimmers and is whatever colour seems right to you. It is the essence of your baby's specialness, their own unique nature that they are too young to express, that makes it glow.

f) You receive the baby into your arms and as you look down on them, you feel enormous love spilling out from you, encircling them, embracing them, filling them up. Your love is a beautiful, pure thing. Now you tell the baby, who is your ultimate love, your darling, everything you love about them, everything you want to say. You can write this down or just say it in your mind or aloud. Let your heart feel expansive as you express your pure love and admiration for your inner baby.

g) When you feel ready, having expressed everything you wanted to, hold your baby to your chest. Feel the love between you and your baby and, as you feel that, feel the love merging. As it does so, feel your heart expanding, finding room for the energy, the being of your inner baby and all that love, inside you. Feel your inner baby taking its rightful place within you and, as it merges with you, feel all the love spilling out, filling your torso and limbs. Feel the sense of being complete and being enough filling your whole body and your mind. Feel the unified sense of knowing that you are enough as the love spreads throughout your whole being.

h) Take a moment and sit with this feeling of being filled up with love, unified with your inner tiny baby, self-acceptance and self-love. Enjoy the feeling of knowing there is nothing you can do to increase the amount of love you deserve, that you deserve as much as will fill you up and more. If you want, you can say something to your inner baby, such as 'I love you and I always will.'

i) When you are ready to end the exercise, take a deep breath in and, breathing out, slowly open your eyes.

How do you feel? Take a moment to think, 'Wow, I am amazing' again, and notice your reaction. Is it different now than before doing the exercise? Going forward you can visualise your inner baby when you are remembering to love and prioritise yourself. It will give you extra permission and a focal point for your intention.

Finding your self-love mentor

The next exercise is also a visualisation, but more of a fun one. You know how little children can have invisible friends? Well, we are going to intentionally create one for ourselves. This friend is going to be our self-love mentor and will help to teach us how to love ourselves, and remind us of this whenever we think of them throughout the day. As with Jung's archetypes (universally understood concepts, such as *mother* or *hero*), I believe you will understand what I mean when I say you are imagining a 'mentor' who has mastered something. This mentor has mastered self-love and we are going to ask them to teach us about it.

And you can let your imagination run wild: during the exercise your mentor can turn out to be a unicorn, an angel, a six-foot teddy bear, a purple monster – whatever pops into your head. On a more mundane level, we could call it a tool for focusing our attention in a specific way. But they are far from mundane: they are brilliant. You can have them look like and be literally anything. Glitter explosions may go off every time they move or they may be a superhero with special powers – whatever feels right to you.

Exercise 6.2: Calling in a self-love mentor

You will want to be somewhere quiet and have a little time to do this. You might want something to write with in case you want to draw your mentor or write down anything they say.

a)   Close your eyes, breathe and relax; do this until you feel comfortable and grounded.

b)   Now I would like you to let a feeling of warmth and love grow in your heart. It can have a colour and a shape if you like. For several breaths, let this colour and feeling grow stronger and clearer.

c)   Imagine a beam shining out from this feeling – it is like a bat signal, but is calling your own perfect self-love mentor. Have the intention of the perfect mentor for you responding to this and reaching out to you. There is no rush, keep breathing and feeling the love until something pops into your mind.

d)   When you do sense or see something, say 'hello' to it in your head and see how it responds (if it is not loving, then this is not your self-love mentor but probably a distraction from your mind; just repeat the step above again).

e)   Ask your mentor if they can fill you with a feeling of love, and just let yourself bask in that for a while.

f)   When you feel ready, you can ask them anything on your mind, but a really good question is how to increase your level of self-love. If you relax and wait with an empty mind, an answer might pop into your head in the form of words, images or feelings. You can ask any other questions you like, including about specific situations.

g)   When you feel that it is time to bring the exercise to an end, slowly open your eyes.

h)   And now, if you like, you can draw your mentor or write out any of the advice they had for you.

Now that you have done this you can visualise your self-love mentor as often as you feel like throughout the day. Their job is to teach you how to love yourself unconditionally, but I also recommend that you ask them to fill you with love at least once a day. I know that it may seem very superficial, imagining something like this, but when we draw on our imagination we also draw on aspects of ourselves, so really this mentor represents the part of us that knows how to love ourselves unconditionally, but which we may not have been able to easily access. So when we ask our mentor how to love ourselves, we are really accessing our own ability to love ourselves, something that would probably have come naturally to us under the perfect circumstances.

If you ever feel like the image of your mentor needs to change, that is fine; the most important thing is their way of being. And in the future you will not need to visualise a mentor at all, you can simply love yourself; however, it is great to have this up your sleeve for times of need.

Self-love and self-care

Doing exercises like the ones above helps as long as we are expanding our self-love in other ways also; for example, in the choices we make, our self-care and how we treat ourselves. We would not want to use an exercise as a way to try to fix a week's work of self-criticism or putting ourselves last. For this reason, we are going to do a short exercise where we will identify the main five things that we want or need right now. Getting in touch with our deeper needs confirms our love for ourselves and helps to make self-kindness a regular habit.

You will want a pen and paper and a bit of peace and quiet, as well as an open mind. For this exercise to work best, it is better not to make assumptions about what we want, but allow our deeper desires to float up to the surface without prompting, whether they are self-care practices or other items or activities.

Exercise 6.3: Self-care is self-love

a)   Breathing in a natural, relaxed way, centre yourself in your heart. Become aware of a feeling of self-love growing there (you can use your self-love mentor to help if you like) – feel the fullness and warmth of it.

b)   Now I would like you to sit with this question, and ask your mind to kindly stay out of the way so the answers can come up from somewhere deeper: 'As someone who deserves love, what is something I can do that will make me feel more loved, and help me in some way?' Sit with an empty mind and wait for the answer, which may be in words, images or an impulse. Repeat this five times until you have up to five answers, writing them down as you go and spending as much time as you need to.

c) If you like you can go through the list and for each item ask yourself, 'How can this increase my self-love?' and again wait for an answer, which you can write down. Take your time.

d) When you feel that you have finished, review what you have written and try to take it in. Think of ways you can meet your wishes and needs which feel right to you.

This exercise can be really fun, because although when we aim for self-care we might think of exercising or getting a haircut, we may actually find we need some quite interesting things. Whatever came up, whether it is bouncing on a space hopper or learning to lip sync, try and make a plan to do it, as long as it is safe. Then when you are doing these things, consciously let the feeling of self-love expand within you. Taking action like this is the practical aspect of self-love and it can reinforce your love for yourself and therefore should always be a part of your life.

Ways of boosting self-love that may be counterproductive

We all crave that warm, full, satisfied feeling of love, but might not realise that that is what we are missing or that it is possible to give it to ourselves. While exercises such as those above are healthy ways of meeting this need, many of us instinctively reach for things that satisfy or distract us in the moment, but do not lead to lasting self-love (although it is a good sign that we are trying to help ourselves). We may try to create the same feeling as love by using alcohol, excessive eating, drugs or meaningless sex, or we might use other addictive, numbing or self-destructive behaviours to distract us from feelings of emptiness within us.

However, it is always best if we go right to the source, which in this case means giving ourselves love, intentionally and consciously, until we are filled up with it and the effects ripple out to all other aspects of our life. No one and nothing else can do this for us, and if we try to use substitutes for self-love we will end up feeling even emptier than before. However, it is never too late to learn to love ourselves and give ourselves permission to be happy.

Motivation for increasing self-love

This is a little section to give you some extra inspiration for your self-love work.

1. You'll inspire others to love themselves

If you love yourself, you will have plenty to give to other people, and you may give many other people in your life permission to love themselves. Loving yourself is far from selfish, therefore; it is an act of graciousness that comes from a place of 'enough for everyone'. Love is not something we can earn; it is a birthright – but because so many of us forget how to love ourselves the more role models we have the better.

2. Self-love keeps us healthy

When we love ourselves then staying healthy, getting the medical care we need or taking care of our emotional needs is a no-brainer. It is also a key factor in helping us to maintain a healthy environment around us, which benefits our friends and families too. Staying healthy in these ways also enables us to be strong and supportive to others.

3. We will have better relationships

Those who lack self-love often experience anxiety in their relationships or a desire to push people away, because true intimacy requires that we let other people in (and for this we need to feel safe and loveable). Through maintaining a good level of self-love, we can receive love from others and give it to them in return, while staying centred in ourselves and present enough to connect to them deeply. We also show others that we deserve love and respect through how we treat ourselves, so having a good level of self-love will help us to avoid unhealthy relationships.

4. Self-love gives us more access to all of ourselves and a strong core

Building a solid foundation of self-love enables us to create a solid sense of self, one that does not implode every time we fail or are rejected. Being strong and integrated at our core makes all of our other self-development work authentic and real. There is no true self-development without self-love because, as the saying goes, 'You can't polish a turd, but you can roll it in glitter.' So without a strong core of self-love, if you believe you are unloveable or worthless at the core, all the self-development done around your periphery will just be glitter, and on the inside you will keep feeling like c$&p.

You instantly know when you meet someone who loves themselves: they have a kind of feeling about them, a glow. That is what we want for ourselves, to feel at home and safe within ourselves, regardless of what is happening outside. This is one of the most important things we can do for ourselves, and we deserve it because, as Byron Katie says: 'Do you want to meet the love of your life? Look in the mirror.'[29]

Self-Esteem

Why we need it

Having healthy levels of self-esteem not only leads us to treat ourselves and others with dignity and respect, it is also crucial for our mental and physical health. For example, it has been found that having high *competence-based self-esteem* (only feeling good about ourselves when

---

[29] Katie 2007

achieving or good at something) is related to heart problems and burn-out, while high *relation-based self-esteem* (only feeling good about our-selves if others like and accept us) may result in issues such as asthma and rheumatoid arthritis.[30] Not only that, but low self-esteem at age eleven to twelve has been linked to developing both eating disorders and psychological problems by the age of fifteen to sixteen.[31] It can affect our behaviour also – low self-esteem in teenagers means they are more likely to engage in risky behaviour (of the bad sort),[32] and has also been linked with aggression, antisocial behaviour and delinquency.[33]

Strangely, although many people are experiencing low self-esteem, narcissism is also on the rise. However, although this may seem an extreme display of self-love, it actually reflects a deep uncertainty of one's worth and there are some fairly big differences between narcissism and high self-esteem. For example, research has shown that although narcis-sists often feel that they are great in terms of qualities like intelligence and extroversion, they do not feel that they are particularly moral or nice, unlike people with high self-esteem.[34] Another way they differ is that nar-cissists much prefer to think of themselves as socially dominant and hav-ing control over other people, but people with high self-esteem do not.[35]

Most of us do not need to worry about being narcissistic, but it is a good idea to avoid using the same methods narcissists use to boost our self-esteem (mainly because they do not work). For example, social-media addiction has been linked to both narcissism and low self-esteem,[36] prob-ably because people are seeking the approval of others to bolster their self-worth. However, this is not a viable way of feeling better about our-selves as it does not 'stick', and when the effect rapidly wears off we need to do something else to elicit approval all over again, making it addictive.

---

[30] Johnson and Rasjuli 2001
[31] Button et al. 1996
[32] Jackman and MacPhee 2015
[33] Donnellan et al. 2005
[34] Campbell et al. 2002
[35] Brown and Zeigler-Hill 2004
[36] Malik and Khan 2015

Remembering that the definition of healthy self-esteem means that we value ourselves regardless of the opinion of other people is very important in this regard. Especially as one out of four teenage girls and 18% of teenage boys in Canada reported having experienced cyberbullying, which was the likely cause of their lower levels of self-esteem.[37]

Therefore, as we work on our self-esteem we should remember that we are looking to reconnect with our intrinsic value, not trying to score points to increase some external estimation of our worth, which leaves us more vulnerable than before. So, to sum up, if we work on building a healthy level of self-esteem we could protect our health, weather life's ups and downs better, and depend more on our own good opinion than anyone else's, which will help us make authentic decisions for our life.

Working on Self-Esteem

Although our levels of self-esteem are usually set early in life, it is possible to work on them to bring them into a healthier range. While there can be a genetic component to low self-esteem, nurture also has quite a strong effect, which means that we can improve our self-esteem through conscious effort.[38] However, unlike self-love, it is not a case of the more the better as when our self-esteem is too high we may believe that we are better than others, be arrogant or feel anxious about sustaining the level of achievement needed to keep our self-esteem that high. On the other hand, when it is too low we may think and act negatively, choose unhealthy relationships, avoid taking chances on things that would make our life better, experience imposter syndrome, and have an all-round rubbish time.

Therefore, we are aiming for a healthy level of self-esteem, one that will allow us to be comfortable with who we are, be able to take constructive criticism and to fail at things without feeling terrible. If you would like to evaluate your level of self-esteem before you try the exercises, you can use the Rosenberg Self-Esteem Scale,[39] which you will find online. Do not

---

[37] Cénat et al. 2014
[38] Nauert 2015
[39] Rosenberg 1965

be hard on yourself if your self-esteem is low, it is always positive to know which areas we can work on to feel better – after all, our current weaknesses are also our areas of future growth.

It does take effort, patience and some courage (change can be scary), because some things that we have been putting up with may no longer feel appropriate, relationships may have to change and we may find ourselves asking for more. If that worries you, then imagining living your whole life without this happening can be a great motivator. Ok, let's start this work by looking at our thoughts.

Our self-esteem and our thoughts about ourselves

Have you read the advice where you speak to yourself only as you would to your best friend? It is good advice, but first we are going to try to excavate a couple of our internal trolls, looking at your self-talk, how it makes you feel and where those thoughts might have come from, before moving on to more positive thoughts.

Exercise 6.4: Our thoughts about ourselves

You will want a pen and paper and some quiet time to do this exercise. There are quite a few steps, because this exercise works on a couple of different levels, so take your time and try to stay open-minded.

a)   Think of some of the harsh things you typically think about yourself and note them down in one column, leaving spaces between them. Be completely honest even about the really ugly things you think. If you need some prompts, think about things you might say to yourself when you fail or make a mistake, someone is unhappy with you, your relationship hits turbulence, or you fail to reach a goal. If you are very self-critical, you can even include negative things you say to yourself when you do well.

b)   Now I would like you to have a think about where each thought might have come from, going down the list one at a time and writing your ideas in a second column. The thoughts might be from parents, siblings, peers, TV, society or yourself. This is not about blame, just detective work – after all, how many babies and toddlers look as though they are treating themselves like that? Generally speaking, you want to go as far back as you can, but you can note down anyone or anything you feel is relevant.

c) In a third column we are going to write down what thought we would think instead, in an ideal world. This is not meant to be rose-tinted, just much more in line with our personality (again, aiming for healthy, not high, levels of self-esteem), so it should be both kind and authentic.

d) Take a moment and read through the two columns of statements. How did each make you feel? Is it more uncomfortable to read the negative or the positive statements about yourself?

e) Now we are going to do something slightly different, and I recommend being relaxed and having an open mind. Read through the statements in the first column, and underneath write the world view that person has (I know it is you, but you might want to imagine it is someone else, just for this step), how they see life, what kind of person they are and what kind of life they have. Take your time and when you have finished, have a read through and ask yourself whether this description matches your world view, your personality, your life. If not, how is it different?

f) Now, staying relaxed, read through the column of more positive statements, and underneath write what kind of world view this person has, how they live, what kind of person they are and how others see them. Take as much time as you need, and when you have finished read it through and see if you feel this description reflects you, your life and others' opinions of you (those people whose opinions you value, anyway) accurately? If not, how is it different? And how does it feel reading through this description?

g) So, now we have looked at our negative thoughts about ourselves, some more positive and realistic thoughts, and how both relate to different ways of seeing life and ourselves. It is important to understand that we have the power to see ourselves for who we actually are, rather than how we have been taught to see ourselves. However, many of the people who accidentally gave us some incorrect thoughts may have given us amazing skills also, so it is a good idea to acknowledge the good, rather than just feeling blame. Go through the list of people one by one, and say something for each along the lines of: 'Thank you for everything you taught me. I forgive you for teaching me this idea that is incorrect and I forgive myself for believing it. I can let it go now and be free.' It is great if you can feel the forgiveness in you, but do not worry if other emotions come up – just feel them too. It can be sad to think of a child being taught they are less than they are, but also great to know that we can correct this.

h) End this exercise by acknowledging all your hard work – I know it is not easy to challenge our deepest beliefs, so really let yourself feel proud. Although you will not change overnight, when you notice yourself thinking negatively about yourself or your life, ask yourself, 'Is this thought authentic to who I am or my life?' What we are really asking is whether our mind is running a rehearsed story or speaking the truth about us. Choose truth – it is a lot more fun.

Living in line with our real value is so important to realising our potential. If we do not address low self-esteem then we can end up feeling bitter, frustrated, depressed, or jealous of others who are living and loving more fully than we are. These unpleasant emotions are actually trying to tell us we deserve more; but if we do not understand that and take action to resolve them they may become our reality instead of transient messages. On the other hand, when we recognise our worth it can give us the space and authority to express different facets of ourselves in a more complete way and be able to receive what we need for fulfilment. Well done on taking this first step towards recognising your true worth. The next step is to get the inner kid on board.

Low self-esteem and our inner child

If we have low self-esteem, the chances are that our inner child is still feeling a little neglected, unseen or unloved. Therefore, in the exercise below we are going to give our inner child some attention, love and praise. Connecting to this part of us is very powerful, so it is important that you treat yourself kindly, just as an amazing parent would.

Exercise 6.5: Inner-child work for self-esteem

You will want some peace and quiet for this exercise, and also I highly recommend that afterwards you write down what you said to your inner child and how you felt. It is good to read this again later when you have had some time to let the self-development dust settle.

a) Sit comfortably and let your breath come and go in an easy way as you relax your body. With each out-breath, let even more tension go.

b) Call to mind an image of yourself as a child, whichever age feels right to you. If you are not sure, I would go with four or five years old. Notice how *little you* is dressed, how they look and their mannerisms. Where are they standing and what are they doing?

c) Now say hello to this child in your mind. They may come up to you and want a hug or to sit on your lap, or may be content to stand or play where they are. I would like you to imagine sending them love, from your heart. This love surrounds them like a warm blanket and you can actually feel them accepting it.

d) Now I would like you to tell your inner child what you really like about them. If you want to, you could write out a list of statements and then, one by one, say them to the child. With each statement, really see the child's reaction. You might see them swell with pride, or feel warm and secure. They won't be about achievements (such as you won that award), but things you like about their personality and maybe even appearance. The statements might look like these, for example:

- *You are really funny*
- *You have a wonderful sense of imagination*
- *You are very clever*
- *You are very brave*
- *You are very interesting*

    I recommend that you really try to let each positive statement into yourself also, basking in the feeling and the connection with your inner child, feeling the love between you.

e) When you have said everything you wanted to, see how your inner child is feeling about themselves. If they are feeling positive, why not let that feeling merge into you, your heart and your mind, and spread out through your whole body. If they are feeling a little low, on the other hand, keep sending them love.

f) If you have anything you would like to say to your inner child before you end the exercise, such as 'I love you' or 'it's so great spending time with you' (whatever feels right, as long as it is positive), say it in your mind and notice their reaction, then let that feeling spread through you also.

Well done on doing this exercise. I know these visualisations can be tricky sometimes – our minds often try to distract us and sometimes part of us may resist doing an exercise like this. That is OK, you can always come back to it later. Sometimes when we start treating ourselves nicely the contrast with how we have been treated in the past can bring up feelings of anger or hurt, or old memories. This is appropriate, honour them by being with them without judgement and giving yourself the time and space to feel them fully (exercise 5.5 in chapter 5, "Acceptance and Self-Acceptance", is on accepting our pain, and may help).

Evidence of our worth

The next exercise is a simple one to balance out the trickier ones above, although simple does not necessarily mean easy! You can do it, though – if you find it hard just stick with it until you finish.

Exercise 6.6: Ten great things

All you will need is a pen and paper and some time to think. This is a great exercise because it helps you to acknowledge your worth. It is important to be kind to yourself, rather than agonising over it – keep things light. Oh, and you cannot repeat the same things every time you do this – that would be too easy! You have to find some new ones each time.

a) Simply check in with how you are feeling in your body and emotions right now, and breathe in a relaxed way.

b) Now list ten things that are great about you.

c) You may find that many of the qualities you listed are mostly good from other people's point of view – e.g. 'I am a great Dad' or 'I am a very giving person.' Just to be nice (because this can be a hard exercise!) you can have up to five that are about how you are kind or helpful to others, but the others have to be exclusively about you – e.g. 'I know how to have fun' or 'I have a great sense of humour.' Do not include superficial things – for example, 'I make £xx a year' – just qualities about you as a person.

d) When you have written out ten things, pay attention to how you are feeling again, both emotionally and physically, and write this down. Notice if your mind attempts to reduce these qualities with self-criticism or sarcasm, and if it does, shift your focus back to the great qualities you have.

While you did this exercise, could you sense the part of you that is in agreement with all of the statements, that knows they are true? That part of you is probably your authentic self and it is good to connect with, and listen to, it regularly. You can do this exercise every day when you are working on your self-esteem, as well as every now and then for a top-up. The easier you find it the higher your self-esteem probably is.

The great thing about this exercise is that you are choosing the statements to make, which is important because, as mentioned before, repeating extremely positive statements has been shown to make those with low self-esteem feel worse. So it is OK if you need to start very small, as long as these statements feel true to you. You can then increase to larger qualities as your self-esteem rises.

Ways of boosting self-esteem that may be counterproductive

There are some methods of boosting self-esteem which, according to logic, seem like they should work, but can actually have the opposite effect. Our minds can be so contrary sometimes!

Positive affirmations

Many people have tried to boost their own self-esteem by repeating positive statements, but research has shown that people with low self-esteem feel worse after using positive affirmations. This may be because it highlights the gap between reality and what they are trying to convince themselves of. However, they do seem to work for people with good self-esteem, so if you feel you are at a healthy level but need a boost then they may work for you.[40] For everyone else, we are going to discuss using 'rational affirmations' instead, in chapter 12, 'Thinking Consciously'.

Praise people like you should

Knowing that self-esteem is important, many well-meaning parents and teachers have attempted to boost it through giving inflated praise, but evidence shows this can be worse for children, leading them to worry more about failure and avoid taking on challenges.[41] Actually giving the appropriate amount of praise for an achievement has been shown to be a lot more successful in boosting children's self-esteem. Although this one is about other people, it may be useful to understand why others trying to make us feel better with overblown compliments does not work.

---

[40] Wood et al. 2009
[41] Brummelman et al. 2014

Trying to bolster our self-esteem with success

Many people's drive to succeed is rooted in a need to prove themselves because they feel that they are not enough as they are. However, chasing achievements or other qualities as a way to bolster self-esteem is a flawed strategy, because then we will only think well of ourselves while achieving or having a certain quality (e.g. good looks) and our self-esteem will be dependent on that.

More often, however, people with low self-esteem achieve great things but cannot believe that their achievement is special in any way or completely a result of their own efforts, often attributing it to luck – this is also known as 'imposter syndrome'. One study of male and female doctors confirmed this connection, finding that subjects with low self-esteem were much more likely to suffer from imposter syndrome.[42]

Ironically, we need good self-esteem in order to be able to receive the praise and recognition we get for our achievements, so achieving in order to feel better never works in the long term. Some people also worry that if they love and accept themselves, they will no longer strive to achieve their goals. However, we are equally capable of creating things out of joy, passion, interest, healthy ambition or a desire to help others, without the incessant yearning for validation that is driven by low self-esteem. Trying to use success to bolster your self-esteem is like trying to fill a bucket of water with a hole in the bottom. Through working on self-esteem we focus on mending the hole instead – much more efficient!

Motivation for increasing self-esteem

Here are a couple of thoughts that may help motivate you whilst working on your self-esteem:

1) If the younger generation see that we are building our success on a solid platform of *feeling enough*, they may do the same. It would

---

[42] Kamarzarrin et al. 2013

be wonderful if more people pursued goals for satisfaction and the desire to make a difference, rather than out of fear of not being enough.

2) When we have good self-esteem, communication and relationships are a lot clearer and cleaner. For example, a friendship between two people with good self-esteem is a meeting of the minds, sharing enjoyment and a free exchange of ideas, whereas when self-esteem is low it might be based on fear, competitiveness or a need to keep the other person down at our level (frenemieships).

3) It is great for healthy intimate relationships because we will not expect our partner to fill us up to make us feel better. It is also much more likely that we will respect them, have good boundaries, be able to be vulnerable and share, and yet know when to take care of ourselves.

4) We will be able to ask for what we want and really believe that we deserve it. This also makes it more likely that we will enjoy the things we receive and avoid feeling bitter.

Feeling that we are enough is essential for us to be the heroes of our own lives – not looking to others for identity or direction, but honouring our own intuition and strengths. Self-esteem and self-love are a major part of this. I recommend that you use one or two of the exercises in this chapter daily over several weeks. If you ever feel like you have slipped backwards, do not beat yourself up – the world is not always geared towards making us feel great about ourselves. We may need to do a little bit of work on this for the rest of our lives, but the results make our effort worthwhile.

The poem 'As I Began to Love Myself' (thought to be by Charlie Chaplin, but there is some doubt around that) sums up how the journeys of learning about ourselves and learning to value and love ourselves are intertwined:

As I began to love myself I found that anguish and emotional suffering are only warning signs that I was living against my own truth. Today, I know, this is 'AUTHENTICITY'.

As I began to love myself I understood how much it can offend somebody if I try to force my desires on this person, even though I knew the time was not right and the person was not ready for it, and even though this person was me. Today I call it 'RESPECT'.

As I began to love myself I stopped craving for a different life, and I could see that everything that surrounded me was inviting me to grow. Today I call it 'MATURITY'.

As I began to love myself I understood that at any circumstance, I am in the right place at the right time, and everything happens at the exactly right moment. So I could be calm. Today I call it 'SELF-CONFIDENCE'.

As I began to love myself I quit stealing my own time, and I stopped designing huge projects for the future. Today, I only do what brings me joy and happiness, things I love to do and that make my heart cheer, and I do them in my own way and in my own rhythm. Today I call it 'SIMPLICITY'.

As I began to love myself I freed myself of anything that is no good for my health – food, people, things, situations, and everything that drew me down and away from myself. At first I called this attitude a healthy egoism. Today I know it is 'LOVE OF ONESELF'.

As I began to love myself I quit trying to always be right, and ever since I was wrong less of the time. Today I discovered that is 'MODESTY'.

As I began to love myself I refused to go on living in the past and worrying about the future. Now, I only live for the moment, where everything is happening. Today I live each day, day by day, and I call it 'FULFILLMENT'.

As I began to love myself I recognized that my mind can disturb me and it can make me sick. But as I connected it to my heart, my mind became a valuable ally. Today I call this connection 'WISDOM OF THE HEART'.

We no longer need to fear arguments, confrontations or any kind of problems with ourselves or others. Even stars collide, and out of their crashing new worlds are born. Today I know 'THAT IS LIFE'![43]

Although we may sometimes feel that loving and valuing ourselves are additional luxuries that we should take care of only after everything else that we need to do, choosing to do so is actually a pivotal attitude which allows us to have faith in ourselves and know that we deserve a full and happy life. I feel that just one person who does this can change a community, even if they live quietly, as the way they treat themselves and others has a powerful ripple effect. And although these people may seem special in some way, we all have the capacity to like, love and value ourselves. Ultimately, the only permission we are waiting for in order to do this is our own. To me this is like choosing freedom and responsibility at the same time because we become free from craving love and respect and acting a certain way to get it, but we also increase our capacity to realise our potential and therefore have a much greater responsibility to step up. Another of the great paradoxes of self-development work.

---

[43] Cited in Noronha 2018

CHAPTER 7

Compassion and Self-Compassion

Sometimes I think that one of the key qualities that make the world a great place instead of a terrible one is compassion. Why compassion rather than love, great communication, free will or human rights, for example? Well, compassion has love mixed into it, and those other things also naturally follow from people having a more compassionate mindset. It is the space filled with grace that we give to ourselves and others, with kindness, understanding, respect, peace and love swirled throughout it. And it does really take the edge off.

There has been a lot of emphasis on compassion recently, both in the media and in schools and workplaces, but how many of us truly understand the concept and know how to intentionally work on it? Many of us have been brought up to treat others respectfully, yet compassion adds something more – an extra dose of humanity, so we will be looking at what it is in more depth and working on it. And for those of us who are very kind to other people but not to ourselves we will also be looking at self-compassion. If you are keen on working on this, I still recommend that you read the whole chapter because if we find self-compassion challenging it can be easier to work on compassion for others first and build from there.

As I have mentioned in the last couple of chapters, there is a lot of crossover between compassion, self-compassion, self-love, self-esteem and acceptance. As you continue with this work, you may feel that at certain points you want to switch back and forth between chapters, which is fine. Let's start with looking at precisely what compassion is.

Compassion

What it is

Compassion tends to give us a sense of warmth, spaciousness and connection with another. We also usually have a feeling of largesse (we have enough for ourselves and for others), love, caring, and a desire for others to be healthy and happy as well as a sense of justice, perhaps. This gentle but powerful feeling is a distinct emotion with its own associated physiological responses and even tones of voice.[44] If we strip it back to its bare bones, we find that it is basically love and a recognition of the humanity of others (and the equivalent of that for animals). Five main aspects of compassion have been suggested: recognising suffering in others, understanding the common humanity in this, feeling emotionally connected to a person who is suffering, tolerating any difficult feelings that may arise, and acting (or wanting to act) to help the person.[45] But most of us are not aware of these separate aspects, just a pull to feel or act a certain way, which is often deep and instinctive.

It is thought that we evolved compassion over time in order to protect our young, as they are vulnerable for much longer than those of other animals, as well as to strengthen the bonds within our communities and relationships. The fact that people often choose compassionate partners makes sense, as they are much more likely to take care of us and any offspring, a preference which further strengthens compassionate tendencies in our gene pool.[46] It is interesting to think of compassion as an evolutionary trait, when it is so often thought of as a mainly spiritual concept. However, perhaps evolution and spirituality are not antithetical, but two sides of the same coin – luckily, we never need to choose!

---

[44] Simon-Thomas et al. 2009
[45] Strauss et al. 2016
[46] Goetz et al. 2010

Although we are all familiar with the feeling of compassion, it can be easy to confuse with empathy. However, these are two very different concepts. And while the root of the word compassion is the Latin *compati*, meaning to suffer with, compassion is not about suffering – there is no point in two people just feeling bad together. Compassion is sympathy and understanding for someone else's suffering. Empathy is closer to the *compati* meaning, as it is feeling what the other person feels; if they are suffering, we feel their pain. However, contrary to popular opinion, a high level of empathy does not always lead to being better at helping people, because boundaries and a clear mind are often more useful than getting deeply involved in others' emotional states.[47] And compassion is actually a much more altruistic emotion because the research shows that people feeling compassion are more inclined to help others than people who are feeling empathy. This is because empathy can make us focus on our own feelings and act to make ourselves feel better, even when it makes the person suffering feel worse.[48] So, with compassion there is more of a healthy distance between our feelings and other peoples', as well as a sense of kindness and a desire to help others.

Compassion may also help to make us more open and present, because to be truly compassionate we need to be fully aware of a situation, completely in the moment, and thinking about how people are affected and what we can do to help. Interestingly, compassion has distinct effect on certain areas of the brain and leads to a specific psychological state. Compassion training has been shown to result in more positive emotions compared with empathy training (even when exposed to the distress of others).[49] Other research has also shown that practising loving-kindness meditation can result in having more positive emotions, more self-acceptance, improved relationships and better health.[50] This may mean that pursuing compassion instead of happiness is more likely to lead to us feeling happy.

---

[47] Bloom 2014
[48] Eisenberg 2000
[49] Singer and Klimecki 2014
[50] Fredrickson et al. 2008

How compassionate are we?

Compassion is a way of being that is very heart-centred; therefore, it encourages us to be kind and respectful and to see the value in others. There is no formal way of measuring compassion yet, but as many of us have an intuitive understanding of this state, with a little self-reflection it is probably obvious whether or not we are compassionate to others. We may find that we are more compassionate towards certain people and groups than others, and reflecting on this may make us aware of any prejudices we have. If we realise that our lives are not really set up for thinking of others, it might be a good idea to create some space for this, not least because it has been shown that altruistic behaviour is very good for our health, happiness and even longevity.[51]

Certain states can temporarily block compassion, including experiencing hardship, being very angry or being stressed. Although it is natural for our level of compassion to vary throughout a year, or even a day, if on average it is quite low it is a good idea to work to raise it consciously, also addressing the imbalance that is making compassion hard for us. It is important to remember that compassion comes from a place of enough, and if we are not feeling that way inside we need to work on that first. *Compassion fatigue* may occur when we have not taken enough care of ourselves and have been overexposed to the suffering of others. In that case, we must first treat ourselves with attentive kindness, taking the time to meet our needs and restore our energy, before we give to others something that we need more of ourselves.

So, to sum up, balanced compassion is well-boundaried, genuine, respectful, loving and without agenda. It cannot authentically be done at the expense of our own emotional health, and when we do it right it is good for both ourselves and others. Now let's look at how we can work on it.

---

[51] Post 2005

Boosting compassion

Because compassion is an innate quality, a lot of being compassionate is just remembering to do it on a regular basis. However, because of the speed that life moves at now, as well as how rare it can be to meaningfully connect with others, it is likely that most of us will have to intentionally work on cultivating this attitude. Luckily, studies have shown that our brains are flexible enough for us to become more compassionate through training, and the exercises in this chapter aim to help you achieve this. The first exercise we are going to use is a simple meditation on compassion to get us in the mood.

Exercise 7.1: Meditation for compassion

In this exercise we will be focusing on feeling compassion within us, before expanding it far out beyond us. It is simple but there are quite a few steps, so feel free to read each one as you go. It is best done with a relaxed, open attitude, so do not worry about doing it wrong or if certain parts feel hard to do, just focus on enjoying the feeling of love and compassion within you. You can repeat this exercise as often as you want to.

a) Sit somewhere comfortable and breathe naturally and easily. Letting any tension drop away from your body, feel yourself relax more and more deeply, and close your eyes.

b) Now sense a feeling of calm growing within you and spreading throughout your body. Feel it grow until it fills your whole body.

c) When your whole body feels full of calm, put your awareness in your heart and notice how it feels.

d) Imagine a feeling of love starting to grow in your heart. Feel the warmth and solidity of it; you can imagine it has a colour, any colour you like.

e) Now see the love in your heart growing and expanding, feeling more and more solid and filling your whole body.

f)   Something enters the love in your body now, an extra quality that turns the love into compassion, and as it does so it may change colour. Again, any colour you like. If you have trouble feeling compassion, imagine that it is also love, but 'love with others in mind'.

g)   Feel the compassion as a warm and solid energy, filling every part of your body. Now, with every breath you take, it grows. Taking your time, visualise it expanding to a metre around your body, then ten metres, then around your local town or city, your part of the country, your entire country, then the whole continent and finally the world. Visualise the whole world filled with the glow of your compassion.

h)   If you like, while you are feeling this compassion and connection with the world, you can say 'I have compassion for every person and animal in the world,' or something similar that feels right to you.

i)   When you feel ready to end the exercise, sense the feeling in your heart and enjoy it. Breathe in slowly and then, breathing out, open your eyes.

Using this exercise on a regular basis can make it easier for us to feel compassion whenever we choose, and you may find that it brings another dimension into your life. Many of us get caught up in to-do lists and day-to-day tasks, but compassion can bring us both the connection and spaciousness we need to feel grounded and present.

Barriers to compassion

As mentioned above, sometimes we are not in the right state of mind to be able feel compassion for others. In this section I would like you to think about times recently and in the past that you have not been compassionate and what you think was stopping you. These factors can be very varied, and may include stress, anger, hunger, long working hours, low energy levels, lack of emotional support or community, prejudices, or issues with our career, relationship or housing. Even caffeine and other substances that affect our state can interfere with our ability to be compassionate.

Exercise 7.2: Dismantling our blocks to compassion

For this exercise you will need something to write with and an open mind.

a) Make a list of the things that you feel are reducing your ability to feel compassion, or things that have blocked it in the past.
b) Beside each item on the list, write how it makes you feel.
c) Now, beside each item also write how you can address it. For example, you might write:

My career status	Makes me feel frustrated and annoyed with myself and I do not have extra energy to care about others	I want to look at the roots of the link between my career and my self-esteem or I want to take steps forward in my career

Even though it may feel normal to you to be stressed, annoyed or very caffeinated, for example, often the states that stop us being compassionate also make us less humane, less able to connect with others and less able to rest and heal physically and emotionally, so they also diminish our ability to live fully and enjoy ourselves. If you found that certain emotions were getting in the way of feeling compassion, you can work on them now before continuing with the rest of the chapter. This is optional, but it may be easier than trying to work on compassion while something else is weighing on you.

Self-expression for compassion

Below is a simple exercise that you can use to remember the good in the world and, although the emphasis is on compassion for others, it is good for us too, especially when we are feeling jaded. Thinking about what we love about humanity is a great remedy for 'not really liking the world right now' (and it is helpful to remember that the media and our minds are skewed towards the negative, so we sometimes have to consciously balance this out).

You are just going to sit down with a pen and paper and write a love letter to humanity, which may sound very saccharine, but it should be authentic to you. So, if you want to write about how clever the physicists are who built the Large Hadron Collider, or about the impressive memory, patience and eyebrows of birdwatchers, it is all good. Anything you love about humanity can go into this freestyle letter.

Exercise 7.3: Love letter to humanity

You will need somewhere comfortable and quiet and a pen and paper for this exercise.

a) Sit quietly and try to relax your mind. Have the intention of writing a letter about everything you love about humanity.

b) Start writing without editing or worrying about spelling. Bear in mind that you are not trying to 'do it right' or present this to others, just to express yourself as fully as possible. Remember, lollypop ladies, pilots, diplomats, doctors, kids tasting lemons for the first time – absolutely anything you love is great. If you find it hard to start, just begin with the first thing that pops into your mind, even if it is a small thing like the person who opened a door for you.

c) If the negative side of your mind wants to put any 'buts' or 'excepts', just ignore it – only put positive things in this love letter. Not to ignore the negative side of life, but I'm pretty sure most of us already have that covered!

I recommend that you sign and date this letter and keep it. When you are having a bad day, you can take it out and remember what you love about the world and the people in it. Come back and repeat this exercise as often as you like.

There is also another, faster way to shift us into a compassionate state, which is to remember a time when we needed compassion ourselves. Maybe we were feeling vulnerable or in need of support and someone else helped us. It is easy to forget this when everything is OK and we are in 'normal-life' mode, but remembering our own vulnerability can be a fast way of reconnecting with our compassionate side.

The key thing with compassion is just to remember to do it. According to psychologist and author Daniel Goleman, it is a question of focus: as soon as we connect with people we are primed to act compassionately; however, many of us are focusing on something else, off in our little bubble, and we forget to do this.[52] So it is important to remember that, even though we may need to work hard and focus on a specific goal sometimes, there are real benefits to ourselves and others from regularly returning to a state of connectedness and compassion.

Self-Compassion

What it is

Self-compassion is simply the same authentic impulse to love and help others as in compassion, just applied to ourselves. And yet it may not feel that simple at all, because so few of us have been taught how to do it. Our critical inner voice often leaves little room for being kind to ourselves and many of us are our own worst enemies in this respect. In this chapter we will be looking at different ways of boosting our self-compassion in order to experience more peace and more connection with ourselves.

Dr Kristin Neff, an expert in self-compassion, defines three main elements that are key to being compassionate to ourselves: self-kindness instead of judging ourselves harshly, remembering that everyone suffers rather than feeling alone in this, and being mindful and accepting of our thoughts instead of getting swept up with them.[53] These three principles can keep us connected to ourselves and to others and give us the

---

[52] Goleman 2007
[53] Neff 2018a

kindness to accept ourselves as we are, gently. This is important because when we criticise and push away certain parts of ourselves we create separation within us, which can lead to a variety of issues. So, self-compassion is a quality that helps us to stay integrated.

Why we need it

> Be kind to yourself. Remember that when you abuse yourself, you will experience the anger, regret, and apathy of the bully as well as the depression, anxiety, and insecurity of the victim. Whatever you do, be kind to yourself.
>
> —Vironika Tugaleva

We could see being self-compassionate as a recognition of both our vulnerability and our worth. Through understanding that we deserve kindness, rest and nurturing and giving that to ourselves, we create an inner space of safety and love. On the other hand, if we are too hard on ourselves, are too self-critical or always pushing ourselves to achieve, then we will not feel safe or loved. The difference in our inner state has an impact on every single aspect of our lives, including our health, relationships and work.

Although some of us may fear that self-compassion will take away our drive or ambition, it is actually self-criticism that has been shown to be detrimental to effectiveness, in various situations. For example, one study into young women athletes found that self-compassion improved performance, but self-criticism did not,[54] while other studies have shown that self-compassion actually leads to greater mastery. This is because it frees students to focus on learning instead of fear of failure, it makes them feel like competent learners, and it fosters 'intrinsic motivation'.[55] This is key to understanding that authentic motivation to succeed does not come

---

[54] Killham 2018
[55] Neff et al. 2005

from fearing failure, but from a belief in oneself and what one is trying to achieve, and self-compassion can help with this.

How self-compassionate are we?

Self-compassion tends to be much rarer than compassion for others, often because people have been raised in a culture that warns against self-indulgence, sloth or arrogance, and these flaws may have been confused with being kind to oneself. Speaking as a British person, historically there has been a fair amount of conditioning towards being stoic and just getting on with things instead of dwelling on our emotional needs. (This does not include complaining about minor things, which for many is an opportunity to talk to strangers or bond with friends, in case you're not British and wonder why we are smiling and grumbling simultaneously!) Unfortunately, this can lead to a mistrust of our own emotions and a reliance on self-criticism as a method of self-improvement, and I'm sure it is not only British people who are susceptible to this (or the only ones to use alcohol or other substances and distractions to temporarily let us cut loose). I have noticed that as mental health moves to the forefront of public awareness, the need for self-compassion is becoming more understood.

Another issue is that even if we understand that we need to be self-compassionate, we may not know how to do it. For example, we may think we are being kind to ourselves when we are actually just avoiding our problems, indulging in addictions or bad habits, avoiding responsibility, or procrastinating. These things are obviously not kind in the long run, but we may think they are because it feels like we are going easy on ourselves. Therefore, it is important to be able to differentiate between true self-compassion that enriches us and substitutes for it that might even harm us in the long run.

Common signs of low self-compassion include being very self-critical, feeling many other people are doing better than you or are happier than you, or being strongly knocked off-centre by negative events. There is a questionnaire for testing how compassionate you are created by Dr Neff.

Here are a couple of statements from it – see if you agree or disagree with them:

- When I fail at something important to me I become consumed by feelings of inadequacy.
- I'm tolerant of my own flaws and inadequacies.[56]

If you find yourself agreeing with the first or disagreeing with the second, this could be a sign that your levels of self-compassion are a bit low. To take the full test, you can visit the website: https://self-compassion. org/test-how-self-compassionate-you-are/. If you find that your self-compassion levels are low, that is OK – this is something we are going to actively work on in this chapter.

Boosting self-compassion

We are going to look at a few different ways of increasing levels of self-compassion, including increasing our awareness of how we are feeling, reducing self-criticism and being kinder to ourselves. It is important to remember that self-compassion is not self-indulgence or weakness. It allows us to meet our own emotional needs and care for ourselves in a way that creates a strong foundation for our sense of self. A sense of self built on self-criticism may fall down with every setback, but a foundation of love will carry us through very difficult times. As Tara Brach says, 'Feeling compassion for ourselves in no way releases us from responsibility for our actions. Rather, it releases us from the self-hatred that prevents us from responding to our life with clarity and balance.'[57]

Let's start with how we are feeling right now.

---

[56] Neff 2018b
[57] Brach 2003, p. 207.

How it makes us feel

To be able to be kind to ourselves we first need to know how we are feeling, otherwise we will not be aware of any emotions or needs that we need to take care of. In this exercise we are first going to check in with how we are doing physically and emotionally and then see how self-criticism and self-compassion affect how we feel. Please note that if you start feeling negative emotions, it is probably just that your awareness of the emotions you already have inside you has increased. Although it is human nature to avoid unpleasantness, the only way out is through, so if you do not feel overwhelmed I recommend that you keep going. If you need a break, that is fine also.

Exercise 7.4: Check-in

a) Sit somewhere comfortable and let yourself breathe naturally. Let any tension in your body fall away and feel yourself relax more with every breath.

b) Now tune into your body and, with an attitude of curiosity, see what physical sensations there are. Whatever you notice, don't try to change it, just acknowledge it and know that it is fine.

c) Now I would like you to bring to mind something you criticise yourself about fairly often, and notice how the feeling in your body changes. Once you have identified a feeling or change, notice if there is an emotion associated with it.

d) And now let go of that feeling, reassuring yourself that everything is fine. Bring yourself back into awareness of your body and let your body relax more with every breath, the tension once again dropping away.

e) When you feel relaxed again, let yourself feel kindness towards yourself that radiates throughout your whole body, like sunshine. Notice how your body responds to this. Do any emotions naturally come up?

It can be very interesting to see how differently these two attitudes affect our emotional and physical feelings and therefore our physical and mental health. And, naturally, I'm sure you can imagine being responsible and effective while also feeling kindness for yourself filling your whole body. Can you also envision how this state of self-compassion might temper your thoughts, words and actions for the better? Now that we know what the state we are aiming for feels like, let's look at dismantling one of the major obstacles to it.

Everyone has an inner critic

As I mentioned above, harsh self-criticism cancels out self-compassion, so identifying the inner voice that criticises and berates us, and then asking it to quieten down, can be a great first step towards being more self-compassionate.

Exercise 7.5: Quietening the critic

You'll just need somewhere quiet to sit and something to write with for this exercise. Although it may seem overly simple, this exercise can be very effective if we do it with a very clear intention of cancelling out the negativity in our attitude to ourselves.

a) Firstly, have a think about a few things you might say to yourself that are critical and write them down. You can aim for around five.

b) Now I want you to look at them, one at a time, while saying to yourself, 'I am perfect as I am right now,' and only move on to the next when that feeling is stronger than the criticism you wrote down.

c) Notice how you feel after doing that for all of them.

d) If your inner critic comes back with more reasons to feel bad and more criticisms, just repeat the phrase above again.

e) Now, breathing in a relaxed and easy way, say to yourself, 'I am perfect as I am right now,' and let that feeling spread through your whole body.

How do you feel now that you have done this? It is not always possible to end the self-criticism habit of a lifetime in just one go, so when your inner critic pops back up again in the future, try gently telling yourself that you are perfect as you are right now.

Putting our critical inner voice in its place can help release us from a self-created purgatory of never ever being able to *be enough*, no matter what we do. If you are you, and the only person who can be you – how could you ever not be enough at it? You are the only one who can do it and you are doing it right now. Can you imagine if animals had these feelings about themselves? And the strange behaviours and adaptations that would spring up as a result? I have a strange mental image of a squirrel standing only in ways that stop its bottom looking big or a beaver accidentally deforesting an area trying to build a dam so gigantic it could finally feel worthwhile. Animals do not doubt that they deserve self-care, and luckily we still have this instinct deep within us. Getting in touch with this powerful instinct to take care of ourselves can really help us as we unlearn some of the negative habits of our minds.

Speaking of which, it might be interesting for you to have a think about who your inner critic sounds like, if anyone, as this may give you a clue about who you picked it up from. Did anyone from your youth say similar things? This is not about blame, just realising that self-criticism can be contagious and sometimes knowing where it came from helps to remind us that it is not authentic to us, just a learned behaviour that can be untangled from the rest of our self.

Other barriers to self-compassion

Just as we have looked at possible blocks to being compassionate, now we are going to look at some things that can stop us being self-compassionate. If we can feel compassion for others but not for ourselves there may be specific issues or beliefs getting in our way, which could include perfectionism, low self-esteem, or a dislike of admitting vulnerability or of feeling our feelings. If you do not like paying attention to your own needs, the exercise below might be a challenge, so take your time and just keep in mind that this work is important and that you do deserve this attention.

Exercise 7.6: Blocks to self-compassion

For this exercise I would like you to think about the times in the past that you have not been compassionate to yourself and what you think was stopping you. You will need something to write with.

a) Make a list of the times that you have not been kind to yourself recently or in the past, and/or the things that stopped you being kind to yourself. For example, failing at something and berating yourself, needing a holiday but pushing through and exhausting yourself, or putting others first at the expense of your own needs. You can put it in a table, as in the example below.

b) Beside each one, write how you felt at that time.

c) Now, for each one, think about whether there is anyone else you know who has a similar block to self-compassion, and note that down. Once again, this is not about blame but understanding where we might have picked up this attitude.

d) Lastly, think about the most authentic approach to overcoming this block to being compassionate to yourself. It should help you to move towards being more in line with who you are, your values and the things you enjoy.

Time I was unkind to myself	How I felt	Who else I know who does this	What I am going to do about it
The time I worked way too hard and didn't take a break	I felt burned out, sad, exhausted, resentful and desperate for time off	Some of my colleagues also work this way – it is the culture in that team at work My sister is also like this	I am going to make sure I take holidays by booking them all in advance and going in spite of any work events

e) Before you end the exercise just allow yourself to have the feeling of being enough as you are and remember that you deserve self-compassion and the time and space you need.

This exercise can help to remind us that, even though we are used to treating ourselves a certain way, we always have a choice and we can start making that choice at any time. If you listed anything that needs to be done, you could schedule it in, or set up reminders for yourself.

Although self-compassion is an attitude, it often expresses itself as an action or habit as self-compassionate people value their thoughts, desires and needs and plan their days accordingly. This is not selfish unless you are always putting others last, because no one else is going to meet your needs for you. And if you think about it, wouldn't you rather hang out with a positive person who is taking care of themselves than an embittered, tired person who isn't? Taking good care of ourselves can be an act of generosity to everyone around us and we will also be in better condition to support others when they need it.

Self-expression for self-compassion

Above, we looked at writing a love letter to humanity to boost our ability to be compassionate. This one is a love letter to ourselves to help us practise self-compassion. It is a little different, however, as we have so much more information about ourselves, so it can be a lot more nuanced and precise.

I want you to write the exact letter you need right now. If you need comforting about a certain thing – for example, if you are grieving a loss or regretting something – then speak to that. If you need praise, affection, attention, consideration, gratitude, honouring, love, admiration or anything – do this through your letter. Above all, it must be kind. Enjoy!

Exercise 7.7: Love letter to yourself

a)   Sit somewhere comfortable and quiet with a pen and paper.

b)   Address the letter to yourself and start anyway you want to. Do not worry if you are stumped for what to write, you can just start with a little list of things you have done well or things you like about yourself and let it go on from there. As with the previous exercise, there is no 'right way' to do this, it is just free-form writing. The only thing you should avoid is criticising yourself. You can write about any time in your life, any quality of yours, or address any need you have right now.

c)   Whenever you feel ready to finish, sign your letter.

Read it through now and allow yourself to feel safe, cared for and valuable. You may want to date this letter and keep it, so when you are having a hard time you can look at it, remembering what you love about yourself and how you want to take care of yourself. You can use this exercise whenever you need a boost, some kindness, or to take yourself out of a harsh internal landscape and put yourself in a cosier one. Like hygge for the soul.

So, in this chapter we have looked at compassion and self-compassion as ways of boosting our humanity, kindness and health. Remember, even though self-compassion may seem like self-indulgence to some, being kind to ourselves is our birthright and the only way to allow ourselves to feel happy and fulfilled as we are. And compassion, rather than meaning we are weak or that we roll over for everyone, allows us to be strong, loving and kind. It also helps us to maintain healthy boundaries with others as well as the internal spaciousness we need so we have room to grow. This sets the perfect tone for our self-development work – not focusing on our flaws and struggling against them to improve, but rather celebrating our strengths and exploring our potential. A path of much less resistance and much more joy.

CHAPTER 8

Recognising Our Emotions

If we want to become more self-aware we might think about meditating, or being more conscious of our thoughts, perhaps. But a vital aspect of this work that often gets brushed over is learning to tune into and identify our emotions, which adds a whole new dimension to our self-understanding. After all, if our thoughts were the lines of a drawing, our emotions would be the colours.

It can be hard for those of us living mostly in our heads, however, to get in touch with our feelings, and when we do we may be tempted to judge them with the logic of our minds. But emotions are not about right and wrong so much as messages from within us, trying to tell us something about our self or our experience that we need to know. In order to be able to receive these messages we need to be able first to be aware of the emotions that are there, to feel them fully and allow them to be as they are without trying to change them or push them away, which is what we will be focusing on in this chapter.

Why Recognising Our Emotions Is Good for Us

Part of being self-aware means taking responsibility for ourselves, and being aware of our feelings means that we can also take responsibility for our emotional state. This is important because some people fear that listening to their feelings means letting them run the show, or acting in emotionally immature ways. In fact, when people are excessively ruled by their emotions or burden others with them it is usually because they have not sat with their own feelings and fully witnessed them.

Witnessing is a powerful act; we know from experiments in quantum mechanics that particles change quite dramatically when they are observed. So do our emotions – maybe because they are messengers that want to be heard. This is partly why fully recognising our feelings is often enough to allow them to transform or resolve themselves completely. However, there are some emotions we resist acknowledging, leading to ongoing issues. We could liken this to having several couriers trying to deliver important information, but you refuse to open the door. This causes you stress because you know they are always outside; they may be putting reminders through your letterbox, knocking, ringing the doorbell, and yet you ignore them. Underneath you always know they are there and it nags at you, but you are so worried about what news they will deliver that you hope distractions and time will make them go away. However, if you would just open the door and receive the messages most of them would leave instantly, leaving you feeling unburdened and lighter.

Some of these messages may be more in-depth and take longer to work out – but since they are affecting you anyway it is better for you to have full awareness of them. On the other hand, if we perpetually refuse to acknowledge our emotions, we are likely to feel stuck and disconnected from our self, while also suffering from the chronic physical and emotional tension created by the effort of suppressing our feelings. Obviously there will be times when we are too raw, too vulnerable or too overwhelmed to feel more than we do right now, and at these times it is appropriate to take a break. But outside of these moments it is best for us to be able to tune into our feelings in real time, and with practice we will find this more and more achievable.

Before we get further in, I just want to mention that the words *feeling* and *emotion* actually have quite different meanings in academic circles (according to neuroscientist Antonio Damasio, an *emotion* is a reaction to something, while a *feeling* occurs only after our brain has made sense of that reaction[58]). However, I use them interchangeably because this book is for the general public, who tend to use these words in this way (and it also means I don't have to keep using the same word over and over). Before we start doing any exercises, let's have a closer look at emotions in general.

About Emotions

People have written whole books on emotion and emotional intelligence, but in this section I want to just touch briefly on a couple of points that I think will be useful for you before we begin.

1. Feelings can be hard to pin down

Identifying intangible things like our feelings can be hard because we may be so 'in the experience' that we lack the perspective to understand what we are feeling completely, we sometimes reflexively push our emotions away before we have had the chance to feel them properly, or they exist beneath our conscious awareness and are affecting us without our knowledge. Generally, we could sum this difficulty up by saying that we are inside ourselves trying to look inside ourselves, which is always tricky! It would be handy if we just had a little console on our arm that announced each emotional state as it arose and its significance, and although there is already AI that supposedly reads the emotions of consumers, for now the rest of us will have to make do with tuning into our feelings through reading the signs within us and a bit of self-expression.

2. Physical sensations, actions, other emotions and thoughts can point to our emotions

The main way we know we are having an emotion is through physical changes and sensations, such as our hairs standing on end, changes in

---

[58] Lenzen 2018

heart rate, butterflies in our stomach or sweating.[59] However, emotions can also create subtler signs, such as a feeling of heaviness or tightness somewhere in our body. Another way we may notice that we are feeling something is when an emotion, reaction or thought we are conscious of points to another feeling deeper within us that we were not aware of. We may also act or speak in a way that is unusual for us and then wonder, 'Where did that come from?' – this comes from a part of us we are not completely connected to, an impulse or emotion that wants attention.

3. There are a lot of emotions and they do not form an orderly queue

One study looked at people's responses to different videos and discovered twenty-seven distinct main emotional states (which was surprising because other theories propose between four and ten basic emotions).[60] There is a great online interactive map showing these emotions as well as the videos that elicited them (you can find it by searching for '27 emotions interactive map'), and this map also illustrates the fact that there is a lot of overlap between different feelings. Because emotions are nuanced, many, interconnected and changing, it is harder to tune into exactly what we are feeling, especially when we are simultaneously experiencing emotions which seem like they should be contradictory. In fact, we can feel emotions as different as delight and sadness at the same time, but most people have been taught they can only have one emotion at a time, so that is all they look for – the loudest or most acceptable one, but not the whole orchestra of emotions that may be alive and moving within us.

4. We learn our relationships to our feelings from the people around us

Families, groups and cultures often have similar relationships to different emotions (including the types of feelings they prefer and how strongly

---

[59] Purves et al. 2017
[60] Cowen and Keltner 2017

they allow themselves to feel), which has a big impact on how aware we are of different emotions. We looked at this in quite a lot of depth in chapter 5, 'Acceptance and Self-Acceptance'. Why not have a think about the 'emotional identity' of your family – which emotions do they like, dislike, reject, seek or fear? And do you find this true within you also? We can easily pick up some less helpful beliefs around emotions, which limit us unnecessarily. However, our ability to feel our full range of emotions doesn't disappear for good, so through making a conscious effort we can uncover any 'lost emotions'.

5. We can catch feelings from others

Not only are our relationships with our feelings greatly affected by others, but our feelings in the moment are too. 'Emotional contagion' is what happens when people catch each other's feelings, just as if a virus had moved between them. Have you ever noticed that making eye contact leads to catching someone else's emotional state faster? I believe this is because we have evolved to be highly attuned to each other's feelings and looking in one another's eyes is part of the way we do this. There is evidence that we even mirror each other's pupil size when making eye contact, as part of an involuntary empathic response to one another.[61] The most important step towards learning how to avoid taking on others' feelings is to be so in tune with our own feelings that it is obvious when someone else's have wandered in.

6. Emotional intelligence is crucial to career, relationships and happiness

In recent years, the importance of developing emotional intelligence has become increasingly clear and the data shows that it is twice as important as IQ or technical skills in terms of performance in business.[62]

---

[61] Harrison et al. 2006
[62] Goleman 2004

Unsurprisingly, emotional intelligence is a big factor in being satisfied in a marriage,[63] probably because the more self-aware we are, the more deeply we can connect with another person, be there for them and grow in maturity. Therefore, although we may have got quite far in life relying mainly on our drive or logic, learning to get in touch with our feelings brings more meaning to our lives by adding depth and allowing us to grow in wisdom and experience, as well as more satisfaction through deepening relationships.

7. Our thoughts and feelings affect each other a lot

Of course, our thoughts also have a massive impact on how we feel. We talk about this in more depth in chapter 12, 'Thinking Consciously', but to sum up: thoughts and feelings flow together, each naturally influencing the other. Have you ever noticed that you were in a mood that was unusual for you and so you started thinking certain thoughts in order to bring you back to a more familiar emotional state? Or that you were feeling anxious and then started to think of things to worry about?

Because our aim is to become more aware of our feelings, learning to step out of the usual current of our thoughts and pay attention to other parts of ourselves is very useful. We may come across resistance from our minds, but with a little practice we can learn to consciously enter a state that allows us to tune into our feelings more easily – a kind of centred awareness – and this is the first thing we are going to be working on, below.

Working on Recognising Our Feelings

There are several approaches we can take to getting in touch with our emotions. In this section we will cover accepting them, finding the right words for them, and tuning into them through physical sensation and self-expression. First, however, we are going to start with creating the right state of mind for this work.

---

[63] Nasiri Zarch et al. 2014

Centred perspective

Because many of us live in a pretty intellectual society we may find that we can think with the ease and grace of a dolphin surfing waves; yet, when it comes to identifying and talking about our feelings, we may be more like a baby fawn taking its first steps. Sensing within ourselves requires that we turn our usually outward-facing attention inwards, but our minds do not always like us accessing parts of ourselves beyond their sovereignty, and may use a stream of thoughts or a story to try to escort us out again. It can be especially tricky to pass inwards beyond this barrier if we are used to thinking a lot. Therefore, learning to peaceably ask our minds to be quieter as we shift focus from our thoughts and outer experience to our inner state and physical sensations is a handy skill.

There are a couple of main aspects to moving our awareness deeper within: one is being OK with silence. When we disengage from our thoughts, the quiet that results may be scary; so it can help to realise that it is there all the time anyway, only now we are paying attention to it, and that we are safe. Another is that when we break our usual thinking habit our thoughts will usually try to get us back on the rollercoaster again. We can simply let them go again each time that happens, and the feeling is not of a struggle, but rather acceptance of the thought and a gentle shifting of focus back to the sensations in our body. It may help to tell our mind we appreciate everything it does for us, but that we are just taking a short break.

Generally, we want to create a feeling of safety and calm within our body, a state of open awareness turned inwards and an uncoupling from our usual train of thought. We are going to give this a go in the exercise below.

Exercise 8.1: Looking beneath our thoughts

We are going to practise stepping into a state of centred awareness, a kind of 'listening' state. If this is new to you then it is completely natural to find it a little challenging. The best approach is self-kindness, knowing that we are perfect as we are, even if we all have some issues, and that it is fine to go at our own pace. We are going to tune in to some physical sensations, but we do not need to judge or understand them at all in this exercise; just to experience them.

a) Close your eyes and breathe in deeply, then, as you breathe out, feel tension and stress leaving your body. Do this for a couple of breaths.

b) Now we are going to sit in stillness for a few breaths, without engaging with our thoughts. I recommend that every time you breathe in you think the word 'centred' and with each out-breath you think the word 'calm'. Each time you become aware of having a thought, accept its presence but let it go and return to focusing on your breath.

c) Continuing to breathe easily, put your attention on the space in your torso between your neck and your pelvis, and just notice how it feels, without judgement. If you find your mind has wandered, let the thoughts go and simply return to your breath and the physical sensations in your torso.

d) To end the exercise take a deep breath in and, as you breathe out, open your eyes.

If you felt this was hard to do – don't worry, as this kind of meditation is like exercising a muscle and you will find that it gets easier with practice. When we find it easier to tune in to our physical sensations and step out of the stream of our thoughts, we will have a much greater capacity to pick up on the whole range, and nuances, of our emotions. But before we dive into connecting to our physical feelings more, let's make sure that we have the words we need to describe our emotions.

Emotional vocabulary

This may seem basic, but it is very hard to be completely attuned to feelings we do not have a word for. I have many clients whose vocabulary for their own current emotions does not extend beyond 'fine', 'stressed' or 'tired', and these are states rather than actual emotions. Therefore, we are going to look at a chart to help us to name emotions in order to boost our vocabulary.

Exercise 8.2: Increasing our emotional vocabulary

Have a look at the chart below, which lists many of the commonest feelings, and use it to try to identify the closest words for what you are feeling right now. It is important to remember that you can be feeling many things at once, so you do not have to limit yourself to one, and also remember seemingly opposite emotions such as happiness and anger can occur at the same time.

I have grouped similar emotions together in each column, but free to make your own chart and move words around, or add new ones. In addition, some of the phrases below are more like the 'three words squashed into one' that Germans use, as English lacks single words for these feelings. Feel free to add some of your own also, like the feeling of satisfaction when taking your shoes off after a long day at work.

Emotions					
Angry	Happy	Peaceful	Afraid	Sad	Proactive
Irritated	Overjoyed	Thoughtful	Anxious	Lonely	Empowered
Annoyed	Excited	Content	Scared	Ashamed	Strong
Rage	Overexcited	Connected	Terrified	Embarrassed	Useful
Hate	Glad	Hopeful	Shock	Guilty	Helpful
Jealous	Sensual	Interested	Isolated	Isolated	Able to make a difference
Competitive	Expressive	Relief	Guarded	Grief	Worthwhile
Resentful	Playful	Calm	On high alert	Depressed	Motivated
Holding a grudge	Spontaneous	Enough	Unsettled	Empty	Wanting to build something
Suspicious	Surprised	Secure	Frozen	Hollow	Organised

Emotions					
Feeling better than others	Creative	Loving	Unable to act	Helpless	Confident
Scornful	Friendly	At home	Paranoid	Useless	Appreciated
Stressed	Kind	Daydreamy	Put on the spot	Stupid	Centred
Confronted	Altruistic	Compassionate	Like an imposter	Flawed	Competent
Grumpy	Grateful	Feeling self-love	Untrusting	Ugly	Relevant
Restless	Amused	Introverted	Pressured	Dejected	Strong and loving
Greedy	Hysterical	Extroverted	Bullied	Overwhelmed	Trusting
Frustrated	Talkative	Poetic	Shy	Hopeless or numb	Having a sense of destiny or purpose
Self-centred and unhappy with self	Having love to share	Safe	Not wanting to be alone	Seeing no point in anything	Inspired or inspiring
Humiliated	Finding things funny	Awe	Jumpy	Missing loved ones	Enthusiastic
Wanting to control others	Seeing a silver lining	Spiritual	Fearful of the future	Vulnerable	Pride

I recommend that you use this chart periodically to help you identify how you are feeling. Sometimes you may not find the exact word for your emotion – that's OK, just try to find the closest one. If you like, you can keep a record of what you feel in your diary. The more you practise identifying your emotions, the easier it will be to understand what you are feeling, even if it is very nuanced. OK, now let's move on to learning to connect with our emotions through our physical feelings.

Tuning in to our feelings through physical sensation

One of the most direct ways of getting in touch with our emotions is through our body. Emotions are always accompanied by a physical sensation, whether we are aware of it or not, and often in areas specific to that emotion (e.g. love in your heart). However, they can also pop up in other places, so let's approach this exercise with a spirit of open enquiry. Remembering how to step out of your thoughts is handy for this exercise, because they do often try to rescue us from uncomfortable feelings, so if this happens we can gently let them go and return to our original focus.

Exercise 8.3: Tuning in to our feelings through physical sensation

When getting in touch with a feeling, unexpected memories, thoughts or other emotions may arise. If it feels like too much at any time, simply stop. I recommend that, as long as you are comfortable, you just go with whatever comes up. You will need something to write with and some time alone.

a) Sitting somewhere quiet and comfortable, just breathe, relax your body and close your eyes.

b) Let the tension go with every out-breath, and start to notice how you are feeling in general.

c) Now notice if there are any sensations in your body that are more in the foreground and more obvious.

d) What are those sensations like? Warm, cool, light, heavy, a ball, knotted, spread out, tense, relaxed or other?

e) Keep noticing the sensations in your body and, with an open mind, notice whether you feel that they have an associated shape and/or colour.

f) Now write out any words that come to mind to describe these sensations and emotions – e.g. dark, fixed, angry, restless, pulsing, heavy, deep, moving, sneaky, orange – whatever comes to mind.

g) When you feel ready to bring the exercise to a close, centre yourself in your body, breathe in a relaxed way and let go of any tension. Then take a deep breath in and, breathing out, open your eyes.

If you want to feel calmer or more centred after doing this exercise, why not use one of the exercises from chapter 4, 'Grounding and Centring'. If you feel that you want to process the emotion you got in touch with, feel free to skip ahead to the next chapter and try exercise 9.1, 'Processing our feelings through physical sensation and a chat', which follows very naturally from this one, and you can then pick this chapter up again where you left off.

If in the course of this exercise you got stuck – for example, if a feeling of resistance came up or you had difficulty focusing on the sensation – do not worry, as that is really common. All you need to do is accept the resistance and gently but firmly bring your attention back to your body. If you cannot move beyond this resistance it may not be the right time for you to get in touch with that feeling, so I recommend revisiting it in the future.

Accepting our feelings

One of the biggest reasons we may repress an emotion is that we just don't like it very much, as we discussed before. After we have pushed it down, it just lives in us somewhere, affecting us and trying various ploys to get our attention. Physical pain is a common way that it does this (although not all physical pain is emotional in origin), and another is by affecting our thoughts, words, actions and choices.

Why would it be hard to accept our feelings? Well, for one thing we might not like what they say about us as people. We have learned all kinds of judgements about 'angry people' and 'selfish people' – cue immediate repression of anger and selfishness. We might also want to avoid a feeling if it tells us something about a person or situation that challenges our beliefs or requires us to act. An attitude that can help us to accept even emotions we find unpleasant is the understanding that everything is both good and bad – absolutely *everything*. Whether it ends up being mostly helpful, harmful or neutral really comes down to how we integrate and use it.

But if, in that initial stage of having the feeling, we categorically reject it then we will not be able to learn from it and it can get stuck inside us.

Generally speaking, feelings teach us about ourselves, because stuff happens, we react to it, and that tells us about our nature, what we want, or what we need to do. For example, when someone bumps into you, anger naturally arises, and this is energy for you to maintain your boundaries with. However, if your parents or carers did not love you having healthy boundaries, then you may have had to reroute the expression of that anger. Maybe you pushed it down, got angry in ways that were acceptable to your family (cynicism, or about politics, for example?), became a bully or started believing you were bad in some way. The problem is not the anger but our reaction to it.

Alienation from our feelings is often also alienation from a part of ourselves. The key is not to 'get rid' of our feelings, but to listen to them; they have really interesting things to say. To continue the messenger analogy, listening to our feelings but not getting swept away by them is like opening the door to receive a letter but not then getting on the back of the motorbike and riding away with the courier. We stay in our home, in our centre, but with the information we needed. Exercise 5.4, 'Spacious welcome', in chapter 5 is great for creating an atmosphere of acceptance within us, if you feel you would like to work on that a little more, while the exercise below helps us to look at opinions and beliefs which may affect our ability to accept our feelings.

Exercise 8.4: Accepting our emotions

Below we are going to look at a few statements around acceptance, and I would like you just to read through them and contemplate them a little – not too intellectually, but with an open mind. Just take your time and notice if you feel any resistance to any of the following statements.

- Acceptance is not just intellectual, it also is an openness in our bodies and hearts.
- Acceptance gives us a sense of space and permission, in this case the permission to feel our feelings.

- Accepting our feelings does not mean giving them control over our actions or words.
- Accepting our feelings means we are open to learning about ourselves, maybe even learning about new sides of ourselves.
- If we are centred in our hearts, it is easier to feel acceptance.
- Acceptance of our emotions does not mean we allow ourselves to become hyper or spiral down into despair – we can accept that those feelings are there and listen to them, but choose to live from a more authentic and centred place.
- Acceptance of our feelings does not weaken us – it strengthens us by making us more self-aware and more grounded in reality.
- When we can accept more of who we are, we gain more access to all of who we are.
- Accepting our feelings can make our thinking a lot clearer.
- When we understand that repressing an emotion does not stop it affecting us, we understand that acceptance is the only way to resolve feelings.
- We can give ourselves permission to accept our feelings and feel them, and we are the only ones who can do this.
- Acceptance gives us the ability to fully explore a feeling and its potential.

You can finish this exercise by thinking to yourself, 'I accept who I am and what I feel.' This phrase may be useful the next time you have a lot of resistance to feeling an emotion.

> When you resent your feelings, you resist the unique form of wisdom that your feelings can provide.
>
> Instead of forcing yourself to be positive about your negative emotions, free yourself to be philosophical about them. In a spirit of open-minded inquiry & non-judgmental compassion, ask yourself 'What are my feelings teaching me?'
>
> —T. K. Coleman, education director and coach[64]

---

[64] Coleman 2018

Drawing our feelings

In the exercise below we will do a simple drawing of anything we feel like. It does not have to be good, or even recognisable; it can be random and abstract. Whatever comes into our mind is fine because this is about being free to express our feelings.

Exercise 8.5: Drawing our feelings

It is important that you do this exercise with an open mind and do not try to control the outcome. And because it is about expression and self-acceptance, it is important that you are not harsh or critical about your drawing; having a feeling of being interested is very helpful. You will need some downtime and a pen and paper ideally, but a device will do if you have nothing else.

a)   Relax your body and give it a little move around, releasing any tension and freeing yourself up a bit. Connect to the feeling in your torso again, as before, simply by being aware of it.

b)   Keeping that awareness of the feelings in your body, start drawing anything and then continue drawing whatever comes naturally. Try not to have any preconceptions about what you should be drawing. If you get stuck, that is OK, just doodle for a bit until you start to draw something else.

c)   When you feel that it is finished, have a look at your picture and write down as many words as you like that come to mind to describe it; for example, happy, scared, small, frightened, angry or joyful.

d)   Keep breathing naturally and looking at your picture. Now, if it shows emotions that are not ideal for you and if you want to, you can draw anything that will help the situation – whatever you feel like. Of course, if you are completely happy in the picture then you may not need to do anything, but if you have a T-Rex on the rampage you could, say, draw roller skates on it – there are no wrong ideas.

e)   When you feel that you have finished this stage, write down all the words that feel most relevant to describe the new, improved scene.

It can take us a little bit of practice to express ourselves this way, but the more we do, the easier it will be. This can be a very fast and simple way of tuning into our feelings as it bypasses our intellect. Because many of us have not drawn much since we were little, it is also a great way to tune in to how our younger selves are feeling – I'm sure they will also appreciate being listened to!

Reasons and Ways We Distance Ourselves from Our Feelings

If you find that feeling your feelings is not the easiest for you, then looking through some of these potential stumbling blocks may help you to understand why.

1. We may have vetoed certain emotions before being old enough to understand that's what we were doing

If we were taught that certain emotions (or states) are taboo, then the risk of being rejected by our caregivers or community might have made us push that feeling deep down. An old-fashioned example might be sensitivity in boys or independence in girls, perhaps. Alternatively, our family may have rejected any outward signs of emotion and, especially if we were emotionally neglected as a result, it is then likely that we will find it harder than others to get in touch with our feelings and express them (because most people learn this from their caregivers). We can still learn this skill as adults but, if you are having trouble with it, then you may find it a lot easier to seek out professional help at first, because breaking through that seal and learning to identify different feelings can be tricky at the start.

Seeing an emotion expressed badly can also teach us to reject and repress that feeling within ourselves. For example, children of a parent who often flew into a rage may never directly express their own anger. Unfortunately, as our suppression of feelings is usually instant and not conscious, it can be tricky to change this tendency. But, on the plus side, when you do realise you have an emotional blind spot, it is often possible to get in touch with that part of you again and learn to start expressing it in a way that is healthy.

2. We don't like feeling uncomfortable

If a feeling is unusual for us, alerting us that something is wrong or making us feel vulnerable, then it can feel a lot easier to pretend it isn't there. As mentioned before, most of us have emotions that we are more comfortable with and seek out, and others that we view with the displeasure of cats surveying a bath full of water. Discomfort is often a prelude to change and growth, so if we allow ourselves to feel it we may discover new feelings and insights. But if we always resist uncomfortable feelings we may remain unnaturally confined and most likely frustrated (and probably blame the wrong things for this frustration). Also, if our emotions are telling us that something is not right and we need to make a change of some kind, we usually feel much better if we act on this.

3. Trauma

In a traumatic situation we can easily feel overwhelmed and freeze, trapping our emotional state inside us. We may recover from the stress of the incident, but that emotion stays buried waiting to be acknowledged and processed. Even if it is not as severe a condition as post-traumatic stress disorder (PTSD), this kind of experience can be 'frozen in time' within us, and will affect us emotionally and physically. Therefore, it is good to work towards releasing it; although, if you have experienced severe trauma it is best to seek help from a professional with experience in this area who will know how to guide you.

You could also explore a method such as TRE (tension and trauma release exercises; using physical exercises to help you release trauma from your body) or you could find a bodyworker who has experience of working with trauma. When I do bodywork or energy work with clients who are in this situation, there seems to come a time when they are ready to go to the place their pain is held. When we visit that place together and their feelings are witnessed and accepted, there is usually an instant change: a release and transformation on several levels, which feels like a return to self. Clients then experience a profound sense of calm, centredness and self-love – as though witnessing their pain was some kind of sacrament. That may sound a bit fantastical, but it is all part of the weird and wonderful world of bodywork and healing. It can be a little harder to bring ourselves to a transformation of this magnitude, as often an experienced guide who creates a safe space and knows the way is key. However, once we have learned some tools from a teacher or therapist, we can also do a lot of this work by ourselves.

4. Disconnect

Disconnecting from our physical sensations and emotions is a safety mechanism that can stop us feeling pain, whether physical or emotional, and it also often happens as a result of trauma. A common way of disconnecting is spacing out, where we do not really feel our bodies or emotions. This is a very effective way of coping in the short term, when we cannot physically get to a place of safety, because it allows us to get at least a *part* of ourselves to a safe place. However, in the long term it hampers our progress as it numbs us and makes it hard for us to connect to other people. To really live, we need to be present, feeling and processing.

The same could probably also be said of medication which numbs emotions. Of course, I am not a psychiatrist and I know that many people genuinely need medication to live a balanced life; however, some people seem to be taking medication just to stop feeling the emotions that are a normal part of life (which may also be trying to alert them to an issue that needs to be addressed). Should we consider it normal that in 2013 one in six people in the United States was taking a psychiatric drug?[65] For some groups the percentage is even higher, with white people and women each at 20%, and older people at 25%. Some of these drugs come with a cost – many people who have taken antidepressants long term face

---

[65] Miller 2016

withdrawal symptoms when they try to stop. One study in New Zealand found that three-quarters of people experienced physical and emotional symptoms from coming off their medication, and 45% felt that they were addicted.[66] I believe that if someone needs medication, then of course they should take it; however, it should not be used as a way for otherwise healthy people to avoid feeling the normal emotions of being a person, because learning to feel and process these is key to knowing ourselves and to building resilience.

> **We cannot selectively numb emotions, when we numb the painful emotions, we also numb the positive emotions.**
>
> —Brené Brown, research professor, author and speaker

Another way of disconnecting is to experience *intellectual bypass*, where we retreat into our heads as a way of avoiding feeling. I expect you know a few people like this, as our society is so geared towards thinking. As soon as an emotion looms, the person runs away up into their head because the mind is safer than unpredictable emotions and 'ideas don't feel.'[67] Because there are rewards for this behaviour in our society, few people get called out for doing it, unless they are sitting on a therapist's couch, where typically they suddenly start to feel very squirmy. This may be the reason that Ernest Hemingway wrote that it was very rare for intelligent people to be happy.[68]

Another less-talked-about form of disconnect is *spiritual bypass*, which is a lot harder to spot because if we are intentionally doing meditation or self-development, then how can we be avoiding our problems? Well, meditation and self-development methods are great in my book (no pun intended!), as long as we use them correctly. They should never be a way of avoiding life or detaching from our emotions. Have you ever heard anyone say that our body is not important as our soul is who we really are,

---

[66] Cartwright et al. 2016

[67] Dunion 2017

[68] Hemingway 1995

or maybe something along the lines of 'It doesn't matter that so-and-so hurt me – I am choosing to live in the light,' or similar? There are many ways to use spirituality to avoid acknowledging pain, our shadow or doing life admin, but it doesn't make these things go away – it just causes an internal rift between what we tell ourselves and what we know to be true deep down.

For this reason, it is important that our spirituality is grounded in reality and is integrated with our body, mind and emotions. If we find ourselves rationalising things instead of putting them right, justifying unhelpful behaviour (from ourselves or others) instead of addressing it or trying to rise above uncomfortable feelings instead of acknowledging them, then we may need to feel our bodies more, move more and be more grounded in reality. Feeling safe helps with this a lot, and you may also find chapter 4, 'Grounding and Centring', and chapter 9, 'Processing Our Emotions', useful.

Through understanding our feelings, we become more self-aware, clear-minded and centred. However, identifying our emotions is only half of this process; we also need to learn how to process our feelings, and in the following chapter we are going to learn to do exactly that.

> When you are grounded in the present –
> feeling your feelings, listening to your body,
> tasting your food, and expressing your ideas –
> you do not build up toxicity.
> You digest your experience as you go.
>
> —Debbie Ford, spiritual teacher and author[69]

---

[69] Ford 2011

CHAPTER 9

Processing Our Emotions

T he reason that directors do not enjoy working with animals or children is pretty much the exact reason that these rapscallions are masters of the art of emotional processing, and they don't even know it. Whereas we self-consciously hold ourselves in a certain way, edit ourselves, and have an internal screening process for what we allow ourselves to feel and express, animals and kids are very much just running around and screaming, laughing or crying in the ball pit of life, feeling what they feel, and letting it all hang out, rather than holding it all in. I am not suggesting we become a director's worst nightmare, but that if we develop some of the skills we need to work through our emotions we can recapture some of that effortless ease of being, creativity, authenticity and self-expression. A very bearable lightness of being.

In this chapter we are going to look at a variety of tools for doing this; feel free to try any you are drawn to in any order. But, just before we start using the exercises, let's first have a look at some of the downsides of not processing our feelings so that we can understand the importance of doing this work. We will also cover some of the less useful ways of expressing emotion, in order to address any that we may be using and gain a better understanding of what healthy emotional processing is.

What Happens if We Do Not Recognise and Express Our Emotions?

Unexpressed emotions will never die. They are buried
alive and will come forth later in uglier ways.

—Sigmund Freud

It can be tough just being a person, never mind being completely clear on our feelings and processing them as we simultaneously try to navigate the complexity of life, so it is understandable that most of us tend to file our emotions away to deal with at a later date. After all, we don't want to break down in tears at work, lose our temper when someone irritates us or jump for joy in public. However, when we do not process emotions they usually go straight into our body, creating patterns of holding, tension, pain and even illness. As an alternative therapist and bodyworker, I often work a bit like a housekeeper on a spring-cleaning mission, helping people to release old, stuck feelings that have been lingering in the body, sometimes for years.

And although storing our feelings in little places throughout our bodies like an Easter-egg hunt for therapists is a pretty effective way of coping in the short term, it is not a great long-term strategy because these feelings stand between us and mental, emotional, spiritual and physical peace and groundedness. That's not to say I'm perfect in this regard at all – I am always amazed when an ache or pain immediately changes or disappears after simply acknowledging my feelings. Learning to be able to do this for myself has made all the difference in being able to understand what I am feeling and why, and to have more perspective on what is mine and what is other people's stuff, which is also key to learning to live more intentionally and take responsibility for myself. This also includes taking responsibility for the effects my emotions are having on those around me, whether I am conscious of them or not. 'What? Surely, if I repress my feelings they can't affect others?', you might say. Unfortunately (or fortunately), this is not the case – even though we think we're hiding our sadness, stress or rage, they come with us everywhere we go; they leak out and touch everyone we interact with. As mentioned in the last chapter, emotions are contagious, and they will piggyback on our body language, the look in our eyes, the tone of our voice and the words that we use. The idea that we can override these living, breathing parts of ourselves, while controlling how we behave and how we come across to others and also being happy and able to connect deeply to others is a myth many of us are brought up with. In reality, our emotions, personality, spirit, body and mind are all fully interconnected. All of these parts of us need to be heard, experienced and appreciated in order for us to live in a complete and honest way.

Interestingly, the connection between our mind and body is so strong that people tend to feel sensations in similar areas when experiencing the same emotion, even in very different cultures.[70] And we can all get ill by supressing our feelings for too long; for example, people who have a condition that stops them recognising and expressing emotion (alexithymia) have been shown to have significantly higher levels of inflammation in their bodies.[71] Also, a potential connection has been found between suppressing emotions and higher cancer mortality.[72] This is obviously a very sensitive area for many people, but if it is true it does not mean that people with cancer are to blame – it just means that expressing our emotions should be high up on our priority list.

Aside from causing health issues, supressing our feelings has a knock-on effect on our relationships and our quality of life in general. One study found that the more likely university students were to suppress their emotions, the more likely they were to have less social support, less closeness in their friendships, and less social satisfaction.[73] And people who habitually repress difficult emotions have a much harder time with intimate relationships because they find it harder to engage with others

---

[70] Nummenmaa et al. 2014
[71] Honkalampi 2011
[72] Chapman et al. 2013
[73] Srivastava et al. 2009

emotionally.[74] This is not to scare you in a Struwwelpeter[75] kind of way, just to highlight how important it is that we do not put off being aware of our feelings and working through them for so long that we become ungrounded, detached (from ourselves and others) or ill.

A Couple of Less Healthy Ways to Feel and Express Emotions

Now that we have looked at a few of the ways that repressing emotions can be bad for us, let's also look at a couple of issues that may result from not being able to process our feelings well. None of us is perfect, so if you find that you sometimes do one or a few of the following things, just remember that many others do also. It is never too late to learn to work with your emotions in order to get to a more centred place, and whether you want to do that work with a counsellor or try to do it by yourself, exercising self-kindness, and making small but significant steps, is a great approach.

1. Projecting on to others

This occurs when we dislike an emotion or aspect of ourselves so much that we allow ourselves see it only in others, and when we do so, we also tend to judge them for it. The problem with this is that we are missing out on an experience of, and connection with, a part of our self. If you find that you are triggered by certain qualities in others that you do not think you have in yourself, you may be storing them in your shadow, that part of ourselves we are unconscious of. When we reconnect with something we have been projecting, it often also helps us to be more understanding towards others and kinder, as well as deepening our experience of ourselves.

---

[74] Goleman 1988

[75] A German cautionary tale warning children of disastrous consequences of misbehaviour

2. Passive aggression

Many people learn this behaviour as a coping mechanism in childhood without realising it, when they find that their needs or boundaries are not valued or acceptable to their caretakers. As we still have these needs or feelings of anger, we may find that expressing them indirectly is a lot safer as a way of unburdening ourselves. Unfortunately, it often leaves an unpleasant feeling in the air, damages our relationships and leaves us feeling insecure – after all, it is not a powerful way to behave. And because people are not usually conscious of their own passive aggression, it can be hard to switch to healthier ways of dealing with anger, even though as an independent adult it is now permissible to express feelings and a need for boundaries.

If you notice that you do not directly communicate your needs or annoyance, or find 'work-around' ways to make people feel your anger, you may be expressing yourself in this way. It is important to get in touch with how you feel and honour this as well as your needs. Do not assume that your needs are not important to other people, or that they will not respect your opinions. Others may not always agree with our feelings, but the ability to express them in an appropriate way means we can have an actual conversation instead of souring the atmosphere with small destructive acts of aggression. Although this is about aggression and anger, there are usually other emotions mixed in – frustration, hurt feelings, a low sense of self-worth – which are also worth addressing. We can watch people who ask for what they want and stand up for themselves, notice how they do it and how they seem to feel about themselves, and then take small steps towards doing this for ourselves.

3. Shutting down

Pretending that our feelings are not there or just pushing them deep down never to be seen again is obviously not a good method of processing our emotions. On the positive side, stoicism can be very useful if we need to be clear-headed or just get through a tough day – we don't want to have a meltdown when operating on someone or giving a presentation, for example – but it is no way to live our whole life. Becoming like a robot may seem to fix the 'problem' of troubling, inconvenient or unpredictable emotions, but it also stops creativity, relating, self-knowledge and any meaningful growth. Many people learn this behaviour from family or the culture around them, and we can also unlearn it. Honouring your humanity, your depth and your worth can be a great approach to starting to open up again. If you find there is a lot in there, it can be a great idea to have a friend to talk to, or to find a support group or therapist. Typically, people who have been emotionally closed down for quite a while have a backlog to work through, and a bit of support is great for perspective and encouragement.

4. Emotional overwhelm

When this happens we cannot get ourselves out of a very charged negative emotional state – we may feel we have been pushed just too far. The key in this situation is self-compassion. I also highly recommend that if you are feeling this way, you seek out a therapist, but if you cannot afford this then you could ask for help from your friends or contact an organisation that offers support. Ways of trying to get out of this that will not work include criticising yourself, punishing yourself, or going over your flaws or problems in your head over and over again. Be kind to yourself, breathe and move your body in a way that feels good to you. If external events are getting you down, you can also try making a plan – preferably one with very small steps, and make the first ones manageable so you can start taking action right away, but also make sure that you take the time to identify and feel your feelings.

5. Holding others hostage

Some people have not learned to feel, process and manage their own emotions in a healthy way. Instead, they put their (predominantly negative) emotions on to others, holding them hostage. Although sharing can be healthy, if we are actively avoiding listening to others while forcing our own feelings and views on to them, expecting them to submit, we are not processing our feelings. This can often leave other people with a feeling of confusion and unease, because the emotion is very charged yet at the same time resists resolution. The other person cannot easily resolve the emotion because it is not theirs, so they cannot make sense of it and work through it. Although many of our friends are happy to do a little bit of 'clean' emotional processing with us, no one wants to have an unresolvable problem forced on to them. Essentially, this is us wanting others to feel as bad as we do.

Because this is a young type of behaviour, adults who do this can seem as tyrannical or changeable as toddlers, maybe even having temper tantrums. Although we all have the occasional outburst, if it is happening often then this may be something that needs addressing as we cannot have healthy adult relationships without an awareness of our own feelings and an ability to manage them ourselves.

Processing Our Emotions

As we have discussed, there are many short-term ways that we can deal with emotions that may not lead to a healthy and balanced state in the long term. Ideally, we want to help our emotions express themselves and move through us in a natural way. A major part of this is the ability to recognise the feeling, accept it, allow it to be present, listen to it (although some are just fleeting and do not have a lot to say) and let it complete itself. However, this does not mean giving our emotions total dominion over us, or chasing a state that we find desirable. So there is a difference between honouring our emotions and handing them the reins. Staying centred and grounded within ourselves as we do this work is very useful.

Interestingly, most emotions contain within them the state we need for their resolution or for healing to occur. For example, sadness makes us feel still enough to reflect on and honour what has happened, anger gives us the energy boost needed to change what is not right and love makes us open up enough to bond with others. In order to tap into this, we just need to develop the ability to be with the feeling and listen to it. Emotions often resolve themselves organically when we do this. It also helps when we express ourselves, breathe freely and move enough. A child can feel, breathe and express like a pro, but it takes the sophistication and experience of an adult's mind to understand the finer points of what an emotion is trying to tell us, as well as the discipline of an adult to take responsibility for clean emotional expression. So the adult and child in us can learn from each other!

An example of having a problem with this process is if someone annoys us but we like them, so we push our anger down by taking shallow breaths to supress the feeling. Or if someone is feeling lonely but distracts themselves with shopping or TV instead of acknowledging the feeling and talking to someone. There are many ways that we halt the process of our feelings moving through us when we feel uncomfortable, and many of them are reflexive and unconscious. Therefore, as we learn to do this work it is important to learn to be with our discomfort, be aware of our reactions to our emotions and also be open to making some changes in the way we deal with them.

In this section we are going to look at several tools we can use to help process our emotions. You will probably find that some work better for you than others, but do keep an open mind because those may just require a little more practice. If you are not used to expressing emotion, or being expressive in general, then you may feel a little silly. However, this is a sign that you are leaving your comfort zone, which is a positive thing as you are more likely to get better results from trying something new than from doing the same old thing you always do.

An open mind is also handy because entering into a dialogue with feelings (whether they are old or new) may challenge some thoughts or beliefs you have. Do not worry if you find you are taking baby steps – babies are great! You are still moving forward, and that is what counts. There is plenty of time, so there is no need to try to process all of your feelings in a day; but do keep it up in the days and months to come – sometimes there is no way out but through. And, as with all of the chapters, if you feel a bit overwhelmed you can stop and do an exercise from chapter 4, 'Grounding and Centring', for a bit instead.

Physical sensation and emotion

Now we are going to tune into our physical sensations as we did in the last chapter, but this time we are also going to see if we can draw an emotion out and ask it to tell us what it needs or what it wants to say. Key things to remember for this exercise are to stay open-minded and try not to *decide* what you are feeling, but *find out*. Our minds will want to create stories or reasons for the way we are feeling – try to let all of those thoughts go, and return to an open-minded, listening state as our goal is to let the feeling speak for itself, rather than letting our mind take over. And that takes concentration sometimes because minds do like to be in control.

Exercise 9.1: Processing our feelings through physical sensation and a chat

The best attitude for this exercise is a relaxed and open, pressure-free one, where we are happy to see where it takes us. As with all of the exercises in this book it is open-ended; there is nowhere you 'should' end up. We are just getting in touch with a feeling that is hanging around for a reason, so let's be open and listen to what it wants to say. You can take your time, and as there are a lot of steps you can read and do them one at a time.

a)   Sitting somewhere quiet and comfortable, just breathe and let your body relax, letting the tension go with every out-breath.

b)   Now pay attention how your body is feeling in general as you continue breathing in a relaxed way and close your eyes.

c)   When you have a sense of this, notice if there are any sensations in your body that are more in the foreground, more obvious. What is that sensation like? Is it warm, cool, light, heavy, a ball, spread out, tense or relaxed, for example?

d) Keep paying attention to that sensation in your body and, with an open mind, notice if you feel that it has a shape and/or colour.

e) Once you are feeling this physical sensation quite clearly and picturing it in your mind's eye, say 'hello' to it in your mind.

f) Now ask it if it wants to say anything and wait with an open mind for its answer. If it does say something, you can have a conversation with it, finding out a little more information regarding what it said. Every time you ask a question you need to wait patiently for the answer; do not let your mind jump in with the answers.

g) Now you can also ask if it needs anything and, again, wait with an open mind for the answer. If it does, you can converse with it a little to find out more, or to discover how you can satisfy those needs. Some things we can even take care of this through the visualisation, such as imagining giving that part of you a hug or attention, or letting it run around pretending to be an aeroplane – anything it is asking for.

h) You can then thank the part of yourself you connected with and ask it if it has anything else it would like to say. When you feel ready to end the exercise, allow a feeling of self-acceptance and love to fill your body and then open your eyes.

This type of exercise can take some practice, so if you found it tricky you are not alone! It is great to revisit it and also try to gently accept any resistance or lack of focus that comes up (which are often natural defence mechanisms). If that happens, just keep bringing your attention back to your physical sensations. You may find that you can only do a little bit at a time, which is also fine. Just do what you can and try to be kind to yourself – this is a gentle, firm enquiry, not the Spanish inquisition.

There are no wrong answers and feelings do not always make logical sense, but be careful that it is not your mind forming and providing the answers – there should be the feeling of the answer arising organically rather than coming from the head down. Our feelings may not be able to be resolved completely in one sitting, especially if we have been carrying them for a long time, so it is fine to use this exercise several times for one emotion; however, I recommend spreading this out over days, weeks or longer.

Accepting our feelings

In the previous chapter we looked at why the ability to accept our feelings was so crucial, and we also started creating space for awareness of our emotions in chapter 5, 'Acceptance and Self-Acceptance'. I just want to reiterate that without acceptance, there can be no complete processing of our emotions. This is because in order to work with a feeling we need to be able to see it all, clearly, and also allow it to be present – both of which are impossible if we are limiting our experience of the emotion by resisting it.

There is no single way to accept all feelings, because our barrier to acceptance can be different for different emotions. Therefore, in this section we are going to look at any prejudices and blocks we have to feeling specific emotions, in order to help us accept having them. If you find you cannot tune in to an emotion at all, or reject the idea of having it, that is a pretty good sign you are not accepting it right now. I recommend mulling over why this might be, and giving yourself time and space to come back to this feeling; but do not try to force any change – our resistance can be formidable. Being interested and open-minded is a more helpful approach.

Exercise 9.2: Accepting our feelings

We are going to look through a list of feelings that some people do not like and select the ones we feel some resistance to working with. It can be hard to call emotions to mind when you are not feeling them right now, so if it helps you can imagine a situation that made you feel that way to get you started. You will be doing all of the steps for each emotion completely before moving on to the next one.

As before, this is an open-ended enquiry with no right or wrong answers – as long as they are authentic to you – so try to give your most honest answer to each question.

a) Sit somewhere quiet and, if you would like to take notes of this exercise, you can make a table as in the example below, but with enough rows to work with up to five emotions.

b) Consider the feelings listed below one at a time, and put any that you feel resistance to in the first column. If you want to work with any other emotions, feel free to add them also.

Anger	Greed	Repulsion
Fear	Hate	Desire to inflict pain
Pain	Self-hate	Hope
Sadness	Humiliation	Love
Suffering	Shame	Pride
Loneliness	Contempt	Self-love
Selfishness	Disgust	Happiness
Competitiveness	Confidence	Joy

c) After picking the emotions you want to work with, start with the first one and note your initial reaction to it. This could be a feeling, thought, belief – anything – just write it down (see the table below for an example).

d) Now in the next column, write how your reaction to this emotion feels in your body.

e) In the following column write down all the negative associations you have with that feeling – essentially, why it is bad.

f) And now write down ways that it could be good. Try to stick with this one even if you feel resistance to it. If you feel the emotion is trying to tell you something, you can put this is in the same column. This is an example of working with anger:

Emotion	Initial reaction	Feeling	Bad aspect	Good aspect
Anger	Don't like it because it takes a lot of effort to resolve and it is embarrassing	Warmth and strength in chest, attachment to it, aggressiveness	It can ruin relationships, it can hurt people and cause pain	Can be used to protect myself and others; it brings some of the truth of a situation out; it makes me want to resolve problems

g)   After you have completed each feeling you want to work on, try and imagine a sense of accepting it and even being grateful for the gift of energy or information it offers you.

Although accepting uncomfortable emotions can be very challenging, it is essential for getting in touch with all of who we are. So the next time you notice yourself pushing a feeling away, try thinking to yourself, 'It's OK, I accept feeling this,' and see what happens. You can use the physical sensation and feeling exercise from the section above, exercise 9.1, to explore it more. In general, the most important thing is to learn to accept our feelings in their entirety.

Breathing into our feelings

Emotions and breath are like peanut butter and jam: they automatically go together. Have you ever tried staying excited while purposefully slowing your breathing or feeling calm while intentionally hyperventilating? It is pretty much impossible because your emotions change your breath and your breathing changes your emotions, which is why breathing in a specific way will elicit a specific emotional state.[76] In the exercise below we are going to use this connection – not to create an emotion, but to help us relate to one and then to help that feeling resolve itself.

Exercise 9.3: Breathing into the feeling

For this free-form exercise I would like you to keep an open mind and, even though it is natural to wish for a certain outcome, it is better not to try to control it. We are going to 'breathe into' a feeling, by which I mean become very aware of it, and then use breath to help process it. The object is not to get worked up or overcome by the emotion, but to allow your feelings to be fully present. With this intention, know that you are safe and calm in addition to experiencing any other feelings that come

---

[76] Philippot, P. et al. 2002

up. If you feel that you want to stop, that is fine; you can also slow and deepen your breath and relax your body to return to a more centred state.

a) Sitting somewhere quiet and comfortable, just breathe, relax into your body and close your eyes.

b) Let any tension go with each out-breath and allow yourself to feel heavy and calm.

c) Notice any more-obvious sensations in your body and, focusing on one, notice what it feels like: warm, cool, light, heavy, a ball, spread out, tense, stuck or pulling, for example?

d) Now, without preconceptions, I would like you to imagine 'breathing into' the most noticeable feeling in your body, by putting your attention on that place and visualising your in-breath going there. As you do this you can also have the intention of giving the feeling the space to be itself, to be noticed without judgement. If your attention ever naturally moves to another spot in your body, that is fine – as long as it does not feel like a distraction from, or avoidance of, a particular feeling.

e) Continuing to breathe 'into' and with the emotion, notice how it changes and where it moves, if at all. Keep breathing with it.

f) Now open your eyes and keep them open as you ask your feeling how it would like you to breathe in order to process it. It's also fine to move your body, open your mouth wide, stretch or make noises if you feel guided to.

g) Stop when you feel that you have done enough for now, and notice how you feel physically and emotionally. Do you find that you are breathing or holding yourself differently than before?

It is incredible how much our breath (and some movement) can liberate a trapped emotion, and even make us feel more alive. In fact, it can allow us to feel more in general. We may not notice how much we are stifling our feelings by controlling our breath day to day, but exercises like this show us just how much we may be diminishing ourselves. Breath is a great way back into our bodies and our feelings.

I also find that the quality and sound of people's breath and the sound of their voices are all incredibly significant in my self-development work with them. When someone only takes little sips of air, or their voice sounds like crying or like bottled aggression, it gives us an indication of their internal state. Breath shows how much we trust the outside world, how free or giving we are, and how easy it is for us to receive. The sound of people's voices tells us how their *instrument is tuned* – because our emotional state creates a complex pattern of tension in our body which shapes the sound of our voice as it comes out. To explore this as a way of releasing emotion, we are going to work with our body as an instrument in the exercise below.

Sounding out our feelings

In chapter 11, 'Our Connection to Our Body', we will use exercise 11.1, 'The Loud Sigh', to try to hear what we are feeling. This is a great tool, which you can also try now to see if you can identify the emotions in you that are shaping the sound. Take a deep breath in and sigh loudly out. The key is not to try too hard to produce a certain sound, and not to modify it or stop it. Just let the sound flow out, loud and uninhibited, all the way to the end, but do not 'push' it out. How did it sound? Normally when people start, they cannot hear anything in particular, and then, little by little, they may start to hear things such as stress, annoyance, sadness or excitement, and this gets easier with practice. But now let's try a more varied tool to help process our feelings.

Exercise 9.4: The sound of our emotions

You will want some alone time in a private place for this exercise, so that you can express yourself freely. Try not to be self-critical or change the sound intentionally, but let whatever is in there come out naturally, also knowing that it does not have to be loud or dramatic to be effective – just real.

a)   Relax in either a seated or standing position, and feel free to change between these at any time in the exercise.

b)   Tuning into your physical feelings, choose the most obvious one, the one most in the foreground.

c)   Now I would like you to tell it that it is allowed to make any sound it wants through you, within reason. Thin walls may lead to you making it a little more quietly, but you can still do it. If you live with other people, you may want to warn them you are doing this first or wait until they have gone out.

d)   If you feel awkward, you can start with a hum or a sigh and let it develop from there. Try to be explorative, but not take charge; let the feeling guide you. Know that there is no 'right' sound, so try to put any self-criticism to the side.

e)   Now that you have made a few noises, ask the feeling if it would like to add any movements. Again, let the feeling guide you, but ensure that you only do what is safe and do not push through pain.

f)   You can breathe, make sounds and also move, until you feel that it is enough, that something has completed, or that you need a break. At this point take a moment to be still, acknowledging your emotions and body and thanking them for doing this with you.

How do you feel now in your body, mind, energy and emotions? Although this is best done in private, you can do a modified, socially acceptable version throughout the day by tuning in to your body and making small movements or quiet sounds. You will probably find that your body starts to feel freer and lighter because many patterns of tension are emotional in origin.

Movement and emotion

Across all cultures you can see that movement and dance are vital to community, bonding, ritual and self-expression. Aside from the psychological and social benefits, because certain aspects of our physiology depend on movement in order to work properly, we need to move to stay healthy. However, as we become more and more sedentary we start to lose our connection to this primal need, and to areas of our body which become numb and disconnected. We need to intentionally shake the cobwebs out of our increasingly stiff and hunched-over bodies through movement – whether that is dance, exercise, stretching or random self-expressive mime.

Because emotions often exist in a place inside us that can be hard to reach with words, they can sometimes be expressed more easily in non-verbal ways, including movement. In the exercise below we are going to liberate any emotions that have become imprisoned and stuck in our body and self, by moving in the way the emotion tells us to. This requires us to tune in to our feelings and to move without a fixed sense of purpose; the polar opposite of what we normally do in society. It is also a great opportunity to scare your neighbours, if you wanted one, or you can draw your curtains if not.

Exercise 9.5: Moving to express emotion

You can do this exercise with or without music. Although it can feel a bit crazy or forced moving without music, you do avoid the issue of your feelings changing and conflicting with the mood of the song you are listening to. So I suggest that if you use music you switch songs as needed.

Please note that you may be surprised by the force of your movements as stronger emotions see their chance to escape. Again, as long as it is not hurting you or unsafe, it is fine. You can make incredibly beautiful or very silly movements, just go with whatever happens and see how your feelings emerge and express themselves.

a) Stand in a private place with enough space to move.
b) If you want to play music, use your intuition to select the right type of music or even a specific song.
c) Now, as you are standing relaxed, tune in to your physical sensations and your feelings. Without forcing anything, let them guide you in making a movement and just keep going.
d) There are no wrong movements, as long as they are safe and you are not dictating or controlling them with your mind. If you are

expressing your feelings then it does not matter if you are doing a moon walk or hopping like a bunny, it is all good.

e) Continue until you feel either that you are finished or that you need a rest; you can always come back to it later.

How do you feel now? It can be a bit tiring sometimes, so if you need a quick nap that is a good idea, even five minutes may help. I also recommend that you do not try to analyse your emotions; just stay with how you feel now and be present. If you feel like it, you can also say thank you to your body for carrying those emotions around for you until you were ready to feel them. Our body does work very hard for us, so a little self-hug and a sense of appreciation can be a nice way of recognising this effort.

Self-expression to free emotions

Self-expression is a wonderful way of tapping into feelings we do not even know we have. And we do not have to be good at writing or even spell correctly to do this, we just need ten minutes, a pen and paper (or device), and an open mind. The advantage of doing this over making sounds and movements with carefree abandon is that we could do it in the middle of a coffee shop or on a bus and no one would know.

As with all of this work, we are not trying to work towards a specific outcome, but to listen to our feelings. Therefore, you do not have to worry that you are doing this wrong, or try to make things go in a certain direction – it is exploratory and free-form. The only wrong way to do this is by being very self-critical or forcing yourself to write about specific things, instead of allowing things to come up as they wish. Often, random things want to come out that we would never have guessed were on our mind; if so, just let them.

Exercise 9.6: Writing our feelings

So, in this last exercise we are going to simply write without pause for ten minutes on the subject of our feelings. We do not pause to correct grammar or collect our thoughts – if at any point you cannot think what to write then you just come back to writing the starting phrase over and over again, which is 'I feel.'

a) Sit somewhere comfortable and quiet, with a pen and paper preferably, but a laptop is OK too.

b) With an open mind, write the phrase 'I feel,' and then if words come naturally just write them down, but if not just keep writing 'I feel I feel I feel' until something starts to comes out. Come back to writing this phrase repeatedly whenever you feel stuck for something to write, until you naturally start writing something else. Continue to write for ten minutes and then stop.

c) As mentioned above, we do not correct spelling or grammar, as this breaks the flow and puts us in the wrong state of mind (critical). Do not worry if what you write does not make sense or is not what you think you should be writing.

How do you feel now that you have done that exercise? If you like, you can date it and keep it in your diary – it may be interesting to you in the future when you look back with more perspective. Freewriting is a tool many writers use to tap into their creativity and overcome blocks, but we can use it to temporarily shrug off the day-to-day thoughts that we have, in order to tune in to our feelings and look at them more deeply. If you ever feel like it, you could take what you wrote and transform it into a poem or some prose. Something beautiful can often come out of our deeper feelings, whether it is truth, art or transformation, and it is always wise to enjoy this if we can.

Well done for your effort in this chapter! Do not worry if you found one or more of the exercises difficult – as I said before, they may take a little more practice, but stick with it. There is nothing quite like working through our feelings for opening us up to more life. No amount of meditation, medication, exercise, education or effort can move us forward in our self-development if we are not processing our feelings – they will always be in the background, affecting all of our self. But by processing them fully we can acknowledge *what is*, and this grounding in the reality of ourselves frees us to live in the moment, often with lighter bodies and clearer minds, and with the unmistakeable sense of certainty that comes from dropping pretence. This is a wonderful state to be in – not being weighed down by the past or dragged by worry into the future, just here in the present, being ourselves and living. What a fantastic relief and immense opportunity.

> Youth is not a time of life; it is a state of mind;
> It is not a matter of rosy cheeks, red lips and supple knees;
> It is a matter of the will, a quality of the imagination,
> a vigor of the emotions;
> It is the freshness of the deep springs of life.

—Samuel Ullman, poet and humanitarian, 'Youth'

CHAPTER 10

Getting in Touch with Our Inner Child

What were you like as a child? Were you fascinated by nature and animals, an artist, a builder or maybe a dedicated performer? Did you love books, cartoons, interpretive dance or exploration? Or maybe all of the above and more? Most of us used to be playful, curious, adventurous, loving, brave and half-wild little tykes, with a startling lack of inhibition about sticking out our big round tummies and streaking almost anywhere. When our spirit had an impulse we heard its call and responded with gusto and joy. We were one seamless, messy, sticky, fidgety whole. Unfortunately, there comes a point where we have to be tamed enough to fit into one of the square, round or triangular holes of society, so that we can achieve goals such as having continence, boundaries, a job and a place in society. This is a pretty big deal; after all, our safety and success depend on being accepted by whichever group we popped up in, but alongside this conditioning often comes self-doubt, loss of our connection to our spirit and feelings of shame, especially in cultures that do not value the qualities of childhood, or have very strong ideas about what an adult *should* be.

This invisible but hefty filter often shuts down our awareness of the whimsy, dreams and needs of our little self, also known as our inner child, with the grace and subtlety of an anvil landing on a badger. And although we do need to behave ourselves a bit, think of others and fit into society *enough*, many of our wonderful childlike qualities make the difference between moving through life as if on a conveyor belt of numbness and blah, and seeing life as exciting and full of possibility. Our inner child remains an essential key to our happiness and ability to be whole throughout our lives, however grown up we tell ourselves we are.

Carl Jung was the first to identify this part of us, at least in the field of psychotherapy, and he believed that our inner child is always within us, wanting our love and attention and always seeking to grow and become whole. So the mini-me lurking within us is not stuck back in the 1920s–noughties (or whichever years we were little) but remains a part of our core personality, which has 'a fundamental impact on one's life as a whole',[77] and which is important for our present and our future also. When we reconnect with our inner child we can not only feel the wonder of childhood again, we can start to address childhood issues that we have carried within us for years. For many of us this gives us a fresh insight into ourselves and a way of healing deep wounds that we may never have experienced before.

Through learning to listen to the little person inside us we have the opportunity to acknowledge their feelings and needs, and through forging a strong, loving connection with them we can develop a stronger connection to our authentic self. Like all self-development work, this is a process with its own schedule and we often progress most easily and completely with an attitude of exploration and openness, just like a child's (at least, one who isn't tired, bored or hungry!), rather than trying to push too fast or being goal-orientated. OK, let's have a look at how we can do this work in a fun and gentle way.

Working with Our Inner Child

Now, you may be wondering how you are going to get in touch with this mysterious midget lurking inside you. If only it was as simple as twisting our top and bottom halves in different directions and opening ourselves like a Russian doll to get to the different ages inside. (What am I saying? That would be terrifying!) Instead, there are three exercises in this chapter and you can use any of them that you feel like. It is best to have an open

---

[77] Firman and Russell 1994, p. 5

mind during all of them, to go at your own pace, and to be positive towards your inner child and yourself because we do not need any extra negativity in there. In fact, being kind to ourselves is especially important because our inner child is often carrying some bruises and scars (one definition sums these up as the: 'anger, hurt, and fear attributable to childhood experiences'[78]). So, in these exercises we are going to approach this part of ourselves with gentleness and understanding (or, we could say, with kid gloves – pun intended).

In addition to this, it is important to bear in mind that our inner child has usually had enough of being told what they *should* be like, what they *should* want or who they *should* be. Can you remember a time when you were little and you felt an adult judging you, making you feel *wrong* some-how, and do you remember how it felt? Did you feel ashamed, angry, hurt or betrayed, perhaps? We do not want to inflict any more rejection or criti-cism on our inner child in this way; we are doing this work to find out what they *do* want and who they *actually* are. So, let's aim to listen kindly to the deepest secrets of our youngest selves and to accept what is revealed whether we find it appropriate to act on or not.

We do not need to wait for our inner child to throw a tantrum or feel very sad to do this work. I only mention this because I have many clients who seem apologetic for coming to a session when their physical or emotional needs are yet not at catastrophic levels. In fact, it is better help ourselves before we need it badly and this is a much healthier attitude in terms of our self-care and self-worth. If it feels right, you can use one or two of the exercises in this chapter as part of your regular self-care routine.

Writing to get in touch with our inner child

This is a surprisingly simple method for reaching our inner child. We are going to write questions from our adult self to our child self – and then, using our other hand, we will write our inner child's response.

---

[78] *Merriam-Webster Unabridged Dictionary* [online], s.v. "Inner Child", accessed 18 June 2018, https://www.merriam-webster.com/dictionary/inner%20child.

As an experiment, I tried typing instead of writing, and although I expected it not to work (because we type with both hands, and so I thought there would be less of a difference between my dominant and non-dominant hands), it was actually OK. I think the intention of using only one hand and then the other is part of what makes the exercise work. However, there is something about writing with a pencil or pen that helps us connect to our emotions more, and it has been shown to increase activity in certain areas of the brain in a way that is similar to meditation.[79] So, if you have the option I recommend you choose writing by hand over typing for this exercise.

Exercise 10.1: Writing with your non-dominant hand

All you need is a pen and paper and some quiet time. When you are writing the answers, it is important to keep an open mind and write down whatever answer comes up naturally; do not try to change it to something you prefer.

a) Start by dividing the page into two columns. Then, in your dominant hand, write a question on the left side of the paper. Just start with something simple, such as: 'What do you like for breakfast?' We can build up to more personal questions later.

b) Now, without any preconceptions of what the answer should be, write the answer that pops into your head with your non-dominant hand on the right side of the page.

c) Do this as many times as you like, making sure to be patient and letting your inner child express themselves fully.

d) After your inner child has told you what they think, make a serious effort to acknowledge them. If they have told you something that they want, try to find a way to give it to them, or, if it is an activity, to do it with them (imagining them there with you as you do it). If what they want is not possible or practical, try to find a way to offer them something close to what they want (there is more on this below).

---

[79] Olson 2016

e)   When you have asked all the questions that you want to, you can end the exercise by telling your inner child that you enjoyed speaking to them and that you love and appreciate them.

Did you find that your inner child said something you didn't expect? Our inner child may be having thoughts and feelings that are quite different to what we are thinking and feeling consciously; and yet their feelings often remind us of our core values and self. This is partly why the work is so valuable: it takes us out of the day to day and reminds us what really matters to us. I am not sure of the exact origin of this exercise, but Lucia Capacchione has written a great book on getting in touch with the inner child,[80] if you want to try some different exercises from the one above.

If your inner child asked for something, you can either visualise doing it (so if they want a hug, imagine hugging them) or do something in the real world and imagine them there with you. This can be anything that you can manage practically – for example, if they wanted to go skydiving, find a compromise that gives them some part of what they wanted, like going on the swings if they wanted to feel free, or a rollercoaster perhaps. Let them know what you are going to do and when, and stick to it as far as possible. While you are doing it, imagine they are there, picture them having fun and enjoy spending time with them.

There will be days when your inner child is more talkative and others when they will be harder to reach, so do not worry if you find this exercise quite different on different days.

Speaking to our inner child

It can be funny, when we start to do this kind of work, imagining a child within us, but then for many of us the memory of how we were as a child returns quite clearly. The clothes we liked, our hairstyle, the way we stood and acted. In the exercise below we are going to call to mind our inner child so that we can speak with them. It can feel really nice to see them again.

---

[80] Capacchione 1991

On some days you may connect with yourself at five years old, on others at nine or sixteen. Usually the first part that comes up is the one that most wants to express itself, so whichever age comes up is fine. For some of us it may bring up strong feelings, so you can stop at any time if you want to. I recommend that if you do stop early, you still do the last step of the exercise.

Exercise 10.2: Speaking to our inner child

You will want some quiet time and a private place for this. It is important to have a kind attitude towards yourself and your inner child, so take this at your own pace and try to enjoy yourself.

a) Start by sitting comfortably. Close your eyes and breathe in a relaxed way.

b) Picture yourself as a child – whichever age comes to mind is fine. Notice their clothes and hair, facial expression, and how they are standing.

c) In your mind's eye say hello to them and then ask them if there is anything they want. Wait for the answer patiently; try not to have any expectations about what you think they 'should' say.

d) If it is possible, you can imagine giving them what they ask for. If they do not want anything, ask if there is anything they would like to say. Again, wait for the response with an open mind.

e) Talk to your inner child as much as you feel is the right amount, always allowing them as much time to respond to questions as they need, and giving them the opportunity to ask questions.

f) When you feel you have finished it is nice to imagine giving them a warm hug and telling them you appreciate and love them.

How do you feel, now you have done that? As with the writing exercise, it can be a surprise to hear what our inner child wants. If there is something specific that they want to do or experience, then I recommend trying to do it as far as possible, if it is practical. For many of us, our inner child will just want love, attention or affection. You can do whatever feels right, from imagining them sitting on your lap and giving them a hug to praising them or giving them attention in other ways. Keep it positive – you are trying to be the ideal parent to yourself.

And now we are going to expand on meeting the emotional needs of our inner child, by looking at what they lacked or were hurt or saddened by when you were little.

Healing for our inner child

All of us experienced difficulties in childhood, whether they were just small events that hurt us or were as serious as trauma and abuse. As children we do not know how to deal with these feelings, so if someone was not able to adequately guide us through understanding and processing our emotions we will have stored it somewhere inside us until we could. This is the emotional equivalent of having an illness and preserving ourselves cryogenically until medical technology is advanced enough to heal us. But it is a bit more of a universal experience and it doesn't cost $200,000+.

Now we are all grown up, we can help our inner child heal that pain, using our greater understanding and experience. Key aspects of this healing include fully witnessing our inner child's pain and having an attitude of self-love and self-acceptance. As children are very sensitive, we should be sensitive towards our inner child and avoid minimising their pain (e.g. a lost teddy bear may not seem like a big deal to us, but it may have been a large part of their world and a big source of comfort to them) or judging them (e.g. for not being strong enough), and reinforce that they have worth, deserve respect and love, and that their feelings are important. For those of us who do not treat our adult selves this way it can be a bit of a challenge, but just do the best you can and that will be enough for now. Healing our inner child very often leads to greater kindness to ourselves as adults, so we may find ourselves on an upward trajectory of self-kindness.

Exercise 10.3: Healing for our inner child

We are now going to use our intention and imagination for healing. If you find this challenging at all, just take your time. We are going to allow whichever age of our inner child wants to be healed to come forward, without judgement. After we work with our inner child of one age, another age may want to be worked on and we can keep going until we feel like we have done enough.

As adults we may have the urge to take charge, or to fix things, but no one likes to be told their feelings are invalid, or are less of an issue than they feel they are. Therefore, first of all it is essential to fully listen to your inner child. Try not to gloss over their feelings or change them too soon just because you feel uncomfortable or you want to stop them hurting. A lot of healing work is fully acknowledging negative influences and events, emotional wounds, and all of the feelings around them. Often, our capacity for healing depends on our ability to let ourselves see the pain that is in us, so if we are not ready to see it we are also not ready to heal it yet. This is about gently allowing the space and time for your inner child to have their experience (not trying to force negative memories, but, equally, allowing them to arise if needed) and then letting them take the lead on when it is time to move on from mostly acknowledging their pain towards healing and positivity.

Finally, I just want to remind you that it is fine to do this exercise one step at a time as this is quite a long one; you do not need to memorise it all. You can stop at any point if you need to; however, I recommend that if you do stop early, you still do the final step.

a) Sit comfortably somewhere quiet and close your eyes.

b) Take a moment to let your breath deepen and expand slightly. Letting the tension drop away from your body, feel a sense of appreciation for this moment.

c) Centre yourself in your heart (putting your attention there and feeling that is the centre of your being) and continue breathing in a relaxed way.

d) Now have the intention of asking the child part of you that would like to be healed to come forward, and help them to feel welcomed and safe. If it takes a little while for a child to come forward, that is fine – they may be shy at first!

e) When your inner child comes forward, have a sense of connecting from your heart to theirs and through that connection send a lot of love to them, with the message that they are welcome, that they are part of you, and that you love and respect them. Just feel that for a while.

f) Now ask them what it is that they would like to have healed and wait with an open mind and heart for their answer. This may not be in the form of words, it may be a feeling, a memory or a picture. As far as you can, follow this by paying attention to it and letting it expand fully until you have the whole idea, image, feeling or memory.

g) Once you have the whole idea, tell your inner child that you understand completely, you see it all, and then acknowledge their emotions and pain. If you have more of an understanding as an adult about what they experienced, you can explain it to them now, as a parent would to a child. For example, if they show you a memory of being hurt, explain that this was wrong, the reason the other person might have been acting badly, and how your inner child is safe from this now because you are taking care of them. After that, if it feels right, you can also tell them about any benefits you gained as a result, such as resilience (but only if you do feel you gained any). Do all this without needing them to stop feeling hurt; allow them to have their feelings for as long as they need to. Equally, there is no need to hold on to that pain if it is ready to go.

h) If it feels helpful, you can also use your imagination for healing. Picturing yourself like a guardian angel, you can take yourself back in time to the moment your inner child is telling you about, so that you can change the situation into a positive one. This could be making the situation safe, more loving, disciplining bullies, righting wrongs, giving affection and attention to our inner child, playing football with them – whatever is needed.

i) You can now ask your inner child if there is anything else they want or need. If they want anything else, you can imagine that you are doing it with them or giving it to them. Also, if another age comes in to be healed you can repeat steps (e) to (i) with them.

j) When their needs are taken care of, imagine hugging them for as long as you both want, and wrapping them in love, safety and gratitude for being part of the foundation of your life. You can tell them that they did well, they are a great person and you are proud of them, or any other positive things you want to say. When you feel ready to, take a deep breath in and, breathing out, slowly open your eyes.

In this exercise we used our imagination as a tool to heal us in the past retroactively – not to gloss over what actually happened or to create a fantasy, but to fully acknowledge what we wanted or needed. This helps our inner child to feel complete, understood and satisfied. However, it is important that we are not masking any leftover negative emotions. If it feels confusing to imagine the past as it would have been in a perfect situation, as well as acknowledging any bad feelings we have, it may help to remember that positive and negative emotions can exist within us at the same time and both be valid.

Doing this kind of work with our inner child can have a profound effect on us, and often leads to us feeling more solid, integrated and happy. Sometimes, with this renewed connection to our core, we may find our emotions and priorities shifting a little, and as long as it feels authentic this is always a good thing. So often when we feel sad, empty or lost we try to fix these feelings by shopping, achieving, eating, drinking or other distractions, when really they may be signs that a deeper part of us is calling out for our attention and love. It is hard for many of us to read these signs and to understand where they come from and what they mean, but if spending some time listening to our inner child and sending them love helps, then there is a good chance that it was their need we were feeling.

We can see this work as parenting our inner child, and they need it just as much as we did when we were little. Although it is sad that many people grow up in situations that are hard in different ways, we have the capacity to heal the part of us that carries that burden, allowing our inner kid to be happy and healthy again. But beyond caring for them, the great thing about hanging out with our inner child is rediscovering the side of us that is excited about life, willing to try things, and to be open, playful, adventurous and interested. Children are usually very firmly rooted in the present, which is a wonderful lesson for us – to be here, where we are, and completely alive. And if we ever start to feel jaded, our inner child is the natural remedy; they will tell us what they want to do, and if we listen we are likely to have a life that is a fun-filled adventure rather than a mundane continuing existence in the adult world.

So take your time, be kind, and above all enjoy hanging out with your inner child. You will have a lot of fun together! (At this point my inner child wanted me to write 'cowabunga!' – and since it *is* her chapter, it would be rude not to.)

> Everything seemed possible, when I looked
> through the eyes of a child.
> And every once in a while; I remember,
> I still have the chance to be that wild.
>
> —Author and Artist Nikki Rowe

CHAPTER 11

Our Connection to Our Body

If you stop to consider it, how many times a day would you say you are aware of your body? Do you ever think about it aside from the times you feel tension, pain or hunger? Although many of us are showing the world more of our bodies than ever, and there are more and more diets and workout routines that focus on our physical state, how many of us are actually connected to our body in a meaningful way?

For many of us, being connected to our body means different things. For some it is being fit and having good coordination, dexterity, balance and proprioception (knowing where we are in space); others think of it as knowing what state our body is in, whether it is tense, comfortable or hydrated, for example; and some think of it as keeping our bodies good-looking and youthful. However, real body awareness not only includes many of the factors above, but extends far beyond them.

Although looks, health and athleticism are great, our physicality is so much more than this. Aside from being an exceptional feat of evolution, it holds aspects of us that we can access only through awareness of it; for example, our ability to stay grounded, primal instincts, sensuality, animal intuition and our emotions. The ability to receive this information depends on us being aware of our body and recognising that it has a kind of intelligence of its own. If we know how to listen to it, our body can tell us what food it wants, what exercise it likes, what posture is good for it, what people it likes, how much rest it needs, where it is comfortable, what feels safe and more. In this way a whole new source of information is opened up to us, which can be a refreshing change from the usual experience of the mind having total dominion in its role as information gatherer and judge.

Think, instead, with our body.

—Taisen Deshimaru, Japanese Zen Buddhist teacher,
Zen and Karma

Our body also houses a lot of information that is passed down for generations. One example of this is the fact that experiencing trauma can affect our DNA, and this change is then passed on to the next generation whether they experience trauma or not.[81] Interestingly, phobias can also be passed down through our genes in a similar way.[82] I will never forget taking my five-year-old god-daughter to an aquarium and helping her stand up on a wall to see into the tank better. Suddenly she became stiff as a board, and I caught her as she fell like timber; she had had a primal freeze reaction to seeing a shark swimming towards us, which must have been pure instinct as she had never had a frightening experience with a shark herself (it was massive, to be fair). It is interesting to think that many of these types of reactions and feelings emerge from our body, while we are often taught to approach issues such as trauma or phobias as if the mind were the only cure.

Aside from responses to fear stored in our DNA, there is also some physiological evidence that emotions are stored predominantly in the body and not in the brain.[83] I have found this to be true through my work with clients, as approaching any issue holistically often yields much more release, integration and change than using one method alone, whether that is through talking, bodywork, energy work or another method. And although for some the term 'holistic' may sound wishy-washy, in this

---

[81] Youseff et al. 2018
[82] Dias and Ressler 2014
[83] Ruff 2014

context it actually means approaching the issue on all of the levels it exists within (physical, emotional, energetic, psychological and more).

Developing Our Connection to Our Body

In this chapter we are going to work through some different ways of building our connection to our body, taking us even closer to an integrated, 360° experience of ourselves. As with all of the exercises in this book, just do what you can comfortably do, as listening to our body is not about pushing hard or ignoring pain. And, as far as possible, try to enjoy yourself!

> It is amazing how many hints and guides and
> intuitions for living come to the sensitive person
> who has ears to hear what his body is saying.

—Rollo May, existential psychologist, *Man's Search for Himself*

Our bodies and sound

Many people find that music and chanting produce a very calming effect on their bodies, relaxing them deeply and helping to put them in a healing state. The purpose of this exercise, however, is not to introduce sound externally, but to let it come up and out from the inside of our body, telling us what is in there and helping us to shift old, stuck emotions.

Exercise 11.1: The loud sigh

This is the fastest way to hear what is going on inside your body in terms of both your emotional and your physical state, and to start moving it through. You will probably want some privacy for this exercise.

a) Take a deep breath and, with a wide-open mouth, sigh, just letting the sound come out. It should not be a controlled breath or sound, as this is not about control but release – visualise letting everything go, letting go of control, surrendering any burdens you have been carrying or stress you have been holding. This is not a sustained out-breath for a number of counts, but a whoosh of air and feeling out.

b) As you sigh out, try to keep your mouth fairly wide open because pursing your lips means you are still controlling your emotions. Try to sigh from a deep place: the very bottom of your lungs, or it may even feel like you are sighing from your belly. It can be hard for some of us to just let it happen, but if you find you are making a tone or sound, then you are probably pushing it out rather than letting it all go. Try to do the latter.

c) Sigh as many times as you feel you need to, and if you feel like moving your head, shoulders or body around while you do so, that is fine – as long as it is safe and it is instinctive rather than something you think you *should* do.

Does your body feel different after doing this exercise? Some people feel physically lighter and that it is easier to move, and often lighter emotionally as well. You can use this tool whenever you want to, to help move stress and emotion out of you. It takes a bit of practice but in time you can also learn to hear what emotions are coming out with your sigh.

About our sigh

As we sigh out, emotions that are stuck in our body may start move through and out of us. We often do not even know those feelings are there until we become aware of them leaving. Many people find that sighing several times deeply is enough to relieve shorter-term pent-up feelings. However, some of us have too much long-standing emotion to release in one go; if you feel that this is you, then you can repeat the practice on a fairly regular basis (maybe once a day) and add one of the other emotion-processing techniques alongside it. This should help to increase your connection to your feelings and body as well as releasing stuck emotions.

The emotions that are held in our body also shape our physical state, creating a type of holding pattern in our body as if it were an instrument tuned in a specific way. This pattern shapes the sound of our sigh, giving us a clue as to how we are feeling. I find that when many people start they can only hear positive aspects of the feeling coming out, such as relief. However, when I am working with people I can often hear stress, frustration, anxiety, anger, sadness or other emotions being set free. The more self-aware people are, the more they can hear the negative emotions being released, maybe because they are not afraid of experiencing these feelings or knowing that side of themselves. So this tool can not only help us to move stuck emotions through us, but can also help us to become more aware of what we are feeling.

If you start crying or laughing that's fine too, as it is another way of releasing pent-up emotions. Let the tears roll and the laughter happen as fully as you feel is right. Putting the brakes on your emotions is what led to them being held in your body in the first place, so you may want to do this exercise in a private place rather than on a train or in the office. I have occasionally advised people to do it in the relative privacy of a bathroom stall, but you should probably use your judgement on this one, as it may sound as though you are having a white-knuckle ride in there. Of course, we are becoming emotionally un-constipated, so maybe that is appropriate!

Physical play

Aside from sighing, we can also use movement as a way to explore how our physical self is feeling. Kids discover lots about their environment and how their bodies work through physical movement and play, which are essential learning tools for their full development. However, as we age social norms cut us off from spontaneous movement so we stop growing in this area quite abruptly, transforming our bodies into automatically moving vehicles for our brains. As Julie Angel, artist, author and movement coach, says: 'How we learn to use our bodies is a way of becoming members of society. Tradition lets us know what is appropriate related to our status, age and gender. All of this is transmitted across generations to make these mechanisms seem "normal", eventually entering the realm of "natural", but they are not.'[84]

Often, the only people who do have a deep awareness of movement are gymnasts, physiotherapists, bodyworkers, dancers, actors and those who are rehabilitating from a medical condition such as a stroke and have to intentionally relearn how to move. But this is not always a given, as many people still interact with their bodies from a very mind-centred place. For example, occasionally manual therapists do not approach the body with the respect and sensitivity it deserves, but handle it as a mechanic would the unfeeling parts of a broken machine. Although sensitivity sometimes gets a bad rap, it is invaluable for increasing our awareness and picking up information, so being sensitive to our body is invaluable. And when we learn how to be sensitive and tune in to our body and move, it becomes an entirely different experience.

In the exercise below we will be remembering what it feels like to move just to feel good, because you have an impulse and then you follow it for its own sake – not to get a flat stomach or because you're late, but for joy and exploration. I recommend an open mind, some privacy if you want it, and comfy clothes that you don't mind getting stretched or a bit grubby.

> Movement [is] a medicine for creating changes
> in a person's physical, emotional, and mental states.
>
> —Carol Welch, neuromuscular therapist[85]

Exercise 11.2: Moving and playing

In this exercise I would like you to explore your body through movement of an unconventional kind. There are no set steps, just some guidance, as this is all about the freedom to move how and when you like. At home, in a park or somewhere that you feel safe, allow yourself to move, sit, walk,

---

[84] Angel 2016, p. 88
[85] Baril 2014

roll, stand and jump in ways you would not normally, but that are safe and easily manageable for your level of health and fitness. Through doing this you will be interacting with your body in a novel way, and therefore your awareness of it will automatically increase several fold. Be playful rather than serious and try not to have a set idea of what to do. Explore through your body, do not dominate it with your mind. Let yourself feel alert, alive, free and open, with your senses clear and sharp and in harmony with your surroundings. This harmony should allow your mind to take more of a back seat, facilitate a return to more natural rhythms and let the unique personality of your body emerge.

For some people who have a chronic injury or other physical issue, it is easy to feel frustrated, sad, embarrassed or let down by their bodies. However, if we focus on what is wrong all the time, we end up being less than we are. Although it is important to acknowledge our feelings, there is also more than enough joy left in whatever movements we can make, that we can be expressive and playful. They say comparison is the thief of joy, and although it is sad that when we age or get injured we can find it harder to make movements we could have made easily before, it is not a foregone conclusion that we have to have only bad feelings about our bodies, or that physical decline is an inevitable part of ageing. Joy and self-expression through movement are available to anyone who can dance in a chair, or move some part of their body.

As you do this exercise you can find out more about how your body works, what it can do, where it is tight, where it is weak, and what movements satisfy you, challenge you or make you feel alive, and you can also find out more about yourself. What new emotions and feelings arise as you move in new ways, how do you see yourself and the world differently? Do you feel the urge to move in a certain way to express an emotion? This can be a lot of fun as there is only so much enjoyment that can be had when sitting, walking or exercising in socially acceptable ways. If you have young kids in your house, then you can enlist their help in relearning how to move and play – they are the real experts.

And if you are thinking of your partner or others and another particular physical activity that a lot of grown-ups find very fun, this exercise will help you in that area too, as increasing your body awareness helps to boost sensitivity to others' bodies and our own sensations, as well as levels of creativity, spontaneity and skill. All good things!

Physical movement and appreciation

Loving our bodies is very hard for many of us as our cultures do not always support a full-on love affair with them, so we will be actively working on that in this section.

Before we dive into an exercise, I'd like to point out a few things that may seem obvious:

- Our body has carried us through our whole life, for many people without even complaining very much. Think of how much airtime your mind gets. Now compare it to how much attention your body gets – for most people this is not even close. And I am not talking about attention on your body's looks, but on its state and the way it feels.
- Whatever you put into your body it has to deal with it – not always without consequences, but it deals with it – alcohol, caffeine, sugar or worse.
- All the late nights, early mornings, sudden workouts, long workouts, hours on the sofa, horrible stress, hours hunched over phones or laptops – your body deals with all of that, too.
- Think about how small your calf and foot muscles are compared with the rest of your body – they are tiny and holding up most of your body weight whenever you are not lying down or sitting on your behind. They don't usually complain at all!
- Your heart is working tirelessly for you, even while you sleep. By the time you reach eighty years old, your heart will have beat close to four billion times.
- Every time we damage ourselves or get ill, our bodies work to recover; they try as hard as they can to be healthy and strong for us.

Can you think of a time you were ever as dedicated and tirelessly hard-working as your body? I think some appreciation is long overdue!

The following exercise is designed for use when you are fit and healthy. If you are not able to do it relatively easily then just do the appreciation side of it, and leave the physical side until it is safe to do it. Do not make any movements that are unsafe or cause pain, of course.

Exercise 11.3: Body awareness and thanks

a) To start with just stand and move your body a little. Notice any areas of tension, pain or restriction and gently move in a way that helps them (without pain). Let a general sense of love and appreciation spread throughout your whole body as you think of everything it does for you.

b) Ask your body if there is any movement it would like to make, and make it. Do this with an open mind and the intention of listening to your body and making it feel heard and appreciated. Enjoy the sense of connection to your body. If it wants to, you can combine this with the sighing, letting your body also express itself through sound.

c) When you feel like it, have a moment of stillness. Be comfortable in yourself and stay aware and open to your body. Let a feeling of warmth and love grow in your heart and spread out through your whole body, bathing it and filling it with a feeling of appreciation and gratitude.

d) You can take this opportunity to say anything you would like to your body. You may think, 'Sorry for being so down on you for having a bit of cellulite/not having enormous biceps,' or 'Thank you for keeping me safe and letting me go anywhere I want to go,' for example – anything that you really feel. I suggest you mainly keep it positive, as this is about creating a better connection between you and your body, but if you need to express anything negative feel free to let that out too.

e) As you continue to sense this feeling of love and appreciation for your body, you can wrap your arms around yourself and give yourself a hug, maybe allowing a sense of pride in everything you have accomplished together to spread throughout your body.

f) Before you finish you can also ask your body what it would like to have more of or to be different in your day-to-day life, and wait quietly with an open mind for the answer.

Take a moment to notice how you feel. Does your body feel happier? Many things in nature have a bias towards the positive, never giving up, and growing up and towards the light, and our bodies are like this. Even though our minds have a negative bias so that we can get ahead of problems, our physical selves are all about the positive. I think that is why when I worked in a pain clinic people often complained, for example, that their shoulder pain was not improving, but when I pointed out that they came in for the back pain that they had had for many years, they found they had completely forgotten about it. Our bodies expect to be healthy.

This is not to say that negative emotions do not move through our bodies, or that we do not get injured, but that our bodies are adapted to enjoy movement and to be loved and valued. It is a shame that the yearning to be considered attractive often eclipses the other beautiful aspects of our physicality, and that function and health are so often sacrificed to form. I'm not certain that spending a lot of time on the internet has had a wonderful influence on our connection to our bodies, especially considering the surge in eating disorders (currently an estimated 1.25 million people in the UK have one[86]). Women reported lower satisfaction with their body image after only ten minutes on social media in one study;[87] therefore, I would recommend that if you do use social media, balance this with healthy, satisfying and affirming activities that bring you back to a sense of appreciation for yourself and how great your body is. Ultimately,

[86] Beat Eating Disorders 2019
[87] Fardouly et al. 2015

our physical self is much more interested in the present moment and being healthy than in reaching for an unobtainable ideal or impressing strangers; actual physicality is all about reality over image.

However, some of us are not actively negative about our bodies, just simply unaware of them. This disconnect may be due to growing up in a culture that does not value a strong body connection, or it could be more of an adaptive response which helped us to deal with trauma in the past. If you think the latter describes you and you would like to reconnect with your body, you could try a method such as Somatic Experiencing (mentioned in the 'Resources' section at the back of this book). But if you feel that it may be more of a general lack of awareness, you can also try mindful practices such as tai chi, yoga, dance or receiving massage to help rebuild your connection to your body.

Feeding ourselves well

Food – a subject potentially more controversial than politics or religion! Whatever your opinion on the best diet, I think we can all agree that our bodies do better with some foods than others. However, the purpose of this section is not to give you a specific diet, but to introduce the concept that the body can tell us what it wants if we know how to listen to it.

One challenge of eating well is to be able to discriminate between a real desire and an addiction or craving. The former is what the body wants in order to work optimally and the latter is what the mind wants in order to produce a certain feeling. Generally speaking, a healthy desire for a food feels positive and happy, and an unhealthy craving feels urgent and like it is controlling you. A great example of addiction is when you are waiting in line for coffee with a friend and they have that simultaneously glazed and focused look in their eyes and cannot converse meaningfully because the caffeine is calling to them like some kind of chemical siren. Compare this with someone buying a bottle of water and we can see that one nourishes us more and the other controls us more. No judgement from me, though; you could lose a finger by getting between me and my morning cup of tea!

So, generally speaking, healthy desires for food lead to us eating things that leave us feeling satisfied, healthy and content afterwards, rather than guilty, unwell or relieved to have satisfied an addiction. In the exercise below we are going to practise asking our body what it wants and listening to the answer.

Exercise 11.4: Tuning in to the body and asking it what it wants

For this exercise you will want to be at a supermarket, farmers market or other source of fresh food (a little variety is helpful). We will be letting our attention and physical reactions guide us in choosing what our body wants (and, of course, we won't choose things we know are bad for us, like things we are allergic to).

a) Start by choosing one of the sections in the supermarket – I recommend starting with fruit and vegetables – and relax your body.

b) Let your eyes wander over all of the different types of food and notice how your body feels as you do so. One food may feel like it has a pull for you, like a magnet, or your body may feel happy or excited looking at it – this is probably a food that is good for you, that your body wants.

c) Continue looking around the different foods, taking your time, relaxing your body and tuning in to it. Try not to have a lot of judgements but let your body be in charge for once – it probably rarely gets a chance to do so.

d) If you want to, you can buy some or all of the foods you felt a pull towards.

e) When you prepare and eat them at home, notice how your body feels – is there a sense of happiness, excitement or anticipation? How do you feel after you eat the food?

Personally, I do not believe that obsessing over food is a good thing – I have seen far too many people staring suspiciously at something as if it were armed and dangerous, rather than just an innocent carb lying on a plate. It is great to enjoy our food, as long as we are eating it in a way that makes us feel better rather than worse, and we are not substituting eating for experiences, affection, attention or self-expression. Our bodies instinctively know how to nourish themselves in a way that is balanced and satisfying. However, we may have to consciously deconstruct some odd habits and biases we have picked up over the years, as we increase our ability to listen to what our body is asking for.

There are myriad wonderful ways to enjoy and connect with our bodies and this is a subject that really deserves a whole book. The thought I want to leave you with is that beyond simply being a tool for getting things done, an object of desire or a way for us to feel pleasure, our body is an important aspect of our self. Through regularly tuning in to it we can develop a strong connection to this part of us, thereby enriching the whole.

Some of the happiest people I know enjoy their bodies rather than fixating on them; they challenge but do not punish themselves; they are sensual but not addicted and they fully inhabit their bodies. They may be dancers or librarians, it doesn't matter. What does matter is that our relationship with our physical side is one of respect, kindness, listening, love and self-expression. I hope this chapter has helped a little in deepening your partnership with your body.

> To connect with our bodies is to learn to
> trust ourselves, and from that comes power.
>
> —Mirka Knaster, *Discovering the Body's Wisdom*

CHAPTER 12

Thinking Consciously

If we have never turned our own enquiring mind inwards to examine itself, most of us will never have challenged the assumption that our thoughts are both fairly logical and an authentic expression of who we are. In reality, however, they are often biased, not telling us the whole story or occurring mainly out of habit. It is also easy for our feelings, limiting beliefs and assumptions (whether personal or cultural) to influence our thoughts without our knowledge because generally we are not aware of the inner workings of our mind – we only pay attention to what comes out, just like hot dogs from a hot-dog factory (although in that case maybe it is for the best, otherwise hot dogs would be ruined for us forever!).

Because our thoughts shape our whole view of reality and have a huge impact on our mental, emotional and physical well-being, it is essential that they mainly reflect our own values, truth and core self. Through taking responsibility for the state of our mind and learning to work with it intentionally, we will also learn to think more consciously. This work includes increasing our awareness of our thoughts, learning to be mindful, and understanding how we can positively influence our own mental state and encourage authentic thoughts, so that we can enter into a more positive and harmonious relationship with our minds.

> Most people believe the mind to be a mirror,
> more or less accurately reflecting the world outside them,
> not realizing on the contrary that the mind is itself
> the principal element of creation.
>
> —Rabindranath Tagore,
> *Personality: Lectures Delivered in America*[88]

Aside from becoming more conscious of our thoughts, we are also going to have a brief look at styles of thinking in order to figure out which ones come naturally to us and which ones we may need to practise more. This can be challenging but rewarding work; it is never too late to learn something new. Before we do all this, however, let's start with an overview of our mind and how it works.

Our Minds and Thoughts

Our brain is an interesting organ. It weighs around 1.3 kilograms in adults (the same as eight to ten apples, or a quarter of an adult elephant's brain) and is made of lots of fat and water, which is probably why it feels a bit like jelly when you hold it.[89] We have trillions of connections between the billions of neurons in our brain and these connections produce on average a signal per second (a few can even produce up to a thousand per second), so it is very busy up there. All this activity is definitely making thoughts; however, defining them precisely is hard. This is because we do not know where thoughts begin and end, or exactly what they are made of, but in general they are viewed as electrochemical reactions in our brain.[90]

Aside from its physiological aspect, it is hard to pin down an exact definition of our mind because it covers not only our thinking style and

---

[88] Tagore was an Indian poet and polymath who won the Nobel Prize for literature in 1913.

[89] Mercola 2009; Voytek 2013

[90] Dougherty 2011

thoughts, but memory, problem-solving, decision-making and many other mental functions. This is not the domain of only psychologists and neuroscientists: philosophers, biologists, social scientists and people developing AI are also exploring this hard-to-define field of study. We do not even know where our mind is located – in the brain, the body or even extending further than that. Luckily for us, we do not need to worry too much about its exact philosophical definition or location, we just have to know how to work with it in a way that improves our lives.

Getting back to more solid ground, it has been proven that if your brain is healthy you can maximise your intelligence and stave off mental disorders such as dementia (one study found that heavy smokers were 44% more likely to develop dementia than non-smokers[91]). Apart from keeping ourselves healthy though sleep, diet and clean living, we would do well to meditate, as it has been shown to have a great effect on our brain, with long-term meditators having much less atrophy in grey matter than non-meditators, which may have important implications for our quality of life as we age.[92]

Interestingly, our attitude can also help us to be more intelligent; it has been shown that by teaching them that intelligence is changeable, students with lower grades are able to significantly improve their results. Therefore, any stereotypes that exist in society about certain groups being more intelligent, or personal feelings of being less intelligent, can be countered with a positive attitude.[93] Do you believe you are clever or do you ever tell yourself you are stupid? If you are doing the latter, stop – and please never tell children that either; believe that they are intelligent and they will rise to meet your expectations.

Our mind is a muscle that we are exercising every day, but what are we training it to do? Our lives now are very different from when we hunted and gathered, surveying the horizon and staying alert to danger from predators or poisons. Very many of us are sedentary, safe and perform

[91] Rusanen et al. 2011

[92] Luders 2015

[93] American Psychological Association 2003

repetitive mental tasks with no obvious connection to the physical world. It is hard to say how our minds respond to this, but it may be no accident that issues such as anxiety are on the rise. In fact, one study showed that, in the same company, office workers were twice as likely to feel anxious as manufacturing employees, and nearly twice as likely to feel depressed.[94] This highlights the importance of the interconnectedness of our mind and body (as well as other aspects of us), so having a positive mental attitude is much easier if we are getting regular exercise.

Before we launch into the exercises, let's have a quick look at what influences may have already shaped the way we think, without our knowing about it.

Conditioning and the Way We Think

No one can think the way we do as adults without training. Our culture, family, peers and education teach us this, and it is essential in order for us to be able to function in society. However, it is a pity that we are not told *how* we are being taught to think, because, without our awareness or consent, we have been moulded. And because our mind is the lens that we see everything through, the way we have learned to think shapes our perception of every single thing that we experience.

Looking at our thinking objectively is useful for self-awareness, because it gives us an idea of what biases we may have and the chance to evaluate our thoughts with a fresh perspective. It also allows us to see if our thoughts and beliefs have kept up with the progress that the rest of us has made, or whether they are out of date and holding us back. As Emily McDowell, writer and illustrator, says:

> 'Finding yourself' is not really how it works. You aren't a ten-dollar bill in last winter's coat pocket. You are also not lost. Your true self is right there, buried under cultural conditioning, other people's opinions, and inaccurate conclusions you drew as a kid

---

[94] Kang et al. 2016

that became your beliefs about who you are. 'Finding yourself' is actually returning to yourself. An unlearning, an excavation, a remembering who you were before the world got its hands on you.[95]

Although this is not always an easy task, we do not need to follow the path of an ascetic to do it. In the following section we are going to look at a few different ways of working with our mind so that we can work towards having thoughts that are authentic and helpful to us.

Creating a Conscious Mind

We could say that we are thinking consciously when we are not just thinking reflexively or on a loop, or getting carried away by stories, but are attuned to our feelings and aware of our thoughts and what they mean. Therefore, this is not about being serene or happy all the time (although if you are that is fine, of course!); it is about having a clear and honest relationship with our mind.

The first real step towards being able to do this is to develop an awareness of what we are thinking, so first we are going to look at mindfulness and then move on to being aware of our thoughts, before learning how to get out of an unhelpful mental state, and then introducing more positive, realistic thoughts. We will also briefly touch on a couple of defence mechanisms that our mind may use to protect us.

As the aim is to use our awareness and intention to make real progress rather than just plastering positive thoughts on top of negative ones, this work is never a quick fix but will require some time and continued effort. And, of course, if you are having unhelpful thoughts you may want to look at the emotions underlying them – maybe using an exercise from chapter 9, 'Processing Our Emotions'– before returning to this work.

---

[95] McDowell 2018

Being mindful

The mindfulness approach to developing self-awareness has its roots in Buddhist practices, but has been simplified for use by people from all walks of life. Jon Kabat Zinn, who has been credited with making this practice accessible and popular in the West, defines mindfulness as 'the awareness that arises from paying attention, on purpose, in the present moment and non-judgmentally'.[96] So you could think of it as simply being with your mind, self and surroundings in the moment, without getting caught up in worries, judgements or stories.

Exercise 12.1: Mindful living

This is a simple technique (but maybe not easy!) for your day-to-day life. As you are going about your normal business, I would like you to practise being mindful. You might be able to do only a few minutes at a time to begin with, but you will be able to build up to more through practice, and you can either do it once or several times throughout the day. This exercise is great for beginners and if you enjoy it then you may want to learn more about this technique or even find a teacher.

There are three main aspects to practising mindfulness, so let's try them now, so that when you want to do it during your normal day you can simply remember to follow these three points.

1. Being mindful and connected to our breath

It is always happening or about to happen, but we are so often unaware of the breath in and out that sustains us; it just happens under the radar. Sitting or standing comfortably, and without changing your breath, just notice it. How does your body move as you breathe? Can you feel the breath on your nose or lips, and how does it feel?

---

[96] Quoted in Booth 2017

As soon as we become aware of our breath, we instantly become more centred, and this is a key aspect of being mindful. We need to be where we are and fully experiencing *this* moment.

2. Not judging things, but really noticing them

Why would it be important not to judge the things we notice? It is good to be discerning, after all – right? Well, discernment is good, but for this practice, we need to be able to see clearly, without getting caught up in explanations or stories. We set the judgement aside so we can simply see things as they are. Getting caught up in our thoughts transports us away from the present moment, but through staying present we become more centred and more aware of what is happening inside and outside of us.

3. Being in the moment

The two points above will hopefully make this a lot easier for you. Just be right where you are, not daydreaming, not worrying, just doing whatever you are doing mindfully. From showering to working to dancing, you can do this pretty much anywhere. When your mind runs down a rabbit hole, gently bring it back to the present moment, and notice your breath and how your body feels. Accept it and notice it. See if you can expand your attention to a wider arc than it normally inhabits. Notice the whole room. And stay centred in yourself and breathing.

How do you feel now that you have tried that? I recommend you give it a spin out in your everyday life and see how it impacts your feelings, mental and physical state, and your day in general. Keep incorporating each of the three aspects as you practise this exercise.

I also want to mention that a very small number of people have an adverse reaction to mindfulness because sometimes full awareness of our feelings is more than we can handle, so there is no need to power on through if you find yourself experiencing this. On the other hand, if mindfulness is making you more aware of negative thoughts or emotions but you are not overwhelmed, then it would be helpful for you to look at the root of these feelings. Through lifting the veil of distraction we may become aware of uncomfortable facts or feelings, giving us the opportunity to do something about them. And, as Buddhist nun and teacher Pema Chödrön says:

The essence of bravery is being without self-deception.[97]

Being aware of our thoughts

Although many of us feel that at least part of our identity is in the thoughts we think, most of us are very much in the passenger's seat when it comes to what our thoughts do, which makes it much easier for us to slip into unhealthy thinking habits. For example, consider those times when we are trying to stop having negative thoughts, relax when we are stressed or not obsess about something. It can feel like we have no choice or that our mind is like a runaway horse that we cannot control.

The first step to having some autonomy in terms of our thoughts is to be aware of them: what we are thinking and any patterns or stories that recur. In the following exercise we are going to practise this, focusing on our most obviously unhelpful thinking patterns.

Tell me the direction of your thoughts and
I will tell you the direction of your life!

—Mehmet Murat Ildan, Turkish playwright,
novelist and thinker

Exercise 12.2: Awareness of unhelpful thoughts

We are going to look at the negative thoughts we have that keep popping up over and over again, and that take us on a ride even when we try to resist. If you really can't think of any such thoughts, then you can try being mindful over the next day or several days of what you are thinking about,

---

[97] Chödrön 2007, ch. 13, p. 1

and then try again. Or maybe you don't have any repetitive thoughts, which is amazing!

This exercise only really works for those thoughts we have that are not authentic, do not offer insight, are repetitive, and keep us small or hold us back in some way. It may feel that they come from somewhere *other* than our core self, like a judge or a critic, or even like someone we know. If, on the other hand, we are thinking negative thoughts based on painful emotions which are genuine, then we should listen to them and look at the feelings they are pointing to instead. If you find it hard to know which types of thoughts are which, you can start the exercise and, when you get to step (c), if you feel that the voice is your own, then these thoughts are maybe just trying to tell you something is wrong and you should look at the feelings underlying them.

a) In a quiet space, reflect on any times recently that repetitive or out-of-control thoughts have made you feel sad, angry, down or deflated. Write out a list of separate occasions if there is more than one. Please note that this is not necessarily about big setbacks, it is about times your thoughts have pulled you down or away from your true self, which might be a disproportionate response to a bump in the road or not even related to an external event at all.

b) Now look at the first situation in as much detail as possible, and write out roughly how the sequence of thoughts normally goes, to the extent you remember (it doesn't have to be perfect). For example:

> I was going to a party but talked myself out of it.
> Thoughts: *I'm going to go; it will be great – unless no one I know is there – I will be standing all by myself looking stupid – just like the time that happened before – and then I felt worse than if I had stayed home – I'm so stupid, why did I think I could go to a party by myself – I'm going to stay home alone where no one can see what a loser I am.*

This example is a bit harsh! But sometimes our thoughts can get quite negative: they know all our weak spots. Complete this step as fully as possible for each of the times you have listed that you found yourself being led down a specific path by your thoughts.

c) And now I would like you to read through each example, and see if the voice of the thoughts reminds you of anyone you know, or maybe even society in general. Is there anywhere you could have picked up this attitude? Or a time in your life when it started? Write all of this down, with any other insights if they come to you.

d) Now I would like you to look at each example, and choose the point where you would have liked to have interrupted the thought pattern, and what you would have interrupted it with. For example:

> I'm going to go; it will be great – unless no one I know is there – INTERRUPT – but that's fine, I'll meet some new people and I can leave whenever I feel like it.

When we interrupt and then channel our thoughts in a new direction, it is great to keep the new thoughts realistic, authentic and adult. I mention this because sometimes when we feel weak we might overcompensate by making out we are incredibly strong, but this can feel flimsy and fake because deep down it does not ring true. So, in the example above, we would not want to say, 'I will be the life of the party, and everyone will love me!', but something more genuine. When we are truthful and in our adult self we are more in line with who we really are, so it is not a massive stretch, just a step out of negativity.

e) Now, looking at each example in turn, imagine what the outcome would have been (whether you may have acted or felt differently) if your thoughts had gone in this direction instead.

f) End this exercise by acknowledging how hard your mind works for you, and with a feeling of gratitude. If you like, you can also set the intention of following chains of thought that genuinely reflect you and your values.

Did you find this exercise hard at all? It can be tricky if we are new to thinking about our own thoughts and starting to taking the reins. Noticing our internal dialogue is a great way of making sure we are being kind and realistic about ourselves, and thinking in a way that helps us to expand and move forward, rather than keeping us small and fearful.

This curating of our internal dialogue helps us to live in line with our values and our true self. So if you found there was room for improvement, keep an eye out for when you are being led somewhere unhelpful by your thoughts and then consciously step in and redirect them, because you are the captain of your ship. And, as I mentioned before, if you feel that you need to do any other work to help with this, whether that is processing feelings, inner-child work or moving your body, it is important to do that also. No aspect of our self is isolated from another.

Changing our mental state

Above, we looked at interrupting a flow of thoughts that is leading us away from who we are deep inside. However, this interruption is not always easy, especially if we are already feeling very invested in our thoughts, angry or down. One of the best ways to interrupt a feeling and thought pattern is by changing our physical state, which can be as simple as sitting up very straight, rubbing or clapping our hands, or jumping up and down. By doing something out of the usual, something our mind is not used to, we can break our thoughts' habitual cycle, and moving helps to shift how we feel. This then gives us the space to choose a different line of thought.

Exercise 12.3: Changing your state

This is a very simple exercise – we are just going to having a go at different ways we can change the feeling in our bodies. Try any that you like, avoiding any that you are not physically up to right now.

- **Loud sigh** – Draw your shoulders up as high as you can while taking a big breath in with your mouth wide open, then sigh out loudly and drop your shoulders. You can also circle your shoulders or wiggle your whole body as you sigh instead.

- **Shimmy** – I like this one because it feels amusing. Just shimmy quite fast and let yourself feel all the emotions that go with that. You can also move your torso back and forth if you want to look like the superstar you are.

- **Rub your hands together** – This is a very convenient one; try to do it fast and strongly.

- **Stretch out** – Stretch in any way you like; this is a great way of releasing stagnant feelings and I like to breathe any way I feel like while doing so.

- **Exercise** – Any form of exercise is good, but if you are looking to cheer up then cardio may be more helpful, or a mix of cardio and resistance training. If you cannot do this, then a walk or chair-based exercises are also great.

- **Self-massaging your shoulders** – Give your shoulders a rub to release tension and bring you back into your body. If you move your shoulders and head around gently at the same time, you can get even more benefit.

- **Jump up and down** – They don't have to be massive jumps so don't hurt yourself, but do enjoy it; or you could make different movements, such as star jumps.

- **Dance** – Do it any way you want to; dancing to music is even better, if possible.

- **Go for a walk** – A brisk walk and a relaxing, contemplative walk are both good; choose whichever helps you most.

- **Rub your ears between your finger and thumb** – If you do this quite fast and strongly, it can also wake you up a bit. Try moving your fingers around to get all of your outer ear (we don't rub the inner ear at all).

How do you feel now? Are you more motivated to pursue a positive train of thought? Although as an introvert I cannot in good conscience say that I believe in being revved up all the time, I do like a physical shake-up as a way of taking back the reins from grumpy brain gremlins. So now you can combine awareness of your thought patterns with this way of interrupting less helpful patterns, and then select a more authentic alternative.

Sometimes people say things like, 'But I did fail,' or 'I am bad at _____,' which is valid. Thinking realistic and positive thoughts is not about being relentlessly positive and being blind to anything negative or ignoring our responsibility. It is more about the usefulness of our thoughts. For example, if you failed then you can use that as a learning opportunity, so your thoughts can be engaged in figuring out a better way forward. However, if they are not doing that and are just putting you down, this is not really authentic but a self-limiting pattern. In this situation we could work on our self-esteem as well as redirecting our thoughts.

Although it can be scary to leave the familiar (even if that is self-denigration or fear), wouldn't it be scarier to live the rest of our life as less than we are, just because we preferred what feels 'normal'? And after a period of adopting a healthier habit, that can become the new normal and feel familiar too; it is just that the initial change can be hard. Some of the most important work we will ever do is creating a healthy mental landscape – this can really set us free to be ourselves, know ourselves and dream big dreams.

> The mind is its own place, and in it self
> Can make a Heav'n of Hell, a Hell of Heav'n.
>
> —Milton, *Paradise Lost*

Positive, realistic thinking

OK, so we have looked at interrupting unhealthy thought patterns, but what exactly should we be thinking instead? I strongly believe in having a balance between positive and negative, because everything has a good side and a bad side, and being blind to one or the other can leave us very wonky. However, our minds have a tendency to lean towards the negative (this is called a negativity bias) because they are looking out for problems to help us survive. If this hadn't been a helpful strategy, we probably would have lost this trait through natural selection, so it must be useful to us. But because twenty-four-hour news channels, the internet, newspapers and other harbingers of doom are constantly supplying us with a stream of upsetting and worrying events, on top of any that occur in our own lives, we need to work harder to balance this out with positive thinking.

However, if we try to only think good thoughts, while secretly having negative emotions, we can end up looking like those people with smiling faces, really intense eyes and bodies full to bursting with the pent-up rage of a thousand suns. Therefore, it is best not to suppress our negative thoughts, but to air them out sometimes and process our feelings around them, so that we are not carrying a lot of charge around. If you find yourself in this situation, make sure that you are working through your feelings. In this section, however, we are going to be focusing on interrupting overly negative thoughts and introducing more balanced and useful ones.

Creating a truly positive mindset is important because it has been shown to significantly boost intelligence, creativity, energy levels and productivity.[98] I have found that the most effective way to do this is through using positive statements that are also realistic because, strangely enough, overblown positivity can make people who have been experiencing negative thoughts feel even more negative. For example, people with low self-esteem felt worse after using positive affirmations than those with low self-esteem who hadn't.[99] Excessive praise can also be unhelpful, sometimes having a negative effect on children's confidence and motivation. For example, praising little girls for *who they are*, instead of *what they do*, reduces their motivation, maybe because it is not based on something they did in reality.[100]

In the exercise below we are going to select some statements that are both positive and realistic, which we can use whenever we need to make a course correction in our thoughts.

---

[98] Achor 2011
[99] Wood 2009
[100] Henderlong Corpus and Lepper 2007

Exercise 12.4: Rational affirmations

You can choose any of the statements below that you like, and feel free to adapt them as you see fit, as long as they are still positive (so, not 'Although I am stupid, I am getting better,' for example, but 'I get a little cleverer every day'). It is important that they feel true to you also, so if one does not, just modify it or choose another one feels right for you.

- I am alive and healthy.
- I am strong.
- I have great friends.
- I have a great partner.
- My family loves me.
- I am loveable.
- I have plenty to eat.
- I have career opportunities ahead of me.
- I am intelligent.
- I am free to come and go as I choose.
- I am the master of my destiny.
- I learn from my mistakes.
- I have hope for the future.
- I have a good effect on my environment.
- I am hardworking.
- I am sensible.
- I am kind.
- I am disciplined.

Feel free to create some of your own, noting that it is best not to focus on things that are too superficial or changeable. For example, 'I have a great job' is a tricky one, because we can lose our job through no fault of our own. But 'I have a great work ethic' can be true whether we are currently employed or not. Similarly, 'I am beautiful' is fine, but looks can change over time or after one bad night's sleep, so how about 'I am a beautiful person,' as inner beauty is more consistent?

Choose two or three of these affirmations, and whenever your mind starts to go down a familiar negative path, shake it off and say one of them, setting your thoughts up for more constructive work.

Thinking something for fun

In this little section, we are going to practise allowing our mind to think something new, without returning to familiar, worn-out thoughts. This is a little exercise in thinking something original for us, and is a great way of remembering what it was like when we had time to think about things just for fun (realistically because there was nothing else to do and tablets were just a form of medicine). If you are not of an age where you got to experience a lot of boredom as a child and teenager, this may take a little more effort, but do stick with it anyway. The mind is a muscle that has to be exercised to become strong.

Exercise 12.5: Staying with one line of thought

The point of this exercise is to follow one chain of thought until you feel that it is completely finished (if it never ends, you can stop after ten minutes if you want to). There are not really any steps, just pointers. Look around you and let your eyes rest on the thing they are most drawn to, and just pause, without jumping into any thoughts. Let thoughts slowly and organically start to come to you and let them evolve naturally. If they seem to be jumping to a different topic but it feels connected, that is fine, stay with it. However, if your mind goes back to familiar repetitive thoughts, haul it back to the object and start again. You may find the progress and evolution of your thoughts happens a little like the blobs in a lava lamp – flowing naturally, sometimes in odd and sometimes beautiful shapes, without any effort on your part.

This exercise is to practise thinking – not reacting or recycling old thoughts, but really thinking. The less of an agenda and the more patience and open-mindedness we have, the better, because, as a missionary bishop said at the beginning of the twentieth century:

> A great many people think they are thinking
> when they are merely rearranging their prejudices.

—Bishop William Fitzjames Oldham, *Zion's Herald*, 1904

You may not have noticed, but I bet this skill has become a lot harder for you since the increased use of smartphones. You may even find you have to fight a lot of resistance to 'check things'; if this is the case don't worry, it is just a little addiction – nothing a bit of discipline can't fix. However, it is important to reclaim this skill with conscious effort, because these concentration muscles can atrophy very quickly without you being aware of it, and that could affect your state of mind and possibly your mental abilities in both the short and long term.

Thought as a Defence Mechanism

Aside from working on what we think, it is also interesting to learn about the defences our minds use to shield us from discomfort. It probably comes as no surprise to you that our minds are capable of doing stuff behind the scenes to try to protect us from various things, including emotional pain, uncertainty or anything that challenges our identity. Let's just have a very brief look at two of the many tricks it can use, and if you are interested in learning about some others you may also want to check out chapter 8, 'Recognising Our Emotions', which touches on both intellectual and spiritual bypass.

Black-and-white thinking

This is a biggie, especially nowadays (thanks, internet!). It means that we think one thing is completely true and another completely untrue; one thing is good and another is bad – but without the shades of grey that reflect the complexity of life. So on social media, for example, *I am right* and *you are wrong*, or *I am informed* and *you are an idiot*. Someone described this to me as a very young way of thinking, highlighting the fact that maturity brings with it an understanding of nuance and an awareness of the impact our opinions may have on others, and maybe even a sense of our responsibility for that. While a child may shout an opinion and feel defensive if challenged, an adult will hopefully look for the truth and therefore welcome more information even if it challenges their existing beliefs.

However, when new ideas feel as though they are a threat to our identity or reality and we refute them reflexively to protect our existing beliefs, then over time we become rigid, outdated and fearful of the change happening around us (which is inevitable, because life is change). This attitude is common in extremists of any persuasion, as their main attitude is 'we are certain', meaning that they are fearful and angry at anything that conflicts with their views, and therefore, deep down, very uncertain. People who are comfortable with what they believe usually do not make a big deal out of it unless put in a position of defending important values.

In order to avoid black-and-white thinking, we need to allow ourselves to see that we are not dealing in absolutes, but everything in between. We can have a dialogue with others and be fine with not agreeing on everything, but still see their point of view. Or we can start trying to answer a question, and stay open-minded until we come to a conclusion that feels correct naturally, rather than rushing the answer in order to feel secure. There are a lot of black-and-white opinions expressed on social media and a lot of comments in ALL CAPS, so it is easy to get caught up in this attitude. Remembering that most of these people are just venting or are enjoying some moral outrage can help us to see that these are not balanced points of view. Some deeper, slower breathing; time in nature; time spent reflecting; and having a sense of kindness to ourselves and others can help us to feel comfortable enough in ourselves to think in a way that deepens our understanding and self-awareness.

Spacing out

This is a very common way that the mind can protect us. Those who have been exposed to some kind of trauma, especially where they couldn't get away physically, may have learned to at least let their mind escape. This is actually pretty effective, as because they disconnect from their physical sensations and emotions they become numb to what is happening. But if they continue to do this long term it stops them from feeling their feelings, standing up for themselves and being fully alive.

Do you ever find yourself 'popping out' of your body and the moment, only to find that the conversation has moved on and you are not really aware of what is going on? Because there are big downsides to regularly running away (we can only really grow as people when we are present, and fun also depends heavily on this), it is important that we work to change this habit. On the plus side, you may discover that you have developed a talent for energy work as a result; however, in this case it is still (actually, especially) important to ground yourself.

The best solution is to practise calling yourself back to the present moment. You may find that mindfulness helps, as well as making movements that help to bring you back into your body, such as the ones we used above for changing our state. Physical exercise can help, through strengthening your connection to your physicality and the present, and you can use exercises from chapter 4, 'Grounding and Centring', and chapter 11, 'Our Connection to Our Body'. You may also need to address some underlying emotion and trauma, which you can get professional help with if you need it. This effort is very worthwhile, as the here and now is the best place to be and the only place that we can integrate our self-development work and feel joy.

Outgrowing defence mechanisms is a sure sign of personal growth. I recommend bucketloads of self-compassion, reading around the subject and taking it slowly. Being aware of what we are doing is the first step, and as our awareness grows we discover more freedom to act and think differently. This is real autonomy, and it is not always comfortable, but it offers so many more opportunities for living. So take your time and don't be too hard on yourself, but also try not to shy away from accountability and self-awareness as you examine your thinking and its effect on yourself and others.

So, in this first half of this chapter we have looked at ways we might improve our mental state and the quality of our thoughts. The key with this work, as always, is being patient and kind to ourselves and making steady, sustainable progress. Although when we do self-development work we are often looking for problems in order to see what needs to be worked on, we want to always focus on moving towards a positive and balanced state. In this way we can avoid making our hard-working mind (a huge part of our self) feel censored or criticised, and instead have an attitude of collaborating together in a lifelong partnership. Within this atmosphere of collaboration and trust, we can work with our mind to co-create a lasting, rich and healthy inner landscape.

Ways of Thinking

Many of us assume that most people think in the same way we do; however, this is often not the case. Some people are more intellectual, others are dreamers and yet others are laser-focused problem solvers. Although it is agreed that there are several different modes of thought (which have been studied and discussed in psychology, neuroscience and philosophy) there is no one standard system for classifying them.

We are going to look at some of the main ways of thinking, and you will probably be able to see which styles of thought you favour just from looking through the following descriptions. However, if you feel that you need some more help, you can also find various questionnaires online to give you a rough idea of what kind of a thinker you are.

It is much easier to think in the way that we are good at and used to – and more challenging to use less familiar styles, but there is a benefit to doing this. Through working on thinking in different ways we gain new tools, which increase our options for how to approach different situations. For each style listed below there is a brief description and then a look at ways you might develop that way of thinking. Please note that this list is not exhaustive – this subject could fill an entire book if explored fully – so I encourage you to do further research if you are interested.

Concrete thinking

Also called 'literal thinking', this is focused on the here and now, is factual, and about real objects and events. Although it would be very limiting if we could think *only* in this way (e.g. if we believed that someone actually threw a baby out with their bathwater, or that a liar's pants were truly on fire), here we are thinking of it in terms of being effective in the physical world. A lot of people who spend time in nature, doing sport or building things are very good at this style of thought. And I don't want to stereotype, but if anything in your wardrobe has actual elbow patches (not just for fashion), there is a chance that you may need to work on this.

Example: Seeing a dog in front of you, but thinking not about the species in general, the concept of owning pets, or the long history between man and dogs – just about that one dog and nothing more.

Practice: This way of thinking is already developed in people as it is the first thing that children learn. However, if you are brilliant academically or creatively but not as good with the here-and-now or practical problems, then working on being more present in the physical world can help you to feel more grounded and to solve practical problems that you may have been ignoring. Maybe take a break from abstract thinking every now and then and do some exercise or build something, without letting your mind wander to more abstract concepts. This can be a wonderful way to reconnect with your environment and your physicality.

Abstract thinking

This includes thinking about ideas and concepts that are not physically present, and which may be theoretical and complex. Abstract thinkers often look for deeper meanings or patterns, looking at how things relate to the whole (*Dirk Gently's Holistic Detective Agency* springs to mind[101]). In order to understand abstract thinking, it may help to know that *to abstract* means to take away from. So we can look at abstract thinking as taking information gained in one area and applying it to another.

Examples: Using a metaphor, imagining rotating a physical object in space (which appears in many IQ tests), or looking at litter in the street and then thinking about a wider pattern of societal issues (while an exclusively concrete thinker would see only the litter).

---

[101] By Douglas Adams; first published in the UK in 1987 by William Heinemann.

Practice: Studying a theoretical subject such as quantum mechanics, algebra or philosophy and using more metaphors can help to develop this skill. In addition to this, you can practise looking for patterns in separate events or issues; for example, seeing people get restless before lunch and then coming home to a restless cat, you might realise the common factor may be hunger. Of course, this is a simple example – you will want to build up to exploring much more complex patterns than that.

Reflective thinking

This is reflecting on our own thinking and actions, leading to learning and better results in the future, and therefore it is a key aspect of self-awareness. It is often talked about in education because students need to be able to evaluate their ideas and thinking processes in order to learn effectively, but it is also important in any area that we want to grow in. It allows us to learn from our experience, develop more accurate theories and ways of doing things, and think critically about what we know in order to develop our knowledge. Therefore, reflective thinking stops us from doing the same thing over and over again hoping for a different result.

Example: You have realised your relationship is not the best right now and you reflect on your behaviour when with your partner. After noticing a couple of less-than-helpful ways of communicating and acting you change these, and your relationship becomes more balanced and happier.

Practice: You can reflect on your actions, and if nothing has happened recently, you can evaluate any actions or beliefs in the past that may have caused an issue, and what happened as a result. For example, you could think about the time something went wrong or went in a direction that you did not anticipate, and think about why that happened. Being open to the idea that some of your beliefs or actions may be incorrect will help a lot. You can also reflect on things that went well and wonder what actions and thoughts helped you and where else they could be applied in a useful way.

Creative thinking

In creative thinking we depart from established rules and ideas in order to find unorthodox solutions and new ideas. When we do this we are very open, looking at a lot of possible solutions without being very critical, which helps us to shift our perspective and open up to more possibilities. It is quite different to analytical thinking, therefore, which is all about being specific and narrowing things down. Some people refer to this as 'thinking outside the box', and it has a lot of crossover with lateral thinking.

Example: You are in an escape room, and stuck on a clue that seems to have no logical answer, so you decide to be imaginative and wonder about all the potential possibilities and connections, regardless of how crazy they are. This change of perspective reveals a clue that allows you to solve the puzzle.

Practice: If you are great at following the rules and doing things a certain way, but not at thinking outside the box, this may help to expand your thinking a little, opening you up to more possibilities. One professor has his students ask three 'if questions' about an existing situation, object or concept to find new ideas.[102] You can also use brainstorming exercises to practise using imagination to create possibilities, or go to escape rooms, which require out-of-the-box thinking to, well, get out of the box.[103]

Analytical thinking

This type of thinking is a systematic and logical style of thought which involves evaluating data and breaking complex information down into separate parts to understand it better. The method includes gathering the relevant data, evaluating it and trying to find the most logical solution to a problem. As it is on the opposite end of the thinking spectrum to intuition, the answer is reached through reasoning, never a gut feeling.

---

[102] Abazov 2015
[103] Salvi 2017

Example: A company has been experiencing a steep fall in sales from its website. The person in charge of looking at this gathers all of the data available about the situation, looks at the steps of the user experience, finds where the visitors to the website are abandoning the process, and from all of this information determines the most likely method of fixing the problem, and then tests it.

Practice: As this skill is methodical and detail-orientated it will require a little patience. If you find that you normally rush this process or skip over details, preferring to trust your gut, then you will need to slow down and try to overcome any aversion you have to looking at things carefully and in detail. To develop your analytical thinking skills, you can also try solving mathematical problems, doing logic puzzles such as crosswords or Sudoku, and playing board games involving strategy.

Critical thinking

This is evaluating information carefully so that we can come to a reasonable conclusion that is logical and not influenced by prejudice. While with analytical thinking we tend to only use information relevant to that specific problem, with critical thinking we may use information from a wider variety of sources to help us make a decision (analytical thinking is part of the critical-thinking process, however). And although it is broader than analytical thinking, it is narrower than creative thinking because it only looks at existing data, rather than creating new information or options. The challenge with this thinking style is that it takes a lot of work and requires us to listen to facts over assumptions, which may be uncomfortable for some of us. The benefit is that we will be very grounded in reality and also it is much harder to manipulate critical thinkers (unless you can control the data they are receiving).

Example: You read an article in the newspaper which includes some shocking facts about a group of people that you are not sure are true. To come to your own conclusion, you gather more information – both from newspapers with a similar political bias and from newspapers with a very different bias, and you also look at relevant statistics and other data.

You systematically evaluate the information and conclude that the newspaper article was voicing opinions without evidence. You form your own, more logical opinion. And you stop buying that newspaper – the only kind of product that should make you work that hard is sports equipment.

Practice: If you find it hard to evaluate information by yourself, take a lot of information at face value or find it hard to solve problems, then it may be helpful to work on your critical-thinking skills. To practise this, you will need a starting point, such as a problem to solve or a piece of information. You will then want to gather information around this, from both sources which support and sources that oppose the information you are looking at. Then you will start to evaluate the data, looking for errors in logic or inconsistencies, and also considering the reliability of the sources: do they have any biases or interests which might influence the information they give, and do the facts support them? Remember, even statistics and the results of studies can be falsely reported or skewed (or the studies can be badly designed), people can be quoted out of context, and meanings can be misconstrued. The critical thinker takes their time to come to a realistic conclusion and, in general, their beliefs are founded on enough research to give them weight; however, they are also not averse to re-examining their beliefs in the light of new information and challenging their own assumptions.

There are many other types of thinking than this, but these are the key ones. You may have noticed that I left out intuitive thinking, but I did so because this is amply covered in the rest of this book. Having read through them, which do you think you favour? Are any of them a noticeable weak point for you? Some places of education, cultures and occupations are better at teaching certain styles of thought than others, but I believe it is never too late to develop a new style of thinking. This gives us much more freedom, as many of our limitations lie within the realm of our mind's ability to adapt its approach. It is wonderful to be able to be flexible and adopt the style of thinking that is most useful for whichever situation we find ourselves in.

The landscape of our mind has an enormous impact on how we make sense of things, approach life, learn, adapt and grow, as well as on our mood, physical state and even our relationship with ourselves. To maintain a healthy, flexible and clear mind means being free to be present and aware in the moment, grounded in reality and, most likely, happy. And like most areas of self-development, if you feel that working on thinking is not really your area then it may hold the most benefit for you. The sum of all of humanity's thoughts is shaping our future, so let's make sure we are thinking well, and consciously!

> A man who as a physical being is always turned toward the outside, thinking that his happiness lies outside him, finally turns inward and discovers that the source is within him.
>
> —Søren Kierkegaard

CHAPTER 13

Expressing Our Spiritual Side

Spirituality is at once one of my favourite topics and one of the hardest to talk about. Intangible and ineffable, it is a state and a quality that is impossible to live without but a bit tough to define. We are all naturally spiritual beings simply by virtue of being alive, but many people are unaware of what this means for them or how to live in a spiritual way. Some believe that this side of us can only be accessed through religion or other specific practices, but actually it is a part of ourselves that is always in play. For the purposes of this book I will look at those aspects of spirituality that are universal and apply to us whatever our background, religion or spiritual tradition.

Although there are many different aspects of spirituality, we will be focusing on just a few: what it is, the ways that science has attempted to get to grips with it and whether some people are more capable of a spiritual connection than others. The second part of the chapter looks at ways of exploring our own spiritual side, including accessing a spiritual state, honouring and caring for our spirit, and being the person we want to be. I hope that looking at spirituality in this way will help you to get a handle on this ephemeral, essential and epic subject. This chapter, unlike the others, does not have very many exercises as the main aim is just to think about certain aspects of spirituality and your spirit in your own time. Let's start by looking at what spirituality is.

What Is Our Spiritual Side?

Regardless of whether we are religious, we are all spiritual beings by virtue of the fact that we all have a spirit. However, as mentioned above, the exact nature of our spirit is a little hard to pin down. At the simplest, most basic level, we can say that it is the thing that leaves our body at the moment of death. I have never been with someone as they died but I have attended a dissection, and the difference between a living person and the body I saw was much greater than I expected: as well as an absence of life, I felt a notable absence of energy. Numerous accounts from eyewitnesses support the idea that there is a spirit which leaves the body after death, including one from Louisa May Alcott, a famous nineteenth-century novelist. She was sitting at her sister Beth's death-bed as she passed away, and later said, 'I saw a light mist rise from the body, and float up and vanish in the air. Mother's eyes followed mine and when I said, "What did you see?" she described the same light mist. Dr G. said it was the life departing visibly.'[104] Many other people have described seeing this phenomenon.

Our spirit is an important aspect of who we are throughout our whole lives, however, not just at the moment that we leave our bodies. It includes our own unique personality, inspiration, hopes, dreams and the shine in our eyes. It is what we diminish when we lie to others and ourselves, when we do things against our own instinct or values, or when we live life in a way that is not meaningful to us. And it is what we replenish through experiencing beauty, self-expression, creativity, aspiring to things we are excited about and doing things that light us up. Although it is intangible, our spirit has a huge impact on our health and happiness. As it is hard to define spirit in absolute terms, in the section below we are going to look at the scientific perspective on consciousness instead, which is closely connected with it.

---

[104] Alcott 1997

The human spirit and consciousness

Looking at consciousness can give us a little inkling of an aspect of spirit that can actually be researched. Although many scientists are trying to define what consciousness is, it seems a lot easier to study the results of it, rather than where it originates (which is the part that really confuses people). The 'hard problem' of consciousness is that scientists are not sure *why* we have a rich inner experience, seemingly just as a result of processing the physical stimuli around us. Although I believe that the physiological mechanism of our consciousness will be discovered, I doubt any scientific discovery could show the *reason* for consciousness, as I believe that resides mainly in the spiritual sphere of life. Although they are connected of course, I feel it will be many years before science and spirituality have developed enough to show how they are describing two different sides of the same story. But it is amazing that that scientists are attempting to pinpoint where consciousness comes from and what it is made of. They are not quite there yet, but some of the research has gone in really interesting directions.

One theory about how consciousness arises is *orchestrated objective reduction*, or Orch-OR, which was created by Roger Penrose, emeritus professor of mathematics at the University of Oxford, and Stuart Hameroff, an anaesthesiologist who studies consciousness (which is interesting because generally it is neuroscientists who lead the charge in terms of trying to figure what consciousness is made of, but it makes sense that you could also gain insight about something through studying its absence). They believe that consciousness is more than just a complicated computation within the mind, and may actually be the result of quantum processes occurring within microtubules in the brain.[105] According to Hameroff, 'consciousness is more like music than computation' because structures in the brain are thought to vibrate as musical instruments do.[106] This theory is controversial amongst other physicists, Stephen Hawking

---

[105] Hameroff and Penrose 2014
[106] Hameroff 2018

wasn't a fan, and there are several other theories of what consciousness is (as well as how it arises and even whether computers can become conscious) but nothing has been proved unequivocally so far.

Another path that people take when exploring the nature of consciousness is looking at near death experiences, or NDEs, which can manifest as an out-of-body experience. For example, one study into people who were resuscitated after a cardiac arrest showed that 45% had memories of visions or experiences they had while clinically dead, and 2% even had a clear memory of events that occurred when they were dead, as if they had been completely conscious.[107] In fact, Jeffrey Long, who looked at 280 cases of people who had NDEs and remembered seeing things from outside their body, said that 98% of these people's experiences were entirely realistic. Of these, 60 people went to check something they had seen while not in their body (a building seen from above, or similar) and found the reality matched what they had seen, even though they had either never been there, or never seen it from that angle before in life.[108]

Personally, I believe that our consciousness and energy are both aspects of our spirit and that there is an interconnected consciousness flowing throughout everything, with our own private pools allowing us an individual experience. However, I think it is up to us all to decide what we think our consciousness and spirit are for ourselves; after all, spirituality is a very personal experience. The main thing is that we take care of our spiritual needs and have some kind of spiritual experience, whether that is meditating, getting out into nature, or something else. Interestingly, although it is natural that there are variations in the ways people express their spirituality, there may also be differences in people's ability to be spiritual in the first place.

Is everyone equally capable of being spiritual?

This is another huge question that could take up its own book. Some people think that being rational and having faith in something that cannot

---

[107] Parnia et al. 2014
[108] Tsakiris 2018

be proven are on opposite sides of the mindset spectrum. From my own experience of working with people, I would say that some people definitely take to spirituality more easily than others. I myself have a brain that is very happy in the intuitive, spiritual world, and have found it more of a challenge being brought up in an analytical culture (yet also very useful). But does this carry across to other people? Well, one study showed that increasing people's reliance on intuition, even temporarily, also increases their belief in God.[109] Another study found that making people more analytical reduces their level of religious belief.[110] So it appears that even temporary changes in how intuitive or analytical we are being can change how 'spiritual' we feel in the moment. Therefore, our state is very important to our experience of spirituality (if we accept that feeling religious is equivalent to feeling spiritual). It is likely that most people's state day to day is shaped by their culture and peers as well as their personality, so certain groups may find it easier to maintain a connection to their spirituality.

Interestingly, a study which used fMRI[111] to monitor brain activity in Carmelite nuns found that their state while in deep contemplation was mediated by several brain regions and systems,[112] which also seems to support the idea of needing to be in a certain state to have a spiritual experience. In my experience, an open-minded, open-hearted, listening, observing and centred state makes it easier to experience our spiritual side. I believe that being in an analytical frame of mind makes this harder because when we are analysing things we are narrow and intent on one specific thing, and (as with doing energy work) feeling analytical is not our friend when we are looking to connect with something universal and greater than ourselves.

So it seems that the opposite side of the spectrum from faith is not being rational – it is being analytical. I feel that the faith/rationality

---

[109] Shenhav et al. 2012

[110] Gervais and Norenzayan 2012

[111] Functional MRI (magnetic resonance imaging) shows where in the brain there is activity.

[112] Beauregard and Paquette 2006

debate is fuelled by sensible people being astonished that others kill each other in the name of religion. But, as I think we all know, it's never about the religion; it is always about territory, tension between different groups, limited resources, money or power, and religion is just an excuse that doesn't sound so selfish. No God who created everyone would say 'No, you're the best ones, I don't even like those guys – wipe them out!' That would be just terrible, terrible parenting! And as people who are following a spiritual path know – this kind of behaviour is anything but spiritual. Therefore, being spiritual does not equate with being irrational, anti-science, anti-progress or against specific groups of people.

There is plenty of space within us for both an understanding of the nuts and bolts of how our environment works (e.g. when we drop something, it falls) and another part that reaches for something greater, which is not completely explainable – they are not mutually exclusive. Yet, if you have never explored your spiritual side, it may seem unfathomable. And this is probably because, as stated above, it requires a very different way of thinking. Analytical thinking cannot make us fall in love or find a higher purpose – it is designed to be impersonal. On the other hand, 'spiritual' thinking will not help us to change a tyre. Ways of thinking and states are like tools – they are each better for certain types of work. And since we all have the capacity to be rational, spiritual and many other things, we can all cultivate a state that allows us to have a spiritual experience if we want to.

Accessing a Spiritual State

Having looked at the way our state affects our openness to spiritual experiences, it is clear that having the right way of being can give us more access to our spiritual side, so that is what we are going to practise here. The following simple exercise looks at purposefully opening ourselves up while in a very positive, uplifting environment, and being completely aware of our experience. As you do this, remembering that spirituality is about connectedness, not just between people but between everything that exists, may help you to create the right state of mind.

Exercise 13.1: Opening to a spiritual experience

This exercise is very free-form because this is such an individual process. I just want to you to go somewhere, spend time with someone or look at something that uplifts you, and be very aware of what happens within you as you do so.

a) Find a thing, place or person that uplifts you.

b) When you are there (or thinking about that place or person), I want you to try to open fully to the experience, being in the moment, not thinking about the future or any problems you have, just be fully aware of where you are. Allow yourself to feel a sense of expanding, and maybe even gratitude and a feeling of being part of something greater than yourself.

c) Now let a feeling of being renewed sweep through your body; let yourself feel inspired, energised and calm as you continue to connect to the thing that lifts you up.

d) When you feel ready to end the exercise, take a couple of deep breaths and maybe have a gentle stretch or move about.

After doing this exercise, do you see yourself differently or did you find that your perspective changed a little? With practice you will be able to tap into this state at will, strengthening your connection to your spiritual side. Until then, it is fine to use uplifting places or people to help you achieve this state.

Connecting with our spirituality is about rising above the humdrum details and irritations of daily life by being uplifted by beauty or inspiration and feeling your connection with other people, the universe, Gaia, God, or whichever other higher power you believe in. You do not need to believe in a higher purpose or creator, but it does help to be able to connect to the feeling of how awesome and majestic the whole universe is. There is often a feeling of being refreshed, optimistic, self-assured, open, grateful, awed and inspired and if you do believe in a benevolent force in the universe, then you may also feel supported and cared for. I believe that everyone is capable of having this kind of experience and it is very good for taking a load off, reminding us of what is important and bringing us back to ourselves.

Honouring and Caring for Our Spirit

Now that we have looked at the kind of state that is needed for a spiritual experience, I would like to look at some of the ways we can care for our spirit. I know it can be hard thinking about all these intangible things, but you can easily see the difference between someone whose spirit is in a good state and someone whose spirit is not. The former is generally in good spirits (excuse the pun), bright and resilient, with a sense of purpose, of who they are, and shiny eyes, and it feels nice to be around them. On the other hand, the latter is often down, tired, unmotivated, jaded, disconnected and complaining, has a grey or pale skin tone and a lack of shine in their eyes, seems to have no purpose or joy, and it can be quite draining to spend time with them.

As our spirit is the spark in us, or our 'energetic personality', it is what moves us to explore, learn, innovate, reach out, try new things, build things and create. It is our life force. When our spirit is in a good state we thrive and grow and when it is not we may go into survival mode. And everything might even still look great from the outside, but we may feel a sense of disconnection, feel lost or find it hard to see the good in things. This is why it is so important to care for our spirit; so with this in mind I have put a couple of simple guidelines below.

1. Listening to our intuition

You spirit may be trying to direct you towards a choice that is more congruent with who you are and your values. If we continually ignore our intuition, we will become more and more disconnected from our spirit and our path. While some may feel that listening to our intuition is irrational or irresponsible, this is not the case – we can sense this side of ourselves whilst also being practical. At the very least we should always be aware of what our intuition is telling us, and where possible we should also follow this guidance. We often find out why only afterwards, sometimes much later.

Look through the eyes of your highest self. What do you see?
—Adrienne Posey, author

2. Associating with people who bring us up

Some people are inspiring and others are tiring. Your energy is connected to your spirit – if you spend it in the wrong places, you will be wearing your spirit out for little benefit instead of applying it to something that will revive and restore you. We want to put energy into things that also give us energy back, so if a certain relationship or behaviour is draining, maybe we should limit the time we engage with it. People whose spirits are in a good state often hang out together, because they empower rather than drain each other. And this does not mean being with maniacally grinning, can't-admit-anything-is-wrong people; we all need to admit when things are not good, or offload sometimes. It really means not hanging around with people who feed on, and breed, negativity or who perpetually have a 'can't-do' attitude.

3. Not ignoring warning signs

Your spirit has stuff it can get behind, and some stuff it can't. I'm not saying that if the company you work for stands for values that are diametrically opposed to your own, it is always 100% bad. However, I have noticed that while some people who work at a company with goals they are morally opposed to believe they will be able to get through by compartmentalising, they do often seem quite troubled to me. We are connected to what we put our energy into – it is our energy, after all. I know sometimes we need to do things to earn a living, but please do consider this point, because in my experience people are affected quite strongly by what they help to create (whether they believe they are or not) and it is not very easy, and sometimes not possible at all, to erase this effect after the fact.

Of course, this does not only apply to our work; we should protect the integrity of our spirit in all aspects of our lives and try not to ignore warning signs that we are failing to do so.

4. Creating an environment that protects and nurtures

If your spirit loves light, beauty, grace and peace but you are living in a dark, messy, loud place, then that is a clear conflict. However, sometimes a dissonance between your spirit and your environment will be much subtler – a piece of art that you feel you should like but don't, a cupboard full of mess, having your work in your bedroom: the things that affect you can be many and may seem innocuous. And what will suit you personally is very individual to you. I recommend that you survey your surroundings and consider if things generally lift you up or bring you down, and if you want to change anything and how. If you are constrained financially and have to live somewhere that does not make you feel good, small touches may help – a potted plant in the corner, a print on the wall. But ideally you will aim to work towards a place that lifts you up. You could also check out Marie Kondo's work on creating an authentic and joyful space (there is a link in the 'Resources' section). The benefits of having a spirit that feels both grounded and uplifted spill over to every area of your life.

5. Living in line with your spirit

Although this has been covered in various ways above, I want to mention a couple of more specific things our spirits do not like. They do not love it when we lie, or when we misrepresent them with our choices. Spirits are quite pure, direct and intentional, so although we may think that small lies are harmless, the discord they create between our self and the world is troubling to our spirit. Over time this can have a dulling effect on our spirit, almost as if it is thinking, 'Why am I here, anyway? If you are just going to ignore me or distort my truth, I may as well tune out.' Although it is important to be sensible and tactful, if our words convey our true meaning then we experience a sense of connectedness that there is no replacement for. This also applies to our actions: by acting in line with our beliefs and desires we can avoid diminishing ourselves.

The effort and energy we put into the world through projects, relationships, talking and playing are connected to the core of our self. If we want that core to be strong and bright, we have to represent it truthfully, and if we do not fully get this from our work we can achieve it through other pursuits and passions. It can take a bit of courage to live in harmony with our spirit because it makes us more noticeable, and this can make us a target for those who feel bad when others feel good. But those are not really the people we're trying to impress, anyway, are they?

Being the Person We Want to Be

A lot of being a *spiritual* person is really about being a *good* person, whatever that means to us. There is a lot of crossover between different cultures' views of ideal values, as well as a few differences. We also differ as individuals – not only regarding which values we aspire to, but which we feel are the most important. I know I have already mentioned values several times in this chapter, but I think it is really important that we occasionally take the time to look at our own. They may change as we grow as people, or they may remain similar – but either way, it is good to be reminded of them because they are a key part of our spirituality.

Values are beliefs or ideals that we consider important, which speak to what we hold dear and the kind of person that we want to be. Being cognisant of them helps us to live in an honest way, creating a life that reflects who we are. A quote attributed to Gandhi (but which may actually have evolved from a Chinese proverb) illustrates this:

> Your beliefs become your thoughts,
> Your thoughts become your words,
> Your words become your actions,
> Your actions become your habits,
> Your habits become your values,
> Your values become your destiny.

The importance of living in accordance with our values cannot be overstated: it is at the centre of having integrity, a quality as precious as it is powerful.

Sometimes it seems that people are ignoring their own values and feel that they are 'getting away with it'. However, it is common for others to pick up on this dissonance, feeling that something is not quite right about the person or that it is hard to trust them, while perceptive people can see clearly that something is wrong. Over time, going against our own values can lead to having a distorted and strange nature, limited relationships and unhappiness. In the very simple exercise below, you are going to look at your core values. If you ever have trouble making an important life decision, it can be helpful to take this list out and reread it.

Exercise 13.2: Core values

In this exercise you are going to write out the ten values you hold to be most important. Even though you may never have consciously thought about them before, once you identify them they will seem obvious, as they are so integral to who you are. If you have trouble identifying your values, think about any time you were annoyed with someone who seemed to lack a key value – what they seemed to lack may be important to you. Some examples of values include honesty, integrity, kindness and hard work.

a)   Sit somewhere quiet and write out your top ten values, taking your time.

b)   Rearrange them in order of importance to you, with the most important at the top, and feel free to reorder your list as needed.

c)   Looking down the list, do you feel you are currently embodying those values? If not, in what ways? Be kind to yourself, especially if you spot areas that need work.

d)   Think of ways that you can bring your life and actions more into line with your core values.

This can be a difficult exercise; we would all like to think we are great people, and I'm sure you are. But none of us are perfect all the time and it can be uncomfortable to think that we may be coming up short in some way. The key thing is just to aim to live a life in harmony with our values and learn from any slips in judgement. It is also important to remember that others may not share our values or place the same importance on them. Finding out what others' values are can really help with communication and understanding. The goal is not really perfection; it is about knowing who we are, what qualities we aspire to have and the way we want to live our life.

This concludes our look at spirituality. Of course, there is so much more out there to learn, and not all of it is right for everyone. Whether you are on a religious or spiritual path or no specific path at all, we are all spiritual beings and developing this side of ourselves can help us draw on a source of strength and inspiration much larger than our own little allotment. A strong connection with our spirit can deepen and enrich our life in unexpected ways, and when the chips are down it can support us through really tough times. But, even more than that, spirituality can give us a sense of connection, infinity, purpose and grace that cannot be found in any other way, and which no one can give to us but ourselves.

> You have to grow from inside out. None can teach you, none can make you spiritual. There is no other teacher but your own soul.
>
> —Swami Vivekananda, nineteenth-century Hindu monk

CHAPTER 14

Continuing Home

Before you put this book back on the shelf or pass it on, it will be useful for you to have a think about how you might carry some of what you've learned forward and apply it in your life. Just like the holiday glow that starts to fade, or the pervasive calm we gained on retreat which goes out the window with the first onslaught of daily life, things we have realised and aspects of our self we've discovered through this work can fall into the shadows again pretty easily.

Yet this is not to say that you need some kind of regimen or disciplined morning routine. I know they say that morning routines are the key to success; yet I am at least a little bit successful and the only thing guaranteed to happen in my morning is a cup of tea, a bit of a yawn and maybe a scratch. So how do we hold on to these ephemeral realisations or aspects of ourselves that have appeared before they merge back into the ether of us? Below I have listed some things you can try if you want to. As I have mentioned a few times, there is nothing in this book you *have* to do – you are the expert, so I would go with your gut.

1. Redo the self-review in chapter 3

We started the book by looking at how we were doing across several different aspects of our self, and then our whole self and way of being. Why not do this again (without reading your initial answers), but as you go consider what you have learned about each area as well as how this may change how you approach life or your relationship with yourself. When you have done that, you can go back and read what you wrote the first time and reflect on any changes that have taken place.

2. Continue to keep a diary

Self-reflection and introspection are great for working on self-development in a way that is very easy to do each day and which easily becomes a habit. If you want to remind yourself of a few crucial things you have learned or habits you want to practise, you can write these at the start of your diary and reflect on them regularly, even making a note of how you have applied them in your life.

3. Create a routine

I am not a massive fan of routines, but I do think that if they work for you then they will be a great way of making sure you are including things in your day-to-day life that lift you up and make you closer to your true self. You can make any of the exercises in this book part of your routine, and you can change this as you see fit. If you do decide to do this and it works for you, please share your experience on social media, as it may help to inspire someone else – thank you!

4. Talk to your friends about what you have learned

There is something special about saying something out loud as it helps you to understand it more completely, as well as gain insight into how you feel about it and its relationship to you. So, by speaking about your experience you may find your understanding deepens; and another plus is that your relationship with others may grow. By circulating information, you may really help your friends and colleagues – often in ways you do not expect. Although I mentioned at the start of this book that people often will not share a deep realisation with you at the depth and profundity you experience it, they may still be able to relate to some aspect of your experience. As always, it is best to avoid being boring or preachy.

5. Start studying or practising a skill

This is a very wide-ranging suggestion. For example, if your inner child wanted to feel free you could start going to the swings regularly, or maybe learning to paraglide. If your spirit wants to be uplifted by being surrounded by beauty you might visit art galleries or start hiking. If you want to self-express more you could go to a creative writing class, or if you want to work on your creative thinking you could become a regular at escape rooms. Like the rest of this book, this is not prescriptive – why not think about how you might regularly practise a new skill or way of being in a way that feels right to you? All new experiences can teach us something about ourselves and often it is not what we expected to learn at the outset.

6. Write notes to your future self

A bit of an odd suggestion, this one. But let's say that a few ideas in this book are really important to you and you do not want them to get swept away in the tidal wave that is life admin. You could write notes to your future self and put them in a certain place, to be read at a date that you mark on your calendar. Or, if you are super fancy with your technical know-how, you could even write them in emails that you schedule to be sent on certain dates. Doing this for each month for a year, for example, would mean you are guaranteed to revisit certain concepts, habits or aspects of yourself that you feel are meaningful, in a spread-out and relaxed way. Another plus is that you will be doing so after you have had time to let it settle for a bit and you may have more perspective.

7. Regular check-ins

There are lots of ways to do this. One that I started doing that was helpful was an annual review around December, when I took some time to reflect on what I felt had gone pretty well and areas that I would like to improve. Then I also thought about what my hopes were for the coming year. Personally, I do not set very rigid goals because of the New-Years-resolution effect, but instead I connect to what inspires and excites me. You can do this, or you can even do a weekly or monthly check-in with yourself. You might ask yourself how you are doing, what upset you, what made you joyful, areas where you feel you want to expand or need some support, and times you felt you did a good job helping others. It can be whatever feels right to you. Although I do reflect on the past, I like to mainly focus on what I want moving forward, in my self-development and in life.

8. Spread the love

It is really good to take the benefits of our self-development work and expand them out into our community, like so much delicious chocolate spread. There is no need to stay completely contained in ourselves, jealously guarding our self-development bounty. But how to share it without preaching, teaching or overreaching (it's true because it rhymes!)? I'd say just being more open, connecting with people a little more, helping where needed and being a compassionate person would make an amazing start. If you feel drawn to helping in a more dedicated way, that is great. You will get a lot out of helping others, which can be easy to forget in our self-contained society. Remembering we are one part of a whole and that other people have very similar needs to ours can take us out of our day-to-day worries and give us the chance to use some of our energy somewhere it matters, which is great for our body and mind. It is also important to avoid overextending ourselves, and through learning to give the amount that is sustainable for us we will be able to be of service to others and our community for a much longer time. I often feel bad that I find committing to a regular volunteer position difficult due to my work taking up a lot of my time, but my thing has turned out to be helping people when I find myself near someone who needs a hand. Your thing may be something completely different. But what is clear is that we are social animals and to be able to feel good we need to help others regularly (which is why it can also be a kindness to accept help).

9. End-of-life meditation

It sounds a bit grim, but bear with me. In this simple visualisation we imagine we are at the end of our life, looking back at it. I imagine I am on my deathbed, but some people are not keen on that, so you can just imagine yourself being very old, sitting somewhere nice. Reflecting back on your life, wonder if there is anything you are particularly proud of, anything you regret doing or regret not doing, and the relationships that are most important to you. This is a great way of evaluating how we are living right now with a lot more perspective. With this perspective we may gain clarity on what is really important to us, where we are putting our energy that may be a waste and what we may be avoiding out of fear but will always regret not trying. We have the time to live our life the way that is meaningful and special to us, and we have the ability – sometimes all we need is a little course correction. Living authentically is the ultimate application of our self-development work because it is us being completely ourselves in real time.

10. Coming home to ourselves

Remember that our birthright is to be happy in ourselves and express who we are into the world – not selfishly, not piously, just naturally. Having this intention of coming home to ourselves can remind us that we are safe, we are whole, and we are loved and deserving of love. This is not a striving or forcing of something that is a massive reach for us. It is a returning to ourselves and reclaiming of all the parts of us waiting to be embraced and enjoyed. We can perform a practice perfectly, yet if we do not believe that we deserve to be loved and happy it will have a very different outcome than if we are able to trust and relax into ourselves.

The journey may be long, it may be difficult, and you may feel lonely or desperate at times. But our centre is always there, it always has everything we need and through learning to listen, we will become the masters of bringing ourselves home.

We are the only ones who can.

Epilogue

Sometimes I look at my clients with amazement. Eyes that were once sad and dull shine with excitement and anticipation of the life to come. A posture that was stooped and apologetic for itself has opened to embrace the completeness of the man, allowing so much of his warmth and power to shine out on those around him. The little girl lost in the woods has become the woman sure of her path and taking it in confident strides, while raising other people up with her. The tender, gentle father, the confident singer, the forgiving hero: so many transformations and so many possibilities. The only common factor is their courage in leaving the familiar in order to find all of the power and life they ever needed, within them.

It makes me happy to be moseying around in the background of all of this in my supporting role to all these rising stars, like some kind of stagehand. I enjoy seeing the process of transformation where suffering turns a corner and becomes mature perspective or fear turns into choosing oneself fully, where realisations burst like fireworks across someone's being or a wounded part of the self living in the past catches up to present time using the elastic power of complete acknowledgement and acceptance. My clients have so much potential in so many directions and you are no different.

How will you use this book to realize yours?

Through my years of working on myself, seeking and searching in books and out in the world, I eventually learned that everything I need is within me, right at my centre. All it took was some tools, some help and some effort and I was able to move closer and closer to this place: my core self, my home. There is clearly still quite far to go, and yet this journey has been such an incredible adventure – the kind that if you wanted to make a movie of it, it would have to have a massive visual-effects budget. Our journeys are all so unique, yet they all start and end at the centre of our being. Through making this journey we grow in so many ways: gaining wisdom, softening into compassion and finding the strength in humility and honesty, we come of age. As we do so, we earn the right to be free, to be autonomous and to powerfully embody our potential. Most surprisingly, through the exploration of so many unfamiliar and difficult territories, moving farther and farther from the habitual in search of the authentic, one day we find we have stumbled upon the one path that will lead us home.

Thank you for reading my book – I hope that you found something of use within its pages! It would be fabulous if you could take the time to leave a review as this is really helpful in letting others know what they can expect and how they might benefit from using this work. Thank you! If you would like to let me know how you're getting on with the book you can find me on social media (Instagram: @suzanne_wylde; Facebook: @Wyldesuzanne). In addition, there are more resources at www.suzannewylde.com, which offer support in a variety of ways.

There is not much more to say, but I would like to leave you with a quote which reminds us that all the answers, qualities and resources we will ever need are not to be found in a guru or a method somewhere out in the world, they are inside us and they always have been:

> Those who hunt after happiness will find it at last,
> if they find it at all, az the old woman did her spectacles,
> which she had lost, perched on her own nose.
>
> —Josh Billings[113]

Whatever your path and potential, I wish you lots of joy, revelations and fun on your epic adventure home!

---

[113] Billings 1904. Josh Billings was an American humorist.

Acknowledgements

I t is quite funny that, although the process of writing is basically hiding away for hours, so many people have helped me to reach the finish line. And for that reason I am very grateful to a lot of people, who have supported me in a wide variety of ways.

I'd like to say a big thank you to my family and other associated miscreants, including Nick and Dorothy for all your support over the years, Matt and Maggie for harbouring a crazy cousin in the attic; Rod and Gill for the great advice; Andy and Karen for the bad jokes and resulting grimaces; Simon and Jen for knowing that a good amount of tea is a metric fudge-ton of tea; George, Joyce (epic pork pies), James, Emily, Jess, the Little Cakes, Danny, Nathan, Maria, Effie and Albie for being lovely and always inspiring me; and Grandma, Nan and the Granddads for being the reason we are all here. I would also like to thank Ann, and also Gary and Sandra Bruce for the kind words of support.

A big thank you to Jon Hutchings and Hannah Niesler at Lotus Publishing for publishing my first book, and then also taking a chance on my second! I am also very grateful to Jonathan and the staff at triyoga, where I have met some wonderful clients and therapists. Thank you to Anna Hunt for the grounding exercise and being a such a great source of light in the world, to Dr Mike J. Meredith for teaching me a lot, and to Maureen for having great perspective. Georgie at Blossom Consulting has been a wonderful help – thank you; and, Marisa Guthrie: your clear advice is very much appreciated. Also a big thank you to Andy Roberts, Laura Ichajapanich and Stan Rechcigl at Breathe Therapies, who have always been very positive and open; I love being a part of your team.

Friends who have been a great support emotionally and have given me feedback (or been human guinea pigs) include Joe Arnold (part-time surfer, full-time dreamer), Adam Bromby, Lily and Sean Cheng, Suzette Chin, Rachel da Cruz Harvey, Greg and Katy Eyre, Simon Gedman, Maya Humphreys, Edmund Ibrahim, Mahf and Desi, Louise and Josh Moondt, and Livia Turco: anytime someone meets any of you they tell me 'You have really nice friends.' You know it – you guys are pulchritudinous (I learned a new word for you!). I would also like to thank actor and writer extraordinaire Genevieve Taricco for her feedback, and Kelly Fischer for casting her expert journalistic eye over the manuscript.

Finally, these lovely people allowed me to quote them or access their work (and if you are not familiar with their work I strongly recommend checking them out because they are very gifted writers, researchers, teachers or therapists): Dr Julie Angel, Coleman Barks, Dr Tara Brach, Dr Brené Brown, Pema Chödrön, T. K. Coleman, Ann Gila, Dr Stuart R. Hameroff, Dr Tom Hollenstein, Byron Katie, Dr Deborah Khoshaba, Dr Mirka Knaster, Emily McDowell, Mehmet Murat Ildan, Dr Kristin Neff, Rasheed Ogunlaru, Scott Raab, Nikki Rowe, J. K. Rowling, Vironika Tugaleva and Carol Welch.

I am also indebted to these associations and publishers, who helped me: the Krishnamurti Foundation, India; BruceLee.com; Black Belt Communications; the University of Georgia Press; Gideon Weil at HarperOne; W. W. Norton and Company; Forgotten Books and Hohm Press.

To list all the people who inspire me could take a chapter instead of a paragraph, but I am very grateful to the authors of all the self-development books I have read over the years that have taught me so much, as well as the many authors who have inspired me through the scope of their imagination and the high quality of their writing.

Although both self-development and writing are very much our own journey, they would have been impossible for me without all the support, inspiration and advice I have received. So, to everyone who has helped me in some way – thank you from the bottom of my heart. Life would not be nearly as entertaining without such funny and delightful company.

References

Introduction

Lee, B. (2009). *Bruce Lee's Wisdom for the Way*, Chicago: Black Belt Communications.

Smiles, S. (2019). *Self Help; with Illustrations of Character and Conduct*. Reproduction of 1863 edition published in Boston by Ticknor and Fields (first published 1859). Online Library of Liberty, accessed 5 February 2019. https://oll.libertyfund.org/titles/smiles-self-help-with-illustrations-of-character-and-conduct.

Chapter 1. A Healthy Attitude to Self-Development Work

Cohen, L. G., and D. K. Sherman (2014). 'The Psychology of Change: Self-Affirmation and Social Psychological Intervention'. *Annual Review of Psychology* 65: 333–71. doi:10.1146/annurev-psych-010213-115137.

Ebert, D. D., S. Nobis, D. Lehr, H. Baumeister, H. Riper, et al. (2016). 'The 6-Month Effectiveness of Internet-Based Guided Self-Help for Depression in Adults with Type 1 and 2 Diabetes Mellitus'. *Diabetic Medicine* 34(1): 99–107. doi:10.1111/dme.13173.

Gandhi, V. (2011). *Kumaré*. New York: Future Bliss Films.

Gebauer, J. E., A. D. Nehrlich, D. Stahlberg, C. Sedikides, A. Hackenschmidt, et al. (2018). 'Mind-Body Practices and the Self: Yoga and Meditation Do Not Quiet the Ego but Instead Boost Self-Enhancement'. *Psychological Science* 29(8): 1299–1308. doi:10.1177/0956797618764621.

Grossman, P., U. Tiefenthaler-Gilmer, A. Raysz and U. Kesper (2007). 'Mindfulness Training as an Intervention for Fibromyalgia: Evidence of Postintervention and 3-Year Follow-Up Benefits in Well-Being'. *Psychotherapy and Psychosomatics* 76: 226–33. doi:10.1159/000101501.

Krishnamurti, J. (2004). *Freedom from the Known*. Chennai, India: Krishnamurti Foundation.

Wilson, B. M., L. Mickes, S. Stolarz-Fantino, M. Evrard and E. Fantino (2015). 'Increased False-Memory Susceptibility after Mindfulness Meditation'. *Psychological Science* 26(10): 1567–73. doi:10.1177/0956797615593705.

Wood, J. V., W. Q. Perunovic and J. W. Lee (2009). 'Positive Self-Statements: Power for Some, Peril for Others'. *Journal of Psychological Science* 20(7): 860–66. doi:10.1111/j.1467-9280.2009.02370.x.

Chapter 2. Key Skills for Self-Development

Sutton, A. (2016). 'Measuring the Effects of Self-Awareness: Construction of the Self-Awareness Outcomes Questionnaire'. *Europe's Journal of Psychology* 12(4): 645–58. doi:10.5964/ejop.v12i4.1178.

Trapnell, P. D., and J. D. Campbell (1999). 'Private Self-Consciousness and the Five Factor Model of Personality: Distinguishing Rumination from Reflection'. *Journal of Personality and Social Psychology* 76(2): 284–304. doi:10.1037//0022-3514.76.2.284.

Chapter 3. Our State

Emerson, R. W. (2018). 'Ralph Waldo Emerson: Essays, First Series[1841] – Self-Reliance'. American Transcendentalism Web, accessed 13 November 2018. https://archive.vcu.edu/english/engweb/transcendentalism/authors/emerson/essays/selfreliance.html.

Lao Tzu (2008). *Laotzu's Tao and Wu Wei: Tao-te Ching*. Translated and interpreted by H. Borel and D. Goddard. London: Forgotten Books.

Petersen, W. (1984). *The NeverEnding Story* [Die Unendliche Geschichte]. Munich: Constantin Film and Bavaria Studios.

Chapter 4. Grounding and Centring

Carrell, S. (2018). 'Scottish GPs to Begin Prescribing Rambling and Birdwatching'. Guardian (online), News, Scotland, 5 October 2018. https://www.theguardian.com/uk-news/2018/oct/05/scottish-gps-nhs-begin-prescribing-rambling-birdwatching.

Frist, B. (2017). 'The Science behind How Nature Affects Your Health'. *Forbes*, 15 June 2017. https://www.forbes.com/sites/billfrist/2017/06/15/the-science-behind-how-nature-affects-your-health/#12960cbc15ae.

Hunt, A. (2018). Anna Hunt's website, accessed 9 October 2018. www.annahunt.com.

Chapter 5. Acceptance and Self-Acceptance

Brach, T. (2003). *Radical Acceptance: Awakening the Love that Heals Fear and Shame*. London: Rider.

Flynn, J. J., T. Hollenstein and A. Mackey (2010). 'The Effect of Suppressing and Not Accepting Emotions on Depressive Symptoms: Is Suppression Different for Men and Women?' *Personality and Individual Differences* 49(6): 582–86. doi:10.1016/j.paid.2010.05.022.

Fox, M. J. (2007). 'What I've Learned: Michael J. Fox'. Interview by Scott Raab. *Esquire*, 17 December 2007. https://www.esquire.com/entertainment/interviews/a4045/michaeljfox0108/.

Fry, P. S., and D. L. Debats (2009). 'Perfectionism and the Five-Factor Personality Traits as Predictors of Mortality in Older Adults'. *Journal of Health Psychology* 14(4): 513–24. doi:10.1177/1359105309103571.

Lewis, J. (2018). *Comedians in Cars Getting Coffee*. Season 5, episode 12, 'Jerry Lewis: Heere's Jerry!' Directed by Jerry Seinfeld. Netflix, 6 July 2018. https://www.netflix.com/watch/80171364?.

Maté, G. (2016). 'Dr Gabor Maté "Conditional Acceptance" 6th Clue'. *YouTube*, 26 April 2016. https://www.youtube.com/watch?v=ErkEQFJusnc.

Ogunlaru, R. (2017). 'Rasheed Ogunlaru > Quotes'. Goodreads.com, accessed 24 November 2018. https://www.goodreads.com/quotes/8617311-there-s-no-beauty-without-difference-and-diversity-love-unconditionally.

Rowling, J. K. (2000). *Harry Potter and the Goblet of Fire*. London: Bloomsbury Children's Books.

Rūmī, Jalāl ad-Dīn Muḥammad (1997). *The Illuminated Rumi*. Translated and with commentary by Coleman Barks. Illustrated by Michael Green. New York: Broadway Books.

Shpancer, N. (2010). 'Emotional Acceptance: Why Feeling Bad is Good'. *Psychology Today* (blog), 8 September 2010. https://www.psychologytoday.com/us/blog/insight-therapy/201009/emotional-acceptance-why-feeling-bad-is-good.

Tugaleva, V. (2017). *The Art of Talking to Yourself: Self-Awareness Meets the Inner Conversation*. Toronto: Soulux.

University of Hertfordshire (2014). 'Self-Acceptance Could Be the Key to a Happier Life, yet It's the Happy Habit Many People Practice the Least'. *ScienceDaily*, 7 March 2014. www.sciencedaily.com/releases/2014/03/140307111016.htm.

Watson, J. B. (1928). *Psychological Care of Infant and Child*. New York: W. W. Norton.

Wikipedia contributors (2018a). 'Mariette Hartley'. *Wikipedia, The Free Encyclopedia*, accessed 16 November 2018. https://en.wikipedia.org/w/index.php?title=Mariette_Hartley&oldid=920404049.

Wikipedia contributors (2018b). 'Muhammad's Wives'. *Wikipedia, The Free Encyclopedia*, accessed 16 November 2018. https://en.wikipedia.org/w/index.php?title=Muhammad%27s_wives&oldid=928876658.

Chapter 6. Self-Love and Self-Esteem

Brown, R., and V. Zeigler-Hill (2004). 'Narcissism and the Non-equivalence of Self-Esteem Measures: A Matter of Dominance?'

Journal of Research in Personality 38(6): 585–92. doi:10.1016/j. jrp.2003.11.002.

Brummelman, E., S. Thomaes, B. Orobio de Castro, G. Overbeek and B. J. Bushman (2014). ' "That's Not Just Beautiful – That's Incredibly Beautiful!": The Adverse Impact of Inflated Praise on Children with Low Self-Esteem'. *Psychological Science* 25(3): 728–35. doi:10.1177/0956797613514251.

Burton, N. (2015). 'Self-Confidence Versus Self-Esteem'. *Psychology Today* (blog), 19 October 2015. https://www.psychologytoday.com/intl/ blog/hide-and-seek/201510/self-confidence-versus-self-esteem.

Button, E. J., E. J. Sonuga-Barke, J. Davies and M. Thompson (1996). 'A Prospective Study of Self-Esteem in the Prediction of Eating Problems in Adolescent Schoolgirls: Questionnaire Findings'. *British Journal of Clinical Psychology* 35(2): 193–203. doi:10.1111/j.2044-8260.1996.tb01176.x.

Campbell, W. K., E. A. Rudich and C. Sedikides (2002). 'Narcissism, Self-Esteem, and the Positivity of Self-Views: Two Portraits of Self-Love'. *Personality and Social Psychology Bulletin* 28(3): 358–68. doi:10.1177/0146167202286007.

Cénat, J. M., M. Hébert, M. Blais, F. Lavoie, M. Guerrier, et al. (2014). 'Cyberbullying, Psychological Distress and Self-Esteem among Youth in Quebec Schools'. *Journal of Affective Disorders* 169: 7–9. doi:10.1016/j.jad.2014.07.019.

Donnellan, M. B., K. H. Trzesniewski, R. W. Robins, T. E. Moffitt and A. Caspi (2005). 'Low Self-Esteem Is Related to Aggression, Antisocial Behavior, and Delinquency'. *Psychological Science* 16(4): 328–35. doi:10.1111/j.0956-7976.2005.01535.x.

Jackman, D. M., and D. MacPhee (2015). 'Self-Esteem and Future Orientation Predict Adolescents' Risk Engagement'. *Journal of Early Adolescence* 37(3): 339–66. doi:10.1177/0272431615602756.

Johnson, M., and S. Rasjuli (2001). 'Contingent Self-Esteem Structures Related to Cardiac, Exhaustive, and Immunological Disease: A Comparison between Groups of Outpatients'. *Cogent Psychology* 4(1): 1391677. doi:10.1080/23311908.2017.1391677.

266 \ The Art of Coming Home

Kamarzarrin, H., M. Khaledian, M. Shooshtari, E. Yousefi and R. Arami (2013). 'A Study of the Relationship between Self-Esteem and the Imposter Phenomenon in the Physicians of Rasht City'. *European Journal of Experimental Biology* 3(2): 363–66. http://www.imedpub. com/articles/a-study-of-the-relationship-between-selfesteem-and-the-imposter-phenomenon-in-the-physicians-of-rasht-city.pdf.

Katie, B. (2007). *Question Your Thinking, Change the World*. Carlsbad, CA: Hay House.

Khoshaba, D. (2012). 'A Seven-Step Prescription for Self-Love'. *Psychology Today* (blog), 27 March 2012. https://www.psychologytoday.com/gb/ blog/get-hardy/201203/seven-step-prescription-self-love.

Malik, S., and M. Khan (2015). 'Impact of Facebook Addiction on Narcissistic Behavior and Self-Esteem among Students'. *Journal of the Pakistan Medical Association* 65(3): 260–63. https://www.ncbi.nlm. nih.gov/pubmed/25933557.

Nauert, R. (2015). 'Gene May Impact Self-Esteem and Optimism'. *PsychCentral*, News, 8 August 2018. https://psychcentral.com/news/2011/09/16/gene-may-impact-self-esteem-and-optimism/29486.html.

Noronha, H. (2018). 'As I Began to Love Myself – Charlie Chaplin'. *Minds Journal*, 24 September 2015. https://themindsjournal.com/ as-i-began-to-love-myself-charlie-chaplin/.

Rosenberg, M. (1965). *Society and the Adolescent Self-Image*. Online facsimile made 2018 by Utrecht University Library of 1965 edition published in Princeton, NJ, by Princeton University Press. https:// www.docdroid.net/Vt9xpBg/society-and-the-adolescent-self-image-morris-rosenberg-1965.pdf#page=3.

Wood, J. V., E. Perunovic and J. W. Lee (2009). 'Positive Self-Statements: Power for Some, Peril for Others'. Psychological Science 20(7): 860–66. doi:10.1111/j.1467-9280.2009.02370.x.

Chapter 7. Compassion and Self-Compassion

Bloom, P. (2014). 'Against Empathy' (forum). *Boston Review*, 10 September, 2014. https://bostonreview.net/forum/paul-bloom-against-empathy.

Brach, T. (2003). *Radical Acceptance: Awakening the Love that Heals Fear and Shame*. London: Rider.

Eisenberg, N. (2000). 'Emotion, Regulation, and Moral Development'. *Annual Review of Psychology* 51(1): 665–97. doi:10.1146/annurev. psych.51.1.665.

Fredrickson, B. L., M. A. Cohn, K. A. Coffey, J. Pek and S. M. Finkel (2008). 'Open Hearts Build Lives: Positive Emotions, Induced through Loving-Kindness Meditation, Build Consequential Personal Resources'. *Journal of Personality and Social Psychology* 95(5): 1045–62. doi:10.1037/a0013262.

Goetz, J. L., D. Keltner and E. Simon-Thomas (2010). 'Compassion: An Evolutionary Analysis and Empirical Review'. *Psychological Bulletin* 136(3): 351–74. doi:10.1037/a0018807.

Goleman, D. (2007). 'Why Aren't We More Compassionate?' (TED Talk). TED website, March 2007. https://www.ted.com/talks/daniel_goleman_on_compassion?language=en.

Killham, M. E., A. D. Mosewich, D. E. Mack, K. E. Gunnell and L. J. Ferguson (2018). 'Women Athletes' Self-Compassion, Self-Criticism, and Perceived Sport Performance'. *Sport, Exercise, and Performance Psychology* 7(3): 297–307. doi:10.1037/spy0000127.

Neff, K. D. (2018a). 'Definition of Self-Compassion'. Self-Compassion. org, accessed 11 December 2018. https://self-compassion.org/the-three-elements-of-self-compassion-2/.

———. (2018b). 'Test How Self-Compassionate You Are'. Self-Compassion.org, accessed 21 August 2018. http://self-compassion. org/test-how-self-compassionate-you-are/#.

Neff, K. D., Y.-P. Hsieh and K. Dejitterat (2005). 'Self-Compassion, Achievement Goals, and Coping with Academic Failure'. *Self and Identity* 4: 263–87. doi:10.1080/13576500444000317.

Post, S. G. (2005). 'Altruism, Happiness, and Health: It's Good to Be Good'. *International Journal of Behavioral Medicine* 12(2): 66–77. doi:10.1207/s15327558ijbm1202_4.

Simon-Thomas, E., D. J. Keltner, D. Sauter and L. Sinicropi-Yao (2009). 'The Voice Conveys Specific Emotions: Evidence from Vocal Burst Displays'. *Emotion* 9(6): 838–46. doi:10.1037/a0017810.

Singer, T., and O. M. Klimecki (2014). 'Empathy and Compassion'. *Current Biology* 24(18): R875–78. doi:10.1016/j.cub.2014.06.054.

Strauss, C., B. L. Taylor, J. Gu, W. Kuyken, R. Baer, et al. (2016). 'What Is Compassion and How Can We Measure It? A Review of Definitions and Measures'. *Clinical Psychology Review* 47: 15–27. doi:10.1016/j.cpr.2016.05.004.

Tugaleva, V. (2018). '17 Quotes to Help You Love Yourself'. Vironika Tugaleva's website, accessed 11 December 2018. https://www.vironika.org/quotes-love-yourself/.

Chapter 8. Recognising Our Emotions

Brown, B. (2010). 'The Power of Vulnerability' (TED Talk, TEDxHouston). TED website, June 2010. https://www.ted.com/talks/brene_brown_on_vulnerability/transcript?fbclid=IwAR1APQHk6ir6iqgnyDu2pCVWaFoTaKfaqEVZBi1GGOI0UyVKZz98wTDVwHk.

Cartwright, C., K. Gibson, J. Read, O. Cowan and T. Dehar (2016). 'Long-Term Antidepressant Use: Patient Perspectives of Benefits and Adverse Effects'. *Patient Preference and Adherence* 10: 1401–7. doi:10.2147/PPA.S110632.

Coleman, T. K. (2018). 'Your Feelings Are Not the Enemy'. T. K. Coleman's blog, 21 June 2018. http://tkcoleman.com/2018/06/21/feelings-not-enemy/.

Cowen, A. S., and D. Keltner (2017). 'Self-Report Captures 27 Distinct Categories of Emotion Bridged by Continuous Gradients'. *Proceedings of the National Academy of Sciences of the USA* 114(38): E7900–E7909. doi:10.1073/pnas.1702247114.

Dunion, P. (2017). 'The Intellectual Bypass'. *HuffPost*, 5 January 2017. https://www.huffingtonpost.com/entry/the-intellectual-bypass_us_586e8c67e4b08052400ee09c.

Ford, D. (2011). *The 21-Day Consciousness Cleanse: A Breakthrough Program for Connecting with Your Soul's Deepest Purpose*. San Francisco: HarperOne.

Goleman, D. (2004). 'What Makes a Leader?' Harvard Business Review, January 2004. https://hbr.org/2004/01/what-makes-a-leader.

Harrison, N. A., T. Singer, P. Rotshtein, R. J. Dolan and H. D. Critchley (2006). 'Pupillary Contagion: Central Mechanisms Engaged in Sadness Processing'. *Social Cognitive and Affective Neuroscience* 1(1): 5–17. doi:10.1093/scan/nsl006.

Hemingway, E. (1995). *The Garden of Eden*. New York: Simon and Schuster.

Lenzen, M. (2018). 'Feeling Our Emotions' (interview with Antonio R. Damasio). *Scientific American*, 1 April 2005. https://www.scientificamerican.com/article/feeling-our-emotions/.

Miller, S. G. (2016). '1 in 6 Americans Takes a Psychiatric Drug'. Scientific American, 13 December 2016. https://www.scientificamerican.com/article/1-in-6-americans-takes-a-psychiatric-drug.

Nasiri Zarch, Z., S. M. Marashi and H. Raji (2014). 'The Relationship between Emotional Intelligence and Marital Satisfaction: 10-Year Outcome of Partners from Three Different Economic Levels'. *Iranian Journal of Psychiatry* 9(4): 188–96. https://www.ncbi.nlm.nih.gov/pmc/articles/PMC4361820/.

Purves, D., G. J. Augustine, D. Fitzpatrick, W. C. Hall, A. S. LaMantia, et al., eds (2017). *Neuroscience*. 6th ed. New York: Oxford University Press.

Chapter 9. Processing Our Emotions

Chapman, B. P., K. Fiscella, I. Kawachi, P. Duberstein and P. Muennig (2013). 'Emotion Suppression and Mortality Risk Over a 12-Year Follow-Up'. Journal of Psychosomatic Research 75(4): 381–85. doi:10.1016/j.jpsychores.2013.07.014.

Freud, S. (2015). 'Sigmund Freud Quotes'. SigmundFreud.net, accessed 13 February 2019. https://www.sigmundfreud.net/quotes.jsp.

Goleman, D. (1988). 'Health; New Studies Report Health Dangers of Repressing Emotional Turmoil'. New York Times, 3 March 1988. https://www.nytimes.com/1988/03/03/us/health-new-studies-report-health-dangers-of-repressing-emotional-turmoil.html.

Honkalampi, K., S. M. Lehto, H. Koivumaa-Honkanen, J. Hintikka, L. Niskanen, et al. (2011). 'Alexithymia and Tissue Inflammation'. *Psychotherapy and Psychosomatics* 80: 359–64. doi:10.1159/000327583.

Nummenmaa, L., E. Glerean, R. Hari and J. K. Hietanen (2014). 'Bodily Maps of Emotions'. *Proceedings of the National Academy of Sciences of the USA* 111(2): 646–51. doi:10.1073/pnas.1321664111.

Philippot, P., G. Chapelle and S. Blairy (2002). 'Respiratory Feedback in the Generation of Emotion'. *Cognition and Emotion* 16(5): 605–27. doi:10.1080/02699930143000392.

Srivastava, S., M. Tamir, K. M. McGonigal, O. P. John and J. J. Gross (2009). 'The Social Costs of Emotional Suppression: A Prospective Study of the Transition to College'. *Journal of Personality and Social Psychology* 96(4): 883–97. doi:10.1037/a0014755.

Ullman, S. (2019). 'Youth'. Samuel Ullman Museum website, accessed 7 January 2019. https://www.uab.edu/ullmanmuseum/.

Chapter 10. Getting in Touch with Our Inner Child

Capacchione, L. (1991). *Recovery of Your Inner Child: The Highly Acclaimed Method for Liberating Your Inner Self*. 1st ed. New York: Simon and Schuster.

Firman, J., and A. Russell (1994). *Opening to the Inner Child: Recovering Authentic Personality*. Palo Alto, CA: Psychosynthesis Palo Alto.

Olson, N. (2016). 'Three Ways that Handwriting with a Pen Positively Affects Your Brain'. *Forbes*, 15 May 2016. https://www.forbes.com/sites/nancyolson/2016/05/15/three-ways-that-writing-with-a-pen-positively-affects-your-brain/#469cada05705.

Rowe, N. (2019). 'Nikki Rowe > Quotes'. Goodreads.com, accessed 8 January 2019. https://www.goodreads.com/author/quotes/7147202.Nikki_Rowe?page=2.

Chapter 11. Our Connection to Our Body

Angel, J. (2016). *Breaking the Jump: The Secret Story of Parkour's High Flying Rebellion*. London: Aurum.

Baril, R. (2014). 'Movement as Medicine: An Interview with Roger Baril & Carol Welch-Baril'. Somaticsmove.com, 12 November 2014. http://somaticsmove.com/movement-medicine-interview-carol-welch-baril-roger-baril/.

Beat Eating Disorders (2019). 'Statistics for Journalists'. Accessed 9 January 2019. https://www.beateatingdisorders.org.uk/media-centre/eating-disorder-statistics.

Deshimaru, T. (2016). *Zen & Karma: Teachings of Roshi Taisen Deshimaru*. 2nd ed. Chino Valley, AZ: Hohm.

Dias, B. G., and K. J. Ressler (2014). 'Parental Olfactory Experience Influences Behavior and Neural Structure in Subsequent Generations'. *Nature Neuroscience* 17(1): 89–96. doi:10.1038/nn.3594.

Fardouly, J., P. C. Diedrichs, L. R. Vartanian and E. Halliwell (2015). 'Social Comparisons on Social Media: The Impact of Facebook on Young Women's Body Image Concerns and Mood'. *Body Image* 13: 38–45. doi:10.1016/j.bodyim.2014.12.002.

Knaster, M. (1998). *Discovering the Body's Wisdom*. New York: Bantam Doubleday Dell.

May, R. (2009). *Man's Search for Himself*. London: W. W. Norton.

Ruff, M. (2014). 'Where Do You Store Your Emotions?' Candace Pert's website, 14 July 2014. http://candacepert.com/articles/where-do-you-store-your-emotions/.

Youseff, N. A., L. Lockwood, S. Su, G. Hao and B.P.F. Rutten (2018). 'The Effects of Trauma, with or without PTSD, on the Transgenerational DNA Methylation Alterations in Human Offsprings'. *Brain Sciences* 8(5): 83. doi:10.3390/brainsci8050083.

Chapter 12. Thinking Consciously

Abazov, R. (2015). '5 Ways to Improve Your Creative Thinking'. *Top Universities* (blog), 11 August 2015. https://www.topuniversities.com/blog/5-ways-improve-your-creative-thinking.

Achor, S. (2011). 'The Happy Secret to Better Work' (TED Talk, TEDxBloomington). TED website, May 2011. https://www.ted.com/talks/shawn_achor_the_happy_secret_to_better_work?.

American Psychological Association (APA) (2003). 'Believing You Can Get Smarter Makes You Smarter'. APA website, Research in Action, 28 May 2003. http://www.apa.org/research/action/smarter.aspx.

Booth, R. (2017). 'Master of Mindfulness, Jon Kabat-Zinn: "People Are Losing Their Minds. That Is What We Need to Wake Up To"'. *Guardian*, 22 October 2017. https://www.theguardian.com/lifeandstyle/2017/oct/22/mindfulness-jon-kabat-zinn-depression-trump-grenfell.

Chödrön, P. (2007). *The Places That Scare You: A Guide to Fearlessness in Difficult Times*. Boulder, CO: Shambhala.

Dougherty, E. (2011). 'What Are Thoughts Made Of?' MIT School of Engineering website, Ask an Engineer, 26 April 2011. https://engineering.mit.edu/engage/ask-an-engineer/what-are-thoughts-made-of/.

Henderlong Corpus, J., and M. R. Lepper (2007). 'The Effects of Person versus Performance Praise on Children's Motivation: Gender and Age as Moderating Factors'. *Education Psychology* 27(4): 487–508. doi:10.1080/01443410601159852.

Ildan, M. M. (2018). 'Quotes and Quotations of Mehmet Murat ildan -63'. Archive for October 2018. Mehmet Murat ildan Quotations on Wordpress.com, accessed 13 January 2019. https://muratildanquotations.wordpress.com.

Kang, W., W.-J. Park, K.-H. Jang, H.-M Lim, J.-S. Ann, et al. (2016). 'Comparison of Anxiety and Depression Status between Office and Manufacturing Job Employees in a Large Manufacturing Company: A Cross Sectional Study'. *Annals of Occupational and Environmental Medicine* 28: 47. doi:10.1186/s40557-016-0134-z.

Luders, E., N. Cherbuin and F. Kurth (2015). 'Forever Young(er): Potential Age-Defying Effects of Long-Term Meditation on Gray Matter Atrophy'. *Frontiers in Psychology* 5: 1551. doi:10.3389/fpsyg.2014.01551.

McDowell, E. (@emilymcdowell) (2018). 'One of my personal inaccurate conclusions that's guided me for as long as I can remember.' Twitter, 19 October 2018. https://twitter.com/emilymcdowell_/status/1053329349527527424.

Mercola, J. (2009). 'Fascinating Facts You Never Knew about the Human Brain'. Mercola website, 22 January 2009. https://articles.mercola.com/sites/articles/archive/2009/01/22/fascinating-facts-you-never-knew-about-the-human-brain.aspx.

Rusanen, M., M. Kivipelto, C. P. Quesenbery, J. Zhour and R. A. Whitmer (2011). 'Heavy Smoking in Midlife and Long-Term Risk of Alzheimer Disease and Vascular Dementia'. *Archives of Internal Medicine* 171(4): 333–39. doi:10.1001/archinternmed.2010.393.

Salvi, C. (2017). 'The Science behind Escape Rooms' (video). RedBull website, 10 March 2017. https://www.redbull.com/int-en/tv/video/AP-1QG5XXKSD1W11/the-science-behind-escape-rooms.

Tagore, R. (1918). *Personality: Lectures Delivered in America*. London: Macmillan.

Voytek, B. (2013). 'What Does It Feel Like to Hold a Human Brain in Your Hands?' *Quora* (blog), 30 October 2013. http://www.slate.com/blogs/quora/2013/10/30/what_does_it_feel_like_to_hold_a_human_brain_in_your_hands.html?via=gdpr-consent.

Wood, J. V., W. Q. Perunovic and J. W. Lee (2009). 'Positive Self-Statements: Power for Some, Peril for Others'. *Journal of Psychological Science* 20(7): 860–66. doi:10.1111/j.1467-9280.2009.02370.x.

Chapter 13. Expressing Our Spiritual Side

Alcott, L. M. (1997). *The Journals of Louisa M. Alcott*. Athens, GA: University of Georgia Press.

Beauregard, M., and V. Paquette (2006). 'Neural Correlates of a Mystical Experience in Carmelite Nuns'. *Neuroscience Letters* 405(3): 186–90. doi:10.1016/j.neulet.2006.06.060.

Gervais, W. M., and A. Norenzayan (2012). 'Analytic Thinking Promotes Religious Disbelief'. *Science* 336(6080): 493–96. doi:10.1126/science.1215647.

Hameroff, S. (2018). 'Overview by SH'. Quantum Consciousness, accessed 9 October 2018. https://www.quantumconsciousness.org/content/overview-sh.

Hameroff, S., and R. Penrose (2014). 'Consciousness in the Universe: A Review of the "Orch OR" Theory'. *Physics of Life Reviews* 11(1): 39–78. doi:10.1016/j.plrev.2013.08.002.

Parnia, S., K. Spearpoint, G. de Vos, P. Fenwick, D. Goldberg, et al. (2014). 'AWARE – AWAreness during REsuscitation – A Prospective Study'. *Resuscitation* 85(12): 1799–1805. doi:10.1016/j.resuscitation.2014.09.004.

Posey, A. D. (2019). 'Quotation Explorer – "A.D. Posey"'. Quotes.schollz.com, accessed 2 February 2019. https://quotes.schollz.com/author/a.d.%20posey.

Shenhav, A., D. G. Rand and J. D. Greene (2012). 'Divine Intuition: Cognitive Style Influences Belief in God'. *Journal of Experimental Psychology: General* 141(3): 423–28. doi:10.1037/a0025391.

Tsakiris, A. (2018). 'Dr. Jeffrey Long's Near-Death Experience Research a "Game Changer" for Science'. Skeptiko, 3 February 2018. https://skeptiko.com/94-jeffrey-long-near-death-experience-research/.

Wikisource contributors (2017). 'The Complete Works of Swami Vivekananda/Volume 5/Sayings and Utterances'. *Wikisource*, 11 October 2018. https://en.wikisource.org/w/index.php?title=The_Complete_Works_of_Swami_Vivekananda/Volume_5/Sayings_and_Utterances&oldid=4851348.

Epilogue

Billings, J. (1904). 'Those who hunt after happiness …'. *St. Louis Republic*, 5 June 1904. Reproduced online by the National Endowment for the Humanities and the Library of Congress. https://chroniclingamerica.loc.gov/lccn/sn84020274/1904-06-05/ed-1/seq-50/.

Resources

There are more resources for your self-development work on my website at www.suzannewylde.com, which I think you will enjoy. In this section you will find some links to different self-development modalities you can try, and below that there are some useful contacts in case you need support from an organisation. Please note that I am not affiliated with any of these teachers, authors or organisations, so I cannot take responsibility for any service they provide. If you need urgent help, it is important that you contact your doctor or the most relevant support service first.

Alternative Resources

Outside of the traditional counselling route there are a number of interesting alternative therapies and other approaches that can help us. As a practising alternative therapist myself, I have seen great progress in people when they use a variety of approaches – not just working with the mind, but the body and spirit also. I recommend that you find a teacher or practitioner that you like, because feeling at ease is very important with all of this work. Here is just a small taste of what is on offer, mostly with my description (not theirs) and a link to a resource which may be one of many for some therapies. There are many other methods you can explore, including acupuncture, bodywork, laughter yoga and more!

5 Rhythms

Emotional self-expression through dance
https://www.5rhythms.com

Mindfulness meditation

Meditation focusing on the breath to stay present
https://www.mindful.org

EFT tapping

Shifting negative thought patterns using affirmations and acupressure
points
https://eftinternational.org

Transformational breathing

Processing trauma and emotions through breathwork
https://www.transformationalbreath.co.uk

Authentic Peruvian shamanism with London-based shaman Anna Hunt

20,000-year-old shamanic healing arts made accessible and relevant to a
modern twenty-first-century audience
https://annahunt.com

Sound therapy

Sound and music to improve health and well-being
https://www.britishacademyofsoundtherapy.com

Art therapy

Emotional expression through art
https://www.baat.org

Somatic experiencing

A way of working with the body to process and release trauma and stress
https://traumahealing.org

TRE

Using simple physical exercises to release trauma from the body
https://traumaprevention.com

Reiki

Energy healing method used to help physical and emotional health
https://www.reikifed.co.uk

Marie Kondo

Tidying and reconnecting with your space
https://konmari.com

Organisations that Offer Support

This list is not exhaustive, so if you are looking for help you might need to do more research to find the best place for you, especially if you live outside of the UK, where many of these organisations are based. Some of these resources are more for education and others for providing group or one-to-one support.

Directory for finding a counsellor or psychotherapist

https://www.counselling-directory.org.uk

Help with depression and other mental health concerns

https://www.samaritans.org (telephone: 116 123)
https://www.mind.org.uk
http://www.sane.org.uk
http://www.supportline.org.uk

Help for people with anxiety

https://www.anxietyuk.org.uk

Support for autistic people, and their family and friends

http://www.autism.org.uk

Support for PTSD

http://www.ptsduk.org

Information for sufferers of different types of trauma

http://www.aftertrauma.org

Help for people who have been the victim of a crime

https://www.victimsupport.org.uk

Support for men and women who have suffered sexual abuse and rape

https://www.safeline.org.uk

Help for women who are suffering/have suffered from domestic abuse

https://www.womensaid.org.uk
http://www.nationaldomesticviolencehelpline.org.uk

Help for men who are suffering/have suffered from domestic abuse

http://www.mensadviceline.org.uk
http://www.mankind.org.uk

Support for black and ethnic minority people who have experienced abuse

You can either use the general services above, or search 'ethnic minority abuse support + *your city*' as there are many regional services. For example:

London, women and girls: http://www.lbwp.online
Scotland, women and children: https://shaktiedinburgh.co.uk
Wales: http://www.bawso.org.uk/our-services

Support for LGBT people who have suffered sexual violence or domestic abuse

http://www.galop.org.uk
http://www.endthefear.co.uk
https://lgbtdap.org.uk

Support for people who have been abusive and want to stop

http://respectphoneline.org.uk

Resilience resources for people exposed to social disadvantage and inequality

https://www.boingboing.org.uk

Help for people who have been in a cult or abusive relationship

https://freedomofmind.com
https://www.decision-making-confidence.com

Index

General Index

Exercise Index

The exercises are numbered by chapter; so, exercise 5.2 is the second exercise in chapter 5.

About the Author

Suzanne Wylde is an alternative therapist, stretching trainer, published author and lifelong self-development junkie who has been featured in national publications and worked with people from very different backgrounds on moving forwards in their self-development and lives. She loves helping people to access and express their full potential and is excited to share some of these powerful tools with you. You will not find her having a cup of tea and reading a book (because she will be well hidden)!

www.suzannewylde.com

Another book by Suzanne Wylde

This easy-to-read guide explains how to overhaul our bodies, boost-ing posture, flexibility and strength by working on our fascia (the dense connective tissue that makes us the shape we are). The Moving Stretch method of resistance stretching is simple and effective, suitable for begin-ners and advanced stretchers alike and holds a wide range of benefits beyond flexibility, including; feeling taller and more open, having more energy, feeling more grounded, improved sports performance, better sleep and feeling more youthful and energised.

Whether you are a yogi or a plank, you will find benefits for your body in these stretches. It only takes just 10-20 minutes of stretching to feel better for the rest of your day!

"It's really very simple and very easy to apply, but above all the benefit is immediate. Sensation of muscular well-being, straightening of stature, it's quite spectacular."

"I am new to stretching, but already feeling the benefits of a more flexible body after just a few days of exercises."

"This is the best book of its kind I have read. The exercises are easy to follow and do."

ISBN 978 1 905367 74 0 | £14.99 | 224 pages |
320 colour photographs | paperback